Documentary Photography

TIME LIFE BOOKS ®

Life World Library
Life Nature Library
Time Reading Program
The Life History of the United States
Life Science Library
Great Ages of Man
Time-Life Library of Art
Time-Life Library of America
Foods of the World
This Fabulous Century
Life Library of Photography
The Time-Life Encyclopedia of Gardening
Family Library
  The Time-Life Book of Family Finance
  The Time-Life Family Legal Guide
The American Wilderness

LIFE LIBRARY OF PHOTOGRAPHY

Documentary Photography

BY THE EDITORS OF TIME-LIFE BOOKS

TIME-LIFE BOOKS, NEW YORK

ON THE COVER: A documentary within a documentary, this picture suggests the way an Alabama tenant farm family lived, and, in the two snapshots tacked to the wall, bears witness to the family's informal documentation of its own experiences. The photograph was taken by Walker Evans in 1936, while he was employed by the Farm Security Administration; it was the powerful and moving record of rural poverty made by him and his FSA colleagues *(pages 66-84)* that popularized the term documentary photography.

Contents

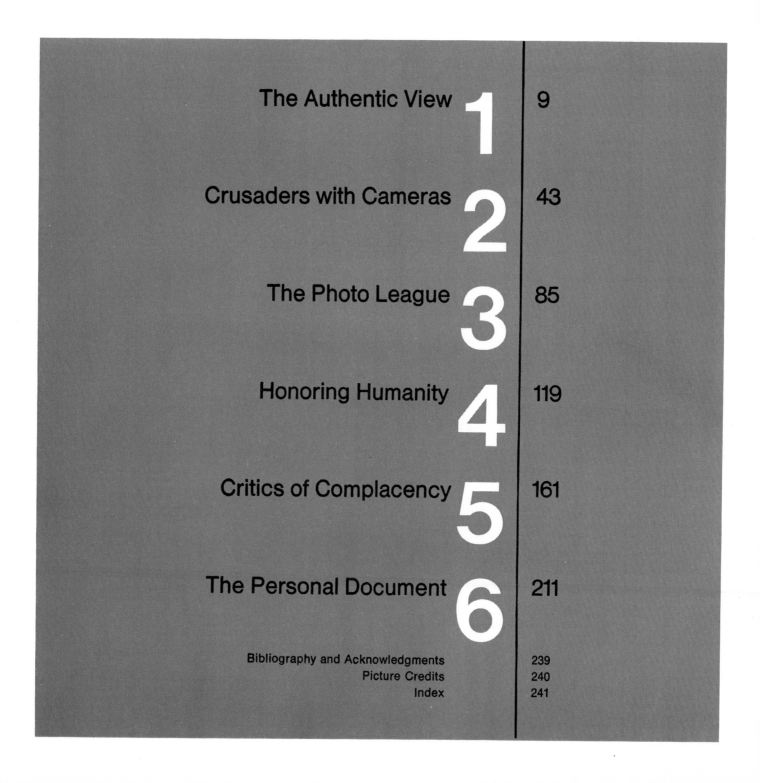

The Authentic View **1** 9

Crusaders with Cameras **2** 43

The Photo League **3** 85

Honoring Humanity **4** 119

Critics of Complacency **5** 161

The Personal Document **6** 211

Bibliography and Acknowledgments 239
Picture Credits 240
Index 241

For help given in the creation of this book, the editors are indebted to Arthur Freed, Assistant Professor of Photography at Pratt Institute, Brooklyn, New York, who served as general consultant in developing the concept of the volume, and assisted in the selection of photographs and the preparation of the text. Valuable aid also was provided by these individuals and departments of Time Inc.: Editorial Production, Norman Airey, Margaret T. Fischer; Library, Peter Draz; Picture Collection, Doris O'Neil; TIME-LIFE News Service, Murray J. Gart; Correspondents Margot Hapgood (London), Maria Vincenza Aloisi (Paris), Elisabeth Kraemer (Bonn), Ann Natanson (Rome).

The term documentary photography came into use during the depression years, when telling pictures of poverty-stricken farmers awakened Americans to the need for social reform. And in many minds this field of photography still suggests pictures of the Dust Bowl, of rural hardship and urban slums.

Yet as this book shows, there is, and always has been, far more to documentary photography than the recording of the world's ills. For there is much more to document than suffering and poverty: faraway places and exotic peoples, quirks of nature and of society, the whole gamut of emotions and relationships. The subject matter is, indeed, almost unlimited.

Then is every photograph a documentary? Not really, for it must convey a message that sets it apart from a landscape, a portrait, a street scene. It may record an event, but the event must have some general significance, more than the specific significance of a news photo. It may record character or emotion—but again, of some general social significance; it is more than personally revelatory, as a portrait is.

Yet whether it shows us family life in Paris or in Maine, the central square of Peking or a stretch of U.S. Route 66, a dive in New York's slums or a village café in Hungary, a sharecropper's cabin or a suburban living room, the documentary photograph tells us something important about our world—and in the best examples, makes us think about the world in a new way.

The Editors

The Authentic View 1

To See, to Record—and to Comment 12

John Thomson: Guide to Far-off Places 16
Benjamin Stone: Chronicler of a Fading Era 22
Jacques-Henri Lartigue: One Boy's Family 28
Eugène Atget: A Romance with Paris 36

ROBERT DOISNEAU: *Tourist at Notre Dame*, 1956

To See, to Record—and to Comment

Documentary photography: a depiction of the real world by a photographer whose intent is to communicate something of importance—to make a comment—that will be understood by the viewer.

That is the definition on which this book is based. It is arbitrary by necessity, since there is no universally accepted definition that suits all aspects of this important and intriguing category. A documentary photograph may be as public as a picture in a mass-circulation magazine, or as private as an intimate view of a loved one. On cursory inspection a good documentary photograph may seem little more than a snapshot. But under more careful scrutiny it generally reveals itself to be a visual representation of a deeply felt moment, as rich in psychological and emotional meaning as a personal experience vividly recalled.

That the attributes of a documentary photograph seem contradictory may be a result of the newness of the term. It was not even coined until the 1930s and then it was linked in the public mind with documentary films—movies that, without fictionalized plot, usually examined the lives of little-known people in remote places. These films, unlike the routine travelogue, were a visual commentary on the world. The same kind of communication had long been provided by still photographs, but until that point they had never been dignified by categorization as something special.

The photographs made by the pioneers of documentary photography look quite different from those being created by many of its modern practitioners. Yet they are fundamentally the same—all comment on reality—and the apparent differences developed logically as the form progressed from the simple to the complex. Documentary photography evolved in several stages, each of which has its own characteristics. The first stage was broad-based and was directly related to the invention of photography itself. With the introduction of the daguerreotype in 1839 came the first relatively simple and inexpensive way to perpetuate images, to fulfill the common desire for a permanent record of the appearance of family, friends and familiar scenes. Record-making became still easier in 1888, when George Eastman brought out his roll-film Kodak: what had been comparatively simple now became so routine that anyone could—and almost everyone did—take personal pictures; the album pasted full of snapshots became a source of family unity and pride. In the broadest sense, these record pictures were documentary photographs: they were scenes from the real world of a subject important to the photographer. And if the photographer was a prodigy like Lartigue, who made photographs of his family, friends and relations before World War I *(pages 28-35),* the results were lighthearted, sophisticated art.

If the familiar made a cherished photographic record, so did the unfamiliar. The early photographers rushed off to capture views of distant, exotic places that could be visited only by the well-to-do and adventurous. Pictures of such romantic sites as Niagara Falls, the Egyptian pyramids and the Alps were purchased to frame and hang on parlor walls; no late-19th Century home was complete without a scene from a faraway place on display. In the 1850s the popularity of the stereoscope, a device in which pictures could be seen in three dimensions, expanded the already booming market for pictures of scenic places. But even without an optical gimmick like the stereoscope, photographs brought the world into the home.

These scenic views won such wide popularity partly because they emphasized a quality, essential to the documentary photograph, that is a basic characteristic of the camera-made image: it provides a clear representation of what the retina of the human eye sees but does not always notice. In the beginning this quality alone seemed miraculous, and the camera was used mainly as a copier of nature. The results were regarded as evidence—as documents—of nature as it exists. Faith in the camera as a literal recorder gave rise to a belief that persists to this day—that the camera does not lie. This trust of the camera provides documentary photography with its greatest psychological strength and its strongest selling point—it tells the truth.

As the camera gained acceptance as a reliable visual reporter, its potential became apparent to photographers who had something more to say than could be communicated by a mere snapshot. A picture of the Alps, if made with sensitivity and skill, could be more than a literal record of a majestic scene. The photograph conveyed ideas beyond the two-dimensional, black-and-gray image of shadows and light. The scene before the lens was reality, but the photographer could make his camera's rendering of the scene generate another reality, deeper and perhaps more important—he could introduce comment. If the first attribute of the documentary photograph was its ability to convey the truth about the real world, its second was its ability to communicate the photographer's comment on that truth.

The first master of this technique was Eugène Atget. He referred to himself simply as a maker of documents—clear, uncluttered views of his beloved turn-of-the-century Paris—which he sold occasionally as reference material for artists and architects. Yet he was a genius at understanding the uses of the camera, particularly its ability to convey his own view. Shots of empty parks *(pages 36-42),* when made by Atget, blended the reality of the scene with its deeper meaning as a part of a city, and with his own feeling for the city. The results are masterworks of documentary photography.

The realization that the camera could communicate truth while commenting upon it led to the second stage in the expanding history of documentary photography: the discovery of the camera's power to hold up a mirror to society, to let the world see its reflection. Jacob Riis, a Danish-born newspaper reporter of the late 19th Century, was one of the first to show how photographs could become social documents. Riis picked up his camera in desperation. He wanted Americans to see for themselves what he had been writing about—the grinding brutality of life in New York City's slums. His pictures were as trenchant as his reporting, exposing to the world the gray, lined face of American poverty. Following soon after Riis came one of the best social documentarians in the history of photography, Lewis W. Hine. Hine was a trained sociologist and schoolteacher whose passionate social awareness took him into factories and down into mines to photograph the inhuman conditions imposed on working-class children and immigrant laborers. His pictures were down-to-earth indictments of early-20th Century American industrial practices, but his talent and compassion made his work do more than arouse indignation; it made the viewer embrace the subjects as fellow human beings and share their hardships. Together, Riis and Hine turned documentary photography to a study of the human condition. This visual comment on the joys and pains of society has to a great extent occupied practitioners in this field ever since.

Through the Depression of the 1930s, the war years of the 1940s and into the postwar recovery period, documentary photographers roamed the world—and examined their own neighborhoods—to capture the special feel of time and place created by each society at a given moment in history. Although these photographers, who included such giants as W. Eugene Smith, André Kertész, Dorothea Lange and Walker Evans, viewed human suffering and despair everywhere they wandered, they also captured the inner strength, dignity and transcendent hope of their subjects. They believed that man was redeemable. Perhaps more important, they felt man was worthy of redemption. Like the Romantic novelists of the 19th Century, these documentary photographers thought that by showing man his follies, they would lead him to correct them. The brooding genius Smith was convinced that once his pictures laid bare the futility, savagery and brute stupidity of war, mankind would be horrified into abolishing warfare for all time.

By the 1950s, however, it was clear that the documentary photographers had achieved no more in reforming society than had the Romantic novelists. Some consciences had been stirred, some laws had even been enacted—Hine's pictures led to the passage of labor legislation that rescued children from servitude in factories. But mankind had not been elevated to a state of greater purity through photographs, and many disillusioned documentarians turned to another approach.

The development of a new concept of documentary photography was signaled by a single event, the publication in 1958 of Robert Frank's book, *The*

Americans. A collection of photographs that Frank made during a tour of the United States, it presented views of the country by an outsider—Frank was born and raised in Switzerland. In his pictures, he saw the patch in the fabric of the American flag *(page 174)*. He set down the tedium of daily life, the polluting residue of industrial society, the frustrations of those Americans caught between the promise of the national rhetoric and its everyday reality. Frank's view was hard-nosed, direct and very personal.

After *The Americans* documentary photography entered the contemporary phase of its evolution. Many photographers turned inward as they withdrew from the rough-and-tumble of public life and actions. Their concern became the recognition—and the problems—of the inner man. Communicating psychological reality became more important than conveying visual reality or social reality. The photographer's emotions, or his experience, became as pivotal to the picture as his view of the world. This charting of the psyche is complex, often treacherous, photography, for it leads to pictures that at first glance may look more like rejects—blurred, strangely framed, empty—than like successful works of art. They demand close interpretation; the viewer must think about them to get the photographer's message.

In its newest form documentary photography is, oddly, returning to its beginnings for subject matter. These modern photographs, like daguerreotypes of old, often show families, friends and homes. But the resemblance to the old family snapshot is only superficial. For within these familiar images today's photographers have found a new reality to record and comment on: their pictures communicate the emotions and interpersonal relationships of private life. From the 19th Century album of snapshots to the 20th Century portfolio of intimate views, documentary photography continues its spiral toward the understanding of society and man. □

John Thomson: Guide to Far-off Places

In the mid-19th Century, England enjoyed a heady new craze—travel and exploration. The Orient and Africa were opened at last to the Western world, and the public devoured the descriptions each traveler felt compelled to write. The flood of books could not satisfy the general curiosity. It took photographs to make the unbelievable real.

Among the first of the photographer-explorers was a practical Scotsman, John Thomson. In 1862 he took his cameras to the Far East, and there for about 10 years, five of them in China, snapped cities and landscapes. Thomson's purpose was clearly documentary; the photograph, he wrote in his introduction to *Illustrations of China and Its People,* "affords the nearest approach that can be made toward placing the reader actually before the scene which is represented."

The book, published in four volumes between 1873 and 1874, was illustrated with 200 of his photographs. In them the enthusiastic public now saw just what Thomson saw: every building stone, every human posture, every detail of clothing. They were so brimming with information that the viewer felt transported to China. Thomson made the photograph serve as the viewer's vicarious experience.

Didactic Victorians took these photographs very seriously—and no one thought of them as "art," least of all Thomson himself. His purpose was simply to instruct. But in documenting the previously undocumented, Thomson did produce a body of work with, to quote Beaumont Newhall, "that sense of the immediacy and authenticity of documentation, which a photograph can impart so forcibly."

Avenue to the Ming Tombs, c. 1865

Camels sculptured from white limestone flank
the Way of the Spirit leading to the tombs of the
Ming Dynasty emperors 30 miles north of Peking.
Two elephants can be seen in the distance. The
greater-than-life-sized statues, thought to be
guarantors of good fortune, date from the 15th
Century. The receding statuary emphasizes the
vastness of the sacred valley, and the standing
man, dwarfed by the statue, seems no more alive
than the animals in this forbidding necropolis.

17

Night Watchman, Peking, c. 1865

*Old Wang, a Manchu guard, beats his wooden
clapper to frighten away thieves. The government
allotted him the sheepskin coat for protection
on winter nights. Ragged and hollow-cheeked,
this functionary provided a shocking glimpse
of a China long hidden from Western eyes.*

View of the Central Street, Chinese Quarter, c. 1865

Thomson climbed to the top of the city wall for this panorama of the central roadway of old Peking. His picture is so clear, and so crammed with information, that the eye can travel endlessly through this strange and wonderful toy town, and at every viewing discover a new detail. In the right rear, beyond the wide, low bridge, tent shops cluster beneath the giant memorial arch; in the foreground, a laborer with buckets suspended from a yoke is about to repair the cobbled road; and far off on the horizon the three rising tiers of the Temple of Heaven are just barely visible.

Thomson found a staggering variety of races and classes in the Orient, and his photographs revealed each sitter to be a member of a unique group; he meticulously recorded costumes or trade implements and posed tableaux to suggest craft or caste. On this page, two Javanese aristocrats at upper left pridefully display their intricate garments, a Hindu barber above sets to work on a client, and a Manchu matron at left models her coiffure, fore and aft. Such detail delighted Thomson, who recommended "careful study of the illustrations" to his "fair readers." The six studio pictures at right were all taken in Singapore, even then (the 1860s) a melting pot; he made no record of who the subjects were.

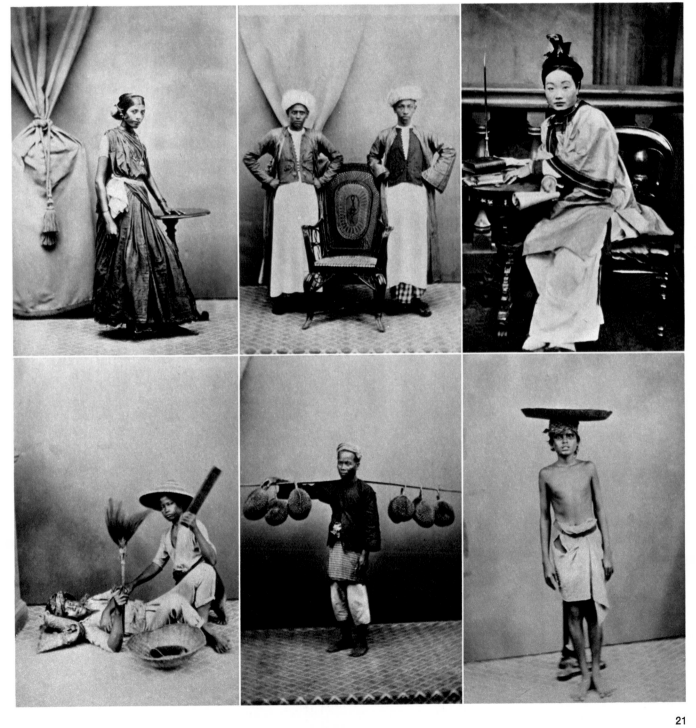

Benjamin Stone: Chronicler of a Fading Era

To the Duke's Health, 1899

Dressed in their Sunday best, neighbors of the Duke of Buccleuch drink his health in rum and milk. By centuries-old custom they paid him a small annual road toll called Wroth Silver, and he provided them a lavish breakfast at the Dun Cow. The arrangement was agreeable to everybody.

Two solemn young people stand framed by a ▶ portal of Westminster Abbey after taking part in the Holy Thursday ceremony at which alms are given to the poor. The observance commemorates the day when Christ washed the feet of His disciples; the white scarves represent the towel He used to dry them. The glow radiating from the scarves may have resulted from halation, the reflection and scattering of light from the back of the glass plate; but the photographer clearly valued its air of supernatural significance.

Sir Benjamin Stone's passion for the photographic record was at least equal to that of his fellows, but he found the close-at-hand world of Victorian and Edwardian England more intriguing than the faraway places that fascinated such predecessors as John Thomson.

Stone was greatly interested in the survival into his day of ancient customs and ceremonies, and he began taking pictures simply because he could not buy the sort he wanted.

"Photographs are the most reliable, the most correct recording means, and therefore they become the most important aid in educating and obtaining instruction," he wrote. And for some 40 years, applying the enormous single-mindedness and the energy that were so eminently Victorian, he catalogued British life, as a contemporary wrote, "to portray for the benefit of future generations the manners and customs, the festivals and pageants, the historic buildings and places of our time."

His dedication to this goal was astonishing. How many photographs he took no one now knows, but more than 25,000 prints survive, all in near-perfect condition. This great body of work was produced in his spare time—Sir Benjamin was also a successful glass manufacturer, a tireless civic leader and a Member of Parliament. Happily, he was wealthy; the £30,000 he spent on photography would be equivalent today to about $750,000.

Famous as a photographer in his own day, Stone has been almost forgotten in ours. Nevertheless the intense honesty of his work as well as its immense value as the chronicle of an age earn him an important niche in the history of documentary photography.

Maundy Thursday Ceremony, 1898

Painswick Churchyard, Gloucestershire, 1902

Stocks at Painswick, 1902

◄ Painswick churchyard is a burial ground, yet in this picture it looks anything but morbid. In the rows of plump, meticulously clipped yew trees —symbols of immortality—and in the tidy pathways, so obviously meant for casual strolling, the photographer found an orderly scene to document, yet one full of airiness and grace.

Outside the same churchyard a young news vendor stands warily beside a set of leg stocks. Confinement to the stocks, once a common form of humiliating punishment for minor offenses, was not imposed after the 1860s, but this set remained as a local relic—perhaps as a warning to the overly high-spirited. And the cautionary effect is heightened by the composition of the picture, its severe horizontal and vertical lines softened only by the billowing yew-tops above.

Charcoal Burner of Worcestershire, 1896

Self-conscious, and perhaps a bit suspicious of
Sir Benjamin's motive in photographing a humble
workman, a charcoal burner poses with his ax and
hand-hewn pyre. To proper Victorians, though,
the hearty old man might have illustrated the
maxim, "the labourer is worthy of his hire."

One moment of an outing down a Cornish lane ▶
will exist as long as this photograph survives. The
enormous amount of information in the picture
—from the carriage and its occupants, dwarfed by
the trees, to the wealth of detail in the branches
and leaves—adds up to a re-creation of reality.

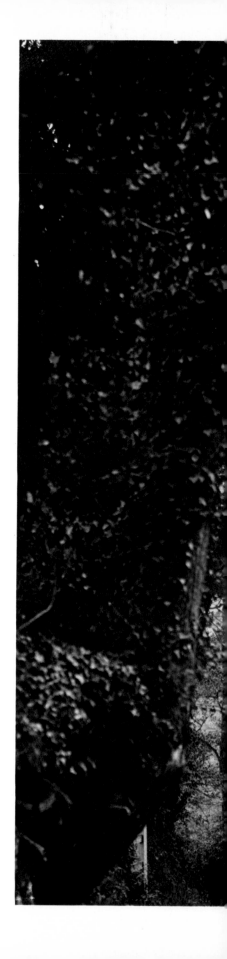

Lane near Penzance, Cornwall, 1893

Jacques-Henri Lartigue: One Boy's Family

By the beginning of the 20th Century, photography had become everyman's toy. The rich and the poor, the esthetically gifted and the insensitive duffers, all used the camera to create visual records of their family histories. But it remained for a seven-year-old boy in France, Jacques-Henri Lartigue, to make the family photo album a work of documentary art.

"My motivation regarding photography is still today, seventy years later, the same: a deep love for a certain period of my life and a desire to freeze its beautiful moments," Lartigue declared when he was nearly eighty. "Photography to me is catching a moment which is passing, and which is true."

Before the young photographer ever owned a camera, he had tried to "be" one himself: by blinking rapidly three times he thought he could fix a scene firmly in his mind. When he found that the pictures were never there when he wanted them, the little boy became so depressed that his parents had to call a doctor. No remedy was found. Then Papa Lartigue, by a stroke of brilliant intuition, bought the boy a camera. A rapid cure was followed by fierce photographic mania.

That Lartigue's life thereafter, as a child and young man, was a turn-of-the-century idyll, untroubled either emotionally or economically, is our luck as well as his. For his pictures of his family and the greater world around him have such spontaneity, such humorous unposed freshness, such generosity of spirit, that we enjoy sharing his private moments. It is his genius that the record of the zany, sports-crazed Lartigue family becomes the family album everyone might long for.

A sumptuously befurred promeneuse, preceded by her brace of fox terriers, sharply eyes the young photographer snapping her from a park bench. Although he clearly admires the elegant lady, his mischievous boy's vision captures something about her that is—just faintly—comic.

Afternoon Walk, Bois de Boulogne, 1911

29

Zissou at the Airfield, 1911

Older brother Maurice, known as Zissou, seems to defy gravity; actually, he is leaning into the wash of air created by a whirling propeller at Buc airfield. "In order to resist the wind of the propeller he had to bend forward," says Lartigue. Zissou's stolid look, dandified outfit and cane accentuate the picture's Chaplinesque air.

Seventeen-year-old cousin Simone, abandoning dignity, rehearses in the park at St.-Cloud for a starring role as acrobat in a circus movie. The film was never made, but the still indicates it would have been lively. Simone was a close friend of Jacques's from childhood and, like all his madcap family, thoroughly used to his camera.

Simone in the Park, 1913

31

Falling Glider at Combegrasse, Auvergne, 1922

Lartigue and his brother Zissou were passionate about airplanes; from early boyhood they cut classes to hang around airfields and they experimented with homemade gliders themselves. In 1922 they journeyed to Auvergne to see the tests of a new glider. Alas, the craft failed to gain altitude and fell almost at once, its launching cables still flapping. Lartigue snapped just as the wing dipped; failure was so rapid the onlookers are just beginning to react to the accident.

Mother's Friends at Pourville, 1906

Corseted ladies in summer dresses promenade above the Norman resort of Pourville-sur-Mer, no doubt to admire the view of beach, pleasure boats and country houses. Their hats are firmly anchored, but the breeze whips at one lady's veil as another pauses to observe the town below.

The gray, muted quality of this photograph is an ▶ abrupt contrast to the gaiety of Lartigue's earlier pictures, an indication of war's effect on the carefree life he recorded so lovingly. The faceless men are not individuals, but soldiers of the French Republic. The airplane, once the object of much excitement, has now become a threat; and as though to emphasize its power, the one in this scene is the only element that is in focus.

Poilus and a Biplane, 1914

Eugène Atget: A Romance with Paris

Iron Gate and Lamppost at St.-Cloud, date unknown

At about the same time that Lartigue began chronicling his happy family's life, Eugène Atget set out on a more serious mission of his own. He intended, a friend later explained, "to create a collection of all that which both in Paris and its surroundings was artistic and picturesque." He began the task in 1898 and kept at it the rest of his life, for 29 years lugging his old-fashioned, heavy view camera all over the city. He documented historic buildings, all-but-hidden architectural details, glimpses of side alleys and ordinary street life —bits and fragments that eventually would fit into the great mosaic he planned as a monumental record of the Paris he knew and loved.

A former sailor and small-time actor, Atget was 41 when he began his new career. His pictures won him no fame in his own lonely lifetime. But his photographs of the lovely parks that surround and embellish Paris are a special part of the work that has become famous since he died. Almost all of them were taken by dawn's early light, when no one else was around. They are documents, clear and uncontrived, of the city's quiet side. That they are also works of art is a tribute to a photographic vision that transcended strict record-making to preserve forever the spirit of a city as well as its appearance.

Like an overgrown fern frond, a lampless light standard rises gracefully from an ironwork gate, one of many such dividers, beautiful as well as utilitarian, that demonstrate the concern for the esthetic that endeared Paris to Atget.

The imposing Tapis Vert (Green Carpet) sweeps ▶ west for 360 yards from the Fountain of Latona. The picture shows a tree and vase prominently in the left foreground; in juxtaposition to the immense but faraway avenue, they emphasize the grandeur of this vista at Versailles.

Tapis Vert from the Fountain of Latona at Versailles, 1901

The Park at St.-Cloud, date unknown

The Park at Sceaux, date unknown

◄ *Just across the Seine from Paris' busiest gate lies the 970-acre park of St.-Cloud (left). Its manicured trees and precisely laid-out walks and fountains, contrasting with the rambling vegetation of Sceaux (above), were more typical of a city where human artistry could be seen on every hand.*

The carefully cared-for estate of Sceaux, confiscated from the Duke of Penthièvre during the French Revolution, had reverted almost to woodland at the time Atget photographed it. The place was soon to be restored as a public garden and before it disappeared forever, the photographer captured a small bit of the wilderness that lent a piquant touch to the sophisticated Paris he loved.

The Hundred Steps at Versailles, date unknown

Ornamental Urn at Versailles, date unknown

Curving lilies and a leaf emerge from a stone urn
on one Versailles path in this record of the
masterly design and craftsmanship of the Sun
King's palace. And the picture, by focusing so
sharply on a detail, provides one small clue to why
Paris became the center of the elegant world.

◄ The Hundred Steps at Versailles rise to a walk
offering a vista of the palace gardens. They
became a setting for the enjoyment of Louis XIV
and his court; the picture shows the scene from the
vantage point of a dwarfed and dazzled subject.

Light weaves among the receding columns of plane trees and statues, and in the foreground shadow dapples the ground and the stone figure. The angle of view on the trees forming an arc around the statuary emphasizes how at Versailles even nature was used to serve the kingly design.

Alley of Plane Trees at Versailles, date unknown

Crusaders with Cameras 2

Rallying the Conscience of Society 46

Jacob Riis: Fighting the Slums 48

Lewis Hine: Abolishing Child Labor 56

The FSA: Crisis on the Farm 66

Walker Evans 68

Ben Shahn 72

Dorothea Lange 78

Russell Lee 82

LEWIS HINE: *Child with Doll*, Paris, 1918

Rallying the Conscience of Society

Once the camera had proved itself a device for showing things as they were, it was inevitably thought of as a tool for changing things to the way they ought to be. Among the first to sense the persuasive power of photography was John Thomson, who turned his camera from exotic China *(pages 16-21)* to the equally exotic—at least to his genteel readers—slums of London *(right)*. Thomson's photographs of lower-class life were sympathetic but, like his Chinese pictures, mainly educational in purpose; they acquainted the public with evils of the slums without urging specific remedial action. It remained for an American to show how the documentary photograph could become an effective weapon in a campaign for reform. He was Jacob Riis, young Danish-born reporter for the New York *Tribune* and later for the *Evening Sun.* And his target, again, was city slums.

In the late 1880s, when New York's immigrant-jammed slums were Riis's beat, they included the most densely crowded urban areas in the world. More than a million people lived in their tenements, and one ward on the Lower East Side had a population density of 334,000 persons per square mile. The death rate was high: nearly 25,000 tenement dwellers died in a single year, and 80,000 were said to be sick at any given moment. The crime rate was equally shocking: in one tenement 102 of the 478 tenants were arrested in a single four-year period.

As a crusading reporter Riis wrote exposé articles in his paper and complained personally to city health officials—with scant results. But he was as resourceful as he was committed, and he no sooner learned that newly invented flashlight powder permitted photographs indoors than he took a camera inside overcrowded flats and filthy cafés.

The pictures that Riis made *(pages 49-55)* resulted in an article in *Scribner's Magazine* and a year later (1890) in a historic book, *How the Other Half Lives.* They had a shocking effect that is hard to imagine today, when pictures are all around; at that time photographs in print were new. Theodore Roosevelt, then a rising young politician, promptly called on Riis and left him a note saying, "I have read your book and I have come to help." When Roosevelt became New York Police Commissioner he did, cracking down on some of the worst abuses. Others joined in an effective reform movement that changed the face of a part of New York and cleaned up many slums. But the indirect results were equally important, for Riis had proved what crusading documentary photography could do.

Two decades later another cause gripped Americans, this time the issue of child labor. Almost two million youngsters between the ages of 10 and 15 were working for a living, and a reform-minded organization called the National Child Labor Committee engaged Lewis Hine, a photographer who had already made a name for himself with poignant photographs of immigrants

Wearing the apron of his trade, the keeper of a London hostel in Drury Lane, where ex-convicts just released from prison could get lodgings or a ha'penny pudding on credit, talks to a customer. The photograph, taken by John Thomson about 1877, appeared in the book titled Street Life in London, a landmark in pictorial persuasion.

arriving at Ellis Island, to do for child labor what Riis had done for the slums. Hine did: by World War I, when he enlisted his camera in the aid of war relief, the tide running against child labor was irreversible.

But it was not until the '30s that the camera became so deeply involved in reform that the term documentary photography often connoted a picture with a social purpose. Photography's commitment to reform was a product of the times. Hard times they were in the United States, with as many as 15 million unemployed, numbers of them homeless and hungry. For the first time a national administration took on broad-scale responsibility for Americans' food and shelter—a step that was unpopular with many citizens, who held to traditional ideas of private incentive and, where necessary, local help for the needy. To win support for the unprecedented federal relief programs, the documentary camera went to Washington.

The United States employed photography in a number of federal agencies, but the one that outperformed them all was a small bureau of a section of the Department of Agriculture charged with dealing with the plight of the farmers, the Farm Security Administration *(pages 66-84)*. Throughout its existence the FSA had hardly more than a dozen photographers all told, and never more than six at a time; yet that small band left a monumental collection of 270,000 photographs documenting the state of the nation at a crucial moment in its history.

The collection stands today in the Library of Congress as one of the finest pictorial records of American life extant, for the photographic bureau of the FSA went far beyond the objective for which it was conceived. The eloquent photographs did a far-reaching job of persuasion in their time; they hung on the walls of galleries, where they revealed to city people the problems their rural countrymen faced, and at county fairs, where they informed farmers about existing federal programs and showed how to qualify for aid. They illustrated dozens of books—including publications of a new kind in which text was incidental and the photographs stood on their own, aided only by slender captions. And in one two-year period pictures distributed on behalf of the FSA appeared in an estimated 175 magazines and newspapers having a total readership of many millions.

So commonplace had the documentary photograph become by then that it was a part of the public's everyday reading matter. The innovation that Riis had introduced was now established tradition, and in the years that followed, the photograph became an instrument of persuasion for every purpose —from winning presidential elections to fighting air pollution, from promoting integration to slowing down war. Today such photographs are so familiar their special character may escape notice, yet they never lose their power to convince or to stimulate action. □

Jacob Riis: Fighting the Slums

On Lincoln's Birthday in 1888, the New York *Sun* carried a chatty item that portended some serious news. "With their way illuminated by spasmodic flashes," the paper reported, "a mysterious party has been startling the town o'nights." The mysterious party consisted of Jacob Riis, two photographers and a health board official. The flashes came from ignited magnesium powder, which had just been found to give off sufficient light for taking photographs in dark places. And the dark places into which this was leading the little group were the slums of New York City.

New York's slums were among the worst in the world. Three quarters of the city's population lived in tenements; those in the Lower East Side's infamous 10th Ward—many of them recent immigrants—were packed together, 522 to the acre. The health board called it the typhus ward; the bureau of vital statistics called it the suicide ward. While the city had not actually given up on it, Riis felt the officials were doing little about it. He believed that the filth and overcrowding of the slums were the causes of their crime and disease, and that the afflictions could be cured only by eliminating the causes.

"The wish kept cropping up in me that there were some way of putting before the people what I saw there," he said. "I wrote, but it seemed to make no impression." He greeted the news of photography by flashpowder "with an outcry that startled my wife, sitting op-

posite. There it was, the thing I had been looking for all these years."

He lost no time in hiring photographers to assist him. But the late hours soon palled on the first two aides, and a third photographer proved unreliable. "There was at last but one way out of it, namely, for me to get a camera myself," Riis concluded. "So I became a photographer, after a fashion."

Photography was neither a pastime nor an art with Riis; "I had a use for it," he said, "and beyond that I never went." That was far enough. His writing, backed up with photographs, exerted an influence on the nation that is still being felt. New York's dreadful police lodging houses—where a "spot" could be had free, but whose filth and overcrowding were as awful as in the five-cent commercial flophouses *(right)* —were abolished. Lights were installed in hallways of tenements. One block, known as The Bend, was torn down and turned into a public park. Playgrounds were built for the schools, classrooms were opened after hours for children's club meetings, and clean water was supplied to the city. Riis helped accomplish all this by means of seven books, plus newspaper stories, magazine articles and lectures. In time he was called Emancipator of the Slums. But photographers remember him as the man who demonstrated the camera's power as a weapon for social reform and gave documentary photography a theme that has preoccupied it to this day.

KENYON COX: *Drawing after "Five Cents a Spot,"* 1889

When Jacob Riis shot the flophouse at right, the reproduction of photographs by photoengraving was in its infancy. To illustrate his article How the Other Half Lives, Scribner's Magazine, in 1889, had Riis's photographs transcribed into drawings that could be reproduced from wood blocks (above). But some of the reality of the squalor was lost. When Riis submitted his account of slum overcrowding to the city health board, he found that his arguments "did not make much of an impression"—until "my negatives, still dripping from the darkroom came to re-enforce them. From them there was no appeal." Thanks to his photographic persuasion, a park replaced the block on which this flophouse stood.

JACOB RIIS: *Five Cents a Spot*, New York, c. 1889

Baxter Street Court, New York, 1888

Bohemian Cigarmakers Working at Home, c. 1890

◄ *Photographs such as the one at left, with children loitering in a slum alley littered with garbage and fallen bricks, helped to bring about truancy laws to keep the young in school, and to provide playgrounds for their use when school was not in session. "Honest play is interdicted in the streets," Riis wrote. "The policeman arrests the ball-tossers, and there is no room in the backyard."*

A great deal of manufacturing—including the family cigarmaking shown above—was carried on at home in the 1890s, enabling employers to evade laws regulating labor conditions. Only when photographs like this were widely published did Americans realize the extent of home labor, and the degree to which it kept youngsters from studying and mothers from caring for children.

Cellar Dwelling on Ludlow Street, New York, c. 1890

*Indoors the reeking tenements had peeling walls,
canted floors and little ventilation. The woman
living in the cramped cellar dwelling shown above
has at last surrendered to the pervasive filth: her
dishes, her floor, even her clothes have clearly
gone long unwashed. "From these tenements,"
the outraged photographer wrote, comes
"the vexed question 'Is life worth living?' "*

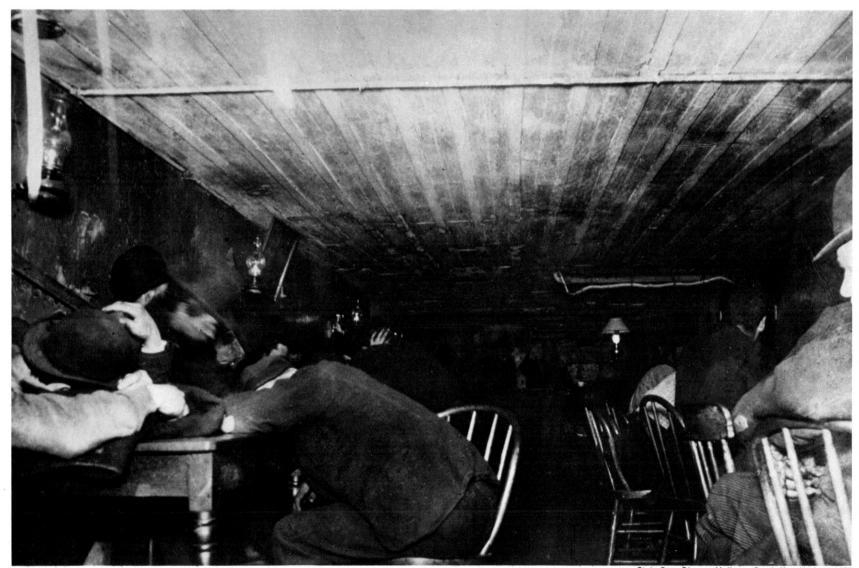

Stale Beer Dive on Mulberry Bend, New York, c. 1890

The infamous Bend—which Riis located "where
Mulberry Street crooks like an elbow"—had a
shockingly high crime rate, some of it emanating
from all-night restaurants like this one, where the
homeless could nap over stale beer, and where
the owner was usually beholden to a political
boss. Of all the changes his pictures effected, Riis
was perhaps proudest of reforming the Bend.

53

Vocational School on West 52nd Street, New York, c. 1894

A simple photograph of children jammed in a classroom obviously meant for half their number becomes a plea for better schools. Then as now, a chance for a decent education, even a measure of vocational training, seemed the best hope for the younger generation to escape the slums.

Night School in Seventh Avenue Lodging House, date unknown

*Night-school students, at a class after working
all day, often found it difficult to pay attention.
Though such situations were hardly ideal,
the reformer-photographer agreed that night
schools, such as those provided by the Children's
Aid Society, were better than no schooling at all.*

Lewis Hine: Abolishing Child Labor

With Lewis Hine, documentary photography moved out of the slums of New York and across the country—wherever contemporary reform movements led the way. One of Hine's major preoccupations was the abuses of child labor, and he documented this widespread evil to provide photographic evidence for the reformers to circulate and to take into the lobbies of state legislatures. To do so he left a position as a science teacher in a New York private school. But he still regarded himself a teacher—and thought of the magazine-reading public as his class.

Unlike Jacob Riis, who considered himself primarily a reporter and who used his pictures solely to supplement his written reportage, Hine relied chiefly on the camera to communicate his message and wrote very little once he had left the classroom. "If I could tell the story in words," he said, "I wouldn't have to lug a camera."

When the National Child Labor Committee enlisted Hine in its crusade in 1908, there was some legislation to protect children from exploitation, but the laws were few, weak and not vigorously enforced. Children worked in coal mines *(opposite);* in West Virginia, for example, they toiled from 7 a.m. to 5:30 p.m., breathing noxious coal gas and in constant danger from rolling rail cars. In the Southern cotton mills they worked even longer, from 6 a.m. until 6 p.m., and were sometimes mutilated by dangerous machinery (whose placards of safety cautions they usually could not read). It was not that all child labor

resulted from insufficient legislation or lack of law enforcement. Sometimes a foreman was inclined to wink at the law because the child's parents—often impoverished immigrants—could not survive unless every member of the family was at work earning at least a few pennies a day.

The job Hine assigned himself was formidable. He often had to overcome the hostility of owners, foremen and guards in factories. Sometimes he got by the gates only by posing as an insurance salesman or a fire inspector. Once inside, he had to make friends with the children to get them to talk while he surreptitiously took notes (he used the buttons on his vest to estimate the child's height). One of his biggest problems was to keep the children at ease even when startled by a burst of magnesium flashlight powder. Somehow, between 1908 and 1921, Hine made 5,000 pictures for the National Child Labor Committee, and the pathetic little drudges he portrayed in factories and mines, mills and tenements, bowling alleys and city streets, persuaded the voting public and legislators of the urgent need for reform.

Not all of Hine's purpose was exposé. During World War I the Red Cross hired him to document its efforts to help war victims—and hence persuade the public of the need for support. The Red Cross later gave him a similar assignment at home. In the performance of that task *(pages 64-65)* Hine turned documentary photography from muckraking to a new and positive role.

Breaker boys—who separated by hand the ▶ useless slate from a mine's yield of coal—gather for Hine's camera before the entrance to a Pennsylvania coal shaft. By the time this picture was taken, many states had laws prohibiting mine operators from hiring boys under 14, but some foremen took them as young as six. At whatever age, the children worked adult hours. Pictures such as this helped point to the evils of child labor, prompting enforcement of laws already on the books and enactment of better ones.

Breaker Boys, Pennsylvania, c. 1910

Messenger Boy, Indianapolis, 1908

*In 1908 this night messenger boy was at work
at 10 p.m. The National Child Labor Committee
claimed that "the messenger's cap is an open
sesame to the underworld." It "enables him to
get liquor at illegal hours or to procure
opium . . . where plain citizens would be refused."*

Newsboy, Washington, D.C., 1912

Children as young as five frequently hawked newspapers, and the photographer reported: "I found them wandering about until 1:00 and 2:00 a.m." Even by daylight the job was dangerous. Opposition newspapers sometimes paid older bullies to harass the little peddlers.

Pin Boys in a Bowling Alley, 1910

◄ The hour was 3 a.m. when these boys were photographed at work in a bowling alley. Three pin boys were kept out of the picture by the boss, presumably because they were even younger.

A casualty of a mill accident, this one-armed boy gamely posed for Hine in about 1910. "We don't have many accidents," one foreman said at the time. "Once in a while a finger is mashed or a foot, but it doesn't amount to anything."

Victim of a Mill Accident, c. 1910

Family Making Garters at Home, c. 1910

Some 13,000 tenement houses in New York City were licensed by the state as places where families could manufacture small articles on a piecework basis. But there were also many unlicensed premises, such as the one at left, where young and old labored day and night to earn less than 10 cents an hour making such things as the sock garters this family is producing. A New York State survey in 1912 found that 25 per cent of those working at home were under 10 years old; 45 per cent of them were under 14.

This youngster in soiled work apron and bare feet, leaning on a thread-spinning frame in a North Carolina cotton mill, was one of approximately 40,000 children under the age of 16 employed in the cotton mills. Despite photographs like this, efforts to legislate reform met resistance. One state officer explained: "The cotton mill people are the poorest paid workers in the country. They have to put their children in the mills."

Spinner at Frame, North Carolina, 1908

63

Parisian Child, 1918

Childish cheer in the midst of disaster—a grinning girl among World War I refugees in Paris— made a touching portrait. Pictures like this were used by the Red Cross to encourage donations.

Documenting the work of the Red Cross closer to home, Hine photographed victims of a drought in Kentucky during the 1930s. He found this young man perched on a school bench, holding a milk bottle given him by the Red Cross.

Undernourished Child, Kentucky, 1933

65

The FSA: Crisis on the Farm

By the 1930s the camera had proved itself a valuable weapon in the reformers' battles against the evils of city slums and child labor. Now came the greatest challenge of all: the Depression. This time, with the nation's entire economic structure in deep trouble, the impetus for reform came from the government itself.

The economic blight of the Depression struck rural America with extra force because it was intensified by a devastating natural blight: drought and dust storms followed the collapse in the market for agricultural products. To help meet the crisis on the farms—on which 33 million Americans, a quarter of the population, lived in 1935—President Franklin D. Roosevelt appointed Rexford Guy Tugwell, a Columbia University economics professor, Assistant Secretary of Agriculture. Tugwell's aid to the farmers included low-interest loans and outright subsidies. The subsidy program was expensive and controversial, and Tugwell realized that photographs could help prove both the extent of the problem and the effectiveness of the cure. To direct the procurement of the pictures he recruited a former protegé named Roy Stryker.

Tugwell's choice was a stroke of genius. As a young economics instructor at Columbia, Stryker had enlivened his classes with photographs, using them to make urban students see the reality behind facts and figures on crops and acreage. In Washington he applied a similar technique. Although his job was only to record the activities of a single branch of the Department of Agriculture, the Resettlement Administration (later the Farm Security Administration), he left behind a collection of pictures that has become a classic archive of documentary photography.

No photographer himself, Stryker recruited a remarkable band of young talents, only a few of whom can be represented in the gallery following. And he exercised his considerable gift for teaching, instructing and cajoling to transform them into anthropologists, economists and historians, as well as reporters and commentators. Carl Mydans, one of that now-famous group, recalls his discussion with Stryker before his first assignment, a trip into the Deep South. Stryker asked casually, "What do you know about cotton?" Mydans replied that he did not know much. "And we sat down and we talked almost all day about cotton," Mydans remembers. "We went to lunch and we went to dinner, and we talked well into the night. We talked about cotton as an agricultural product, the history of cotton in the South, what cotton did to the history of the U.S.A. and how it affected areas outside the U.S.A. By the end of that evening, I was ready to go off and photograph cotton."

Although Stryker and his photographers were accused of boondoggling, the pictures fulfilled the government's initial aims, by documenting both the need for the farm relief programs and their ultimate success. For photography the pictures did far more. They were not only eloquent records but such compelling works of art that they drew public attention to a form of photography that had been taken for granted. They were the first documentary photographs to be known as such; thus the FSA men and women who made them were the first people ever called documentary photographers.

The unrelenting realism that became a hallmark ▶ of FSA photographs is plain in every detail of this fact-crammed picture of an Alabama sharecropper's family: shoeless feet; tattered, dirty clothing; a peeling bedstead supporting a rumpled bed; a bare and cracked floor. Touches of sad beauty, such as the eyes of the young girl, gave such scenes the power to shock America with the plight of "one third of a nation." But they also offered desperately needed reassurance. For in the midst of misery this photograph finds strength: eager-faced boy, steely-eyed grandmother, even grim-faced father and mother proclaiming an unconquerable will to survive.

WALKER EVANS: *Alabama*, 1936

Walker Evans

Kitchen Wall, Hale County, Alabama, 1936

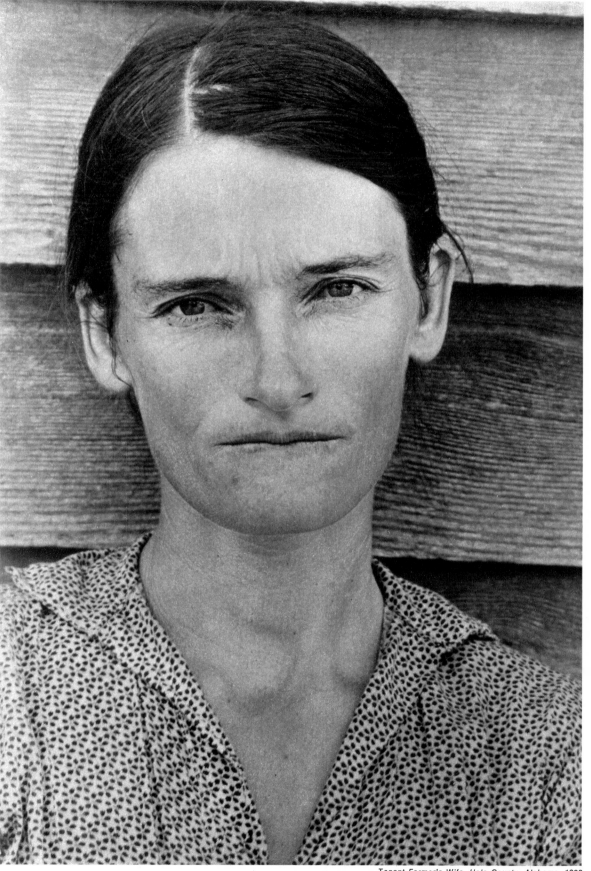

The least sentimental and in terms of the art of photography the most influential of all the FSA photographers was Walker Evans. Among other things, Evans helped set the FSA style of documentary simplicity and directness. One of his favorite subjects was architecture; but whether the subject was a peeling billboard, a cabin wall *(left)* or a family group *(page 67),* his photographs resemble still lifes.

Evans is a symbolist: he makes the temporal seem eternal and the specific seem general. In his days with the FSA team he achieved his effects—strikingly spare and stunningly textured—by shooting head on, rarely from an angle, and by using an 8 x 10 view camera set at a small aperture, which gave his pictures amazingly fine detail and crisp focus that conveyed coldly sharp realism. Evans was the only FSA photographer who regularly used such a large negative size, and although others emulated his style, none quite duplicated the effect. Even after the passage of a generation has obscured the wounds of the Depression, Walker Evans' pictures of the most wretched subject matter still have a starkly evocative beauty.

◄ *Making the most of the fine detail that is attainable only with a large view camera set at a small aperture, the photographer recorded the spare beauty of line and texture on this rude cabin wall, where a tenant farmer's wife has hung her meager assortment of kitchen utensils against the rough splintered boards.*

A cotton farmer's wife stands before her tenant cabin like a specimen pinned to a wooden wall, her bleak and immobile stare fixed on the photographer's camera—as though her miseries had rendered her incapable of expression.

Tenant Farmer's Wife, Hale County, Alabama, 1936

Mealtime, Forrest City, Arkansas, 1937

Empty plates clasped by anonymous hands in a jammed queue speak tersely of hunger in a time of disaster. The figures, waiting for food at a camp for flood refugees, are reminders of the persistent paradox of scarcity in the land of plenty.

Street Scene, Atlanta, Georgia, 1936

In an acid comment by Evans on the gap between reality and the American dream, two bleakly similar houses on a dreary Atlanta street form a backdrop for billboard promises of celluloid romance. The irony is heightened by one billboard showing a current movie star, Carole Lombard, with the blackened eye her role called for.

Ben Shahn

FSA Rehabilitation Clients, Boone County, Arkansas, 1935

Ben Shahn came to the FSA through a side door. A renowned painter, he was contributing paintings and posters to the FSA, and was lured into Roy Stryker's orbit partly because he had once shared a studio with Walker Evans and partly because he had found the camera useful as an instant sketch pad.

For the FSA, Shahn took a three-month excursion through the South and Southwest and returned so excited by photography that he thought of making it his life's work. He did not, but after he returned to painting, he acknowledged that his FSA experience with the camera influenced his later art. His photography also made a great contribution to the FSA, for his painter's conception made many of his photographs persuasive works of art.

Framed by the spare lines of the cabin that seem to indicate the limits of their life, an Arkansas farm woman and her daughter (above) seem to be stopped in motion, yet with nowhere to go.

In another example of life suddenly frozen into ▶ immobility, the artist-photographer caught this couple and child as they passed in front of a soda fountain. The family is arrested in one of those moments of uneasiness so characteristic of the depressed times when even the Sunday best that should bespeak confidence and tranquillity could not mask fear of the future.

Man, Woman and Child, Smithland, Kentucky, 1935

73

Cotton Pickers at Work, Pulaski County, Arkansas, 1935

*The artist's eye spotted these sacks as they trailed
like regal trains behind the cotton pickers,
who, painfully stooped, trudged up and down along
the rows to gather the harvest for wages
that sometimes were as low as 45 cents a day.*

Cotton Pickers, Pulaski County, Arkansas, 1935

*Warily confronting the camera, cotton pickers are
photographed against the rough backdrop of
a wooden shed. Shahn used to meet the workers
at 5:30 in the morning, photograph them
during their long working day, and then drive
them to the company store where, he recalled,
they would buy soft drinks and "drink up
in one sweep one-quarter of their earnings."*

75

Sharecroppers' Children on Sunday, Little Rock, Arkansas, 1935

Sunday clothes sharpen the message of poverty conveyed by the warped boards of the cabin and the splintery, rickety bench. Yet there is art as well as social significance in Shahn's picture. The range of facial expressions and bodily contours is united by the classical triangular composition in which the family have arranged themselves.

A woman and a girl waiting in line for relief ▶ payments outside an office in Urbana, Ohio, look in different directions, pointing up a series of opposites: age and youth, contemplation and observation. Yet they are drawn together in their common engagement, waiting for the relief money that will keep them alive through jobless times.

On Relief, Urbana, Ohio, 1938

77

Dorothea Lange

Of all the photographers who served the Farm Security Administration, none had a greater effect than Dorothea Lange, a petite woman with a soft voice that could scarcely be heard across a room. In the earliest days of the FSA, Roy Stryker saw a portfolio of her pictures of migrant farm laborers in California; they moved him to hire her forthwith. As a consummate artist she served thereafter as an exemplar for many other FSA photographers.

Dorothea Lange's pictures had an epic quality, with an added human and almost romantic vitality. Her subjects came alive; even her landscapes were vivid reminders of the sufferings of the human tenants who had given up and fled the worn-out acres. And if ever photographs succeeded at persuasion, Dorothea Lange's did; her pictures of farmers made homeless by the dust storms, for example, are credited with being largely responsible for the government's setting up camps for the migrants in 1935.

A tobacco sharecropper in Georgia looks up from his task of patching an inner tube, while his children wait to get moving again. Like a migrant laborer, a tenant farmer found a car important to his work—without it, he couldn't get his crop to market—but much of his time was spent fixing it.

Seemingly impassive as stone monuments, ▶ members of a gang of migrant laborers bend to a crop of lettuce in a posture they maintained all day long. But the physical torment so graphically rendered in this picture is only part of its subject, for it also celebrates the durability of spirit that enabled people to survive under such conditions.

Sharecropper and Family, Georgia, 1938

Lettuce Cutters, Salinas Valley, California, 1935

Child and Her Mother, Washington State, 1939

A forlorn child leans against barbed wire on the Yakima Valley farm where her family subsists with government aid, while her mother watches her from behind the fencing that separates them from the world outside. Federal loans helped such families buy seed, stock and fertilizer.

Behind another barbed-wire fence (right), no ▶ longer serving its purpose, the parched Dust Bowl stretches beyond empty buildings to the horizon. Photographer Lange managed to convey as poignant a message in this lifeless scene as in the picture of mother and daughter above.

Portrait of the Dust Bowl, Texas, 1938

Russell Lee

Mother and Child, Oklahoma, 1939

A small girl watches with tender concern as her sick mother, a farm laborer, lies down to rest on a stony patch of ground. The poignant scene gains much of its realism and immediacy from the harsh lighting, deliberately created with a flash bulb.

To the technical skill, artistry and compassion that had enriched the FSA pictures, Russell Lee added another value. He recognized the need for communication between groups of Americans separated by social class and geography, and he possessed the depth of human understanding to make photographs that filled that need. "America was very provincial in those days," he said. "City people didn't know about people living in the country; rural people didn't know about the city. One of our jobs was to acquaint city dwellers with the rural way of life."

To that task Lee brought a journalist's eye for the significant and a tongue for friendly persuasion. When a woman in the Midwest resisted his efforts to photograph her, he told her reassuringly: "Lady, you're having a hard time, and a lot of people don't think you're having such a hard time. We want to show them that you're a human being, a nice human being, but you're having troubles." Lee got not only the pictures he set out after, but others of several of her friends—and invitations to share their meager meals. Such understanding enabled Lee to get some of the most revealing and poignant studies of rural America made in the '30s.

A stolid farm mother permits a glimpse into a bitter life as she stands in her cabin doorway, holding her crying infant while an older child looks on from the emptiness of their poor home.

Sharecropper's Wife and Children, Missouri, 1938

Fourth of July Picnic, Vale, Oregon, 1941

Lee found this family celebrating America's
birthday with a quiet but crowded outing in a park.
Here, cut off from other celebrants by parked
cars, the mother serves up a homemade picnic
to her brood while the father smokes in silence.

The Photo League **3**

"A True Image of the World" 88

Sol Libsohn 90

Walter Rosenblum 92

Sid Grossman 94

Jerome Liebling 96

Jack Manning 98

Morris Huberland 100

Aaron Siskind 102

Ruth Orkin 104

Eliot Elisofon 106

Arthur Leipzig 108

Morris Engel 110

Dan Weiner 112

Lou Bernstein 114

Bill Witt 116

Lester Talkington 118

SID GROSSMAN: *San Gennaro Festival,* 1949

"A True Image of the World"

In 1928, the year before the stock market crashed and the Great Depression began to spread over the country, a group of New York City motion-picture and still photographers formed an organization called the Film and Photo League. Their major aim was to record events of social significance that were often not reported in the commercial press: street demonstrations against unemployment and for home relief and, since much of their work was commissioned by unions, labor strife—strikes, picket lines, clashes between police and pickets. In 1936 the motion-picture men broke away from the group, some going on to produce documentary films, others continuing to make newsreels. The rest renamed themselves the Photo League and based their documentary work on a broadly conceived credo. It read in part:

"Photography has tremendous social value. Upon the photographer rests the responsibility and duty of recording a true image of the world as it is today. . . . The Photo League [works] in keeping with the traditions set by Stieglitz, Strand, Abbott and Weston. Photography has long suffered . . . from the stultifying influence of the pictorialists. . . . The Photo League's task is to put the camera back in the hands of honest photographers, who will use it to photograph America."

Though hampered by a lack of money (some League members were still in school, others held low-paying clerical jobs, a few eked out a living photographing for merchandise catalogues), they scraped together the rent for a loft, which they remodeled to serve as exhibition room, lecture hall, classroom and darkroom all in one. They approached such big-name photographers as Paul Strand, Berenice Abbott and Margaret Bourke-White to form a board of advisers. Their spirit was infectious, and the big names consented. Encouraged, the youngsters began persuading other members of the photographic elite—Roy Stryker, Edward Weston, Robert Capa, Dorothea Lange—to speak at the League and to allow their work to be exhibited there. Soon they began issuing a monthly mimeographed bulletin, "Photo Notes," devoted to documentary photography. It contained original articles, reviews of current shows and reprints of essays on the subject, as well as news of League events. Distributed free to galleries, museums and photographers, "Photo Notes" had wide influence and drew more members into the League, where for no charge they could hear and interview such professionals as Henri Cartier-Bresson, Ansel Adams or Lewis Hine. After Hine died in 1940, most of his work was given to the League.

A major part of the League was its school, where students were taught the history, techniques and esthetics of photography. Just as membership dues were kept low (seven dollars a year), the school's tuition was about $30 for a 12-session semester, and no one was turned away for lack of funds. Probably the school's most important course was a workshop on documentary photography taught by the late Sid Grossman *(pages 94-95),* a gifted if controversial instructor. Former League members describe him as "brilliant," "a man you either loved or hated," "authoritarian and demanding but at the same time a sentimentalist," "rough on everybody but underneath gentle." His analyses of students' work could be abrasive, and some students weathered only one class, but a survivor expresses the graduates' general opinion: "Grossman excited you about photography; he was a great teacher."

The workshop developed group projects that sent students out to photograph the neighborhoods of Manhattan, for, as a publicity pamphlet put it, "The streets of New York . . . are the League's most important studios." Many of the students were city born and bred, many knew the tenement areas first hand, and they brought the insider's sensitivity to bear on their work. From these projects came the Photo League Documents: series of pictures that interpreted photographically the people of certain areas—Pitt Street, Chelsea, Park Avenue, Harlem—and their way of life.

During World War II, though most of its members were in the armed forces overseas, the League produced documentary photographs for the Red Cross and servicemen's organizations. By 1947 the organization could boast that more than 1,500 photographers had been trained in its school and darkrooms. Money was always in short supply, but at the end of that year, after strenuous fund-raising, the group had substantially more than 100 members and was preparing to move to larger quarters in the basement of a Greenwich Village hotel. Then an event occurred that stunned its membership: in December the Photo League appeared on a list, issued by Attorney General Tom Clark, of organizations the Department of Justice had found to be subversive to the United States. The League was shocked; it categorically denied the charge of disloyalty, describing itself as "a photographic and not a political organization." Membership took a sudden leap, as photographers from as far away as California rallied to the League's support; and for a time things went well. But in May 1949, a former member, testifying at a trial of Communist leaders, implied that the League was a Communist-front organization. The League challenged anyone to "present an iota of evidence to prove our activities as subversive," and reiterated its stand that it was a purely photographic group. By this time, however, political tensions brought about by the Cold War had increased, and some League members, facing serious professional ostracism, felt compelled to resign. Young people, more affluent than the League generation had been and with a variety of photographic schools to choose from, did not replace the members who left. By 1951 the Photo League had ceased to exist. The essay that follows presents the work of some of its members, along with their comments about the League and the influential documentary photography it produced.   □

Washington's Birthday, 1940

"These pictures," explains Sol Libsohn, a leader in the Photo League from its early days, "combine two ideas we had—one, that by its nature the camera actually sees more sharply than the eye, and that this quality of the medium should not be discarded lightly as we believed the pictorialists had done. And secondly, that unless you feel an involvement with people, with the human condition, you should not photograph them at all. I took the one above at a holiday sale at a large department store in Manhattan. They were selling radios for a penny, things like that. I was struck by the visual juxtaposition of these people, strangers, closed in against each other for warmth against the chill February air. They were there for bargains, but what fascinated me was an instinct I had that they really seemed to need something completely different, something spiritual, even if they didn't know it.

"The picture on the right was taken on the Lower East Side. I had a deep interest in the ordinary people who lived there then, and when I saw that group I was overcome by another feeling I often have: that streets are like stage settings, and sometimes you can catch people on those stages in very penetrating tableaux."

Rivington Street, 1945

Walter Rosenblum

Pitt Street, 1939

"The Photo League had a community darkroom, and that's why I joined," says Walter Rosenblum. "I had learned photography at a Boys' Club, and when I started going to college at night in 1937, I heard about this group that charged a small membership fee and whose members had access to a darkroom that was always open. The equipment was old but serviceable; you paid 10 cents for the chemicals and supplied your own paper. There were always other people working, and I got to know them and began taking classes and doing odd jobs, and finally I was hired as office secretary for $10 a week. I found teachers, took registration, collected dues, arranged exhibits. I was there all the time—it became my life. Later I became editor of 'Photo Notes' and was president of the League for several terms between 1941 and 1948.

"The picture at left was part of my Pitt Street Document, done for a workshop conducted by Sid Grossman. I took pictures of the kids who hung around the candy store on the Lower East Side block for six months, so I knew them pretty well, including this boy. I made his portrait with an old hand-held folding view camera called a Maximar that is no longer manufactured. I wanted to express the strength of character in his face, the toughness his spirit had developed, growing up among those tenements in the background. The Puerto Rican girls at right are from a series I did on 105th Street in Spanish Harlem. It was an off-the-cuff shot with an early Nikon. I didn't know them, but they were such beautiful youngsters—one about eight and the other around 15—that when I saw them I was instantly captivated."

105th Street, 1946

Sid Grossman was 21 years old, fresh out of City College of New York and working as a pick-and-shovel man on a Works Progress Administration street-repair crew in 1936, when he joined and helped reorganize the Photo League. He later became the director of the Photo League School, whose aim he said was "to help the student to develop a personal approach to photography . . . to make his individual interpretations of his immediate world."

Grossman applied this aim in his own photographs of such familiar subjects as the Coney Island bathers shown on these pages. His style, recalls a former League member, "was really revolutionary at the time. Sid was one of the first photographers to chop off pieces of bodies—heads and arms and legs. He would practically get on top of the subject, moving up to what seemed like only a few inches away. It was as if he couldn't get close enough to what he was trying to say." In the picture at lower right, he seems to have joined the tangle of merrymakers, to have gotten so intimate that he is one of them and they are no longer aware of his camera.

Grossman, who died in 1955, once said, "The function of the photographer is to help people understand the world about them." He would ask his students if they ever took pictures just for themselves. He would answer for them: "No, you don't," and add that he did not himself, "though I have boxes of pictures that nobody wants to buy. . . . I know the time will come that they will be usable and I will have won."

Coney Island, 1947-1948

Jerome Liebling

East Side Windows, 1948

"I was about 22, a World War II vet studying photography on the GI Bill at Brooklyn College in 1947 when my teacher, Walter Rosenblum, suggested I join the Photo League," Jerome Liebling recalls. "Since I was a city boy I liked the League idea of going into the streets to photograph New York.

"I took the picture at left with a 2¼ x 2¼ Super Ikonta B, a camera with a convenient eye-level rangefinder viewer, when I revisited my old East Side neighborhood. It was changing and becoming an artists'-colony extension of Greenwich Village, but I managed to find this view of the traditional tenement architecture and the woman in the classical tenement-dweller's pose —leaning out of the window to get some air and to watch the life going on in the street.

"In 1949 I was in Paul Strand's class at the Photo League, where we documented the area near Knickerbocker Village, a Manhattan housing project that had been built in 1934 on the site of a notorious slum. By the time we photographed it 15 years later, new decay was evident. By shooting this youngster *[right]* without much environmental detail, I wanted to invite the viewer's sympathetic interest in him, from his curious gaze to his gracefully crossed hands to the poverty betrayed by his cheaply made, broken shoes."

Knickerbocker Village, 1949

Jack Manning

Boy with Cymbals, 1938

"The Photo League was a few blocks from the high school I went to in 1937, so I used to visit their exhibits," says Jack Manning, now a photographer for *The New York Times.* "I had a Rollei and I had begun to teach myself photography. One day I showed Aaron Siskind some of my pictures, and he invited me to join the League's Harlem Document group *[pages 102, 110],* which he headed. You had to know your craft for that project because you went out and worked on your own. I was with the project for two years and I liked it so well that in my spare time I still shoot the same kind of documentaries—I've done them on the slums of Puerto Rico, on the Puerto Ricans in New York City and on the people of Spain.

"The picture at left was part of a series I took of 20 kids at a settlement house in Harlem who were forming a band. The one at right was taken on an Easter Sunday—I approached the young lady and told her about the Document project and then asked her if I could take her picture, and she was very willing to pose for me.

"I learned from the League that a documentary photographer has to be technically good enough so that he can concentrate on content, in order to make honest statements with his camera that will serve to help people. The critics disparaged us by calling us the Ashcan School of Photography—but I liked the title, and was happy to be identified as an Ashcan photographer."

Easter Sunday in Harlem, 1938

Three Women, 1955

Morris Huberland says: "When I joined the Photo League around 1940, LIFE and *Look* magazines were developing the photo essay, and I went to the League to hear photojournalists like Eliot Elisofon lecture on this new form.

"Of all the activities at the League, the esthetic criticism at the symposiums was most important to me. The talk was broadly based; we knew the history of photography, and we studied the nature pictures done by Edward Weston and Ansel Adams as well as the documentary work of Atget *(pages 36-42)* and Lewis Hine *(pages 56-65)*.

"I define documentary photography as an expression of how people relate to their environment. I easily identified with the street documentaries I saw at the League, for I had pictures like that in my own files. I had been brought to New York as a child from Germany and was a product of the ghetto, and what I loved about the city was that it was a series of ethnic neighborhoods, each with its distinct flavor. I roamed those neighborhoods, photographing the various national groups. In the early days I used a somewhat bulky Voigtlander-Avis view camera. But for street pictures I switched to smaller cameras when they became available since they made it easier to capture the passing moment. A Rollei took the picture of the boy at right in Hell's Kitchen, a predominantly Irish area—his extraordinarily expressive eyes made him stand out from the other kids. I used the even smaller 35mm Pentax to take the picture at left of Puerto Rican women in Spanish Harlem. Just as I snapped the shutter, the girl in the middle noticed me and became perplexed. But I chatted with them and we parted friends."

City Boy, 1948

Aaron Siskind

Harlem Cabaret, 1938

"I was a schoolteacher who used to take pictures as a hobby with a little 12-dollar camera in 1932 when I went to an exhibit at the old Film and Photo League, and the pictures of men made homeless by the Depression stirred me," Aaron Siskind remembers. "So I joined and some years later organized the Feature Group, where rank beginners went out to document city areas. A black journalist suggested we do a study of Harlem, and that's how the Harlem Document came about.

"I went out just as the others did, even though I was directing the project. These pictures were taken with a 40-dollar Voigtlander-Avis camera and two lights set on stands. The shot on the left was made at a little nightclub—in those hard times there were very few customers and those few were white. The picture at right was at the Savoy Ballroom, where every night for 50 cents people could shag and stomp to two dance bands. I set up my gear on the edge of the floor and then I induced this couple to dance into the area.

"To me documentary photography means making a picture so that the viewer doesn't think about the man who made the picture. At its esthetic core is a very old tradition in art: naturalism. And its purpose is to document all facets of social relationships."

Dancers at the Savoy Ballroom, 1937

Summer Afternoon in the Slums, 1948

104

Ruth Orkin's connection with the Photo League was formalized by politics. She recalls: "I had been going to forums at the League for quite a while, but I became an actual member as an act of principle, two weeks after the Attorney General's list *[page 89]* came out. I never took any classes—that was a good thing about the League, it wasn't strictly classroom. It was also someplace for photographers to get together and learn from each other informally, like cafés in European cities where artists meet to keep up with what's going on. To me, documentary photography is what's real. And reality is what moves people in the long run.

"This picture is a study of the bleak, decaying streets in an old section of Greenwich Village. The building on the left, a warehouse, was clattering with noise all the time. The street wasn't well paved—the cobblestones went back to the 18th Century and the dirt lodged between them. In the right background is a wholesale meat market, which added to the street litter.

"I took the picture just as a gust of wind came up and blew grit swirling around the people who were sunning themselves on the corner. They were Polish and Irish, very poor, who lived there. It was a neighborhood that was always alive with people, even in the midst of the dirt and decay."

Eliot Elisofon

Third Avenue Elevated, 1936

Eliot Elisofon, once president of the Photo League, remembers these pictures as being "made at a time when I was learning how to record the New York scene—what it looked like, where the people were. It was a way of saying, 'This is New York.' I took both of them with a 3¼ x 4¼ Speed Graphic, a slightly smaller version of the hand-held view camera press photographers then used, and in this picture *[left]* what interested me was the design that the structure of the elevated lent itself to. There was also the repetition of the words of the toothpaste ad under each step—in themselves the words were almost meaningless, but the pattern they formed reinforced the design.

"What fascinated me about the shoe-shine man *[right]* was the fact that he had printed the passages from the Bible letter by letter with rubber stamps. He was a man of deep religious feeling, and he had put his message in the window of his booth for everyone to read.

"I came to the Photo League around 1935, after I had been photographing for a year or two. I wanted to learn formal technique combined with meaningful subject matter—social conditions interested me. I remember there were all kinds of heated discussions about technique and craftsmanship as well as esthetics. In retrospect I suppose we were pretty square, but we were just trying to say something with a camera."

Shoeshine Man, 1936

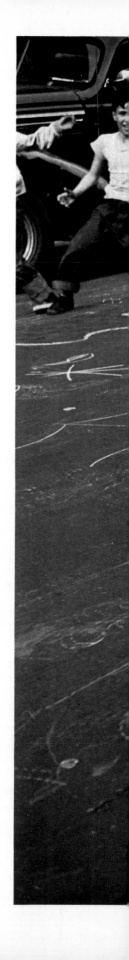

Watching Santa, 1944

"I took these pictures of kids in Brooklyn, where I was born and brought up," says Arthur Leipzig. "To make the one above, I stood inside a store window, hidden behind a Christmas display, and shot the kids looking through the window at a mechanical Santa Claus. The one at right is from a series on street games in the city. My inspiration was a picture by Pieter Bruegel, the Flemish painter, called 'Children's Games.' It shows scores of half-grown kids, playing some 80 different games. Some of them, I found as I wandered around, were still being played today, even though the painting was done in 1560.

But mainly I noticed that poor kids in urban areas have their imaginations and very little else to work with. In this picture, the kids had some chalk, so they made up chalk games.

"I wouldn't label my work documentary," Leipzig says. "I just photograph the way I feel—but the League helped me to learn to do that." He joined the Photo League as a beginning photographer in 1942, attracted by its low fees. He recalls: "Two weeks in Sid Grossman's class, and I knew what I wanted to be. Six months later I got a job as a newspaper photographer, but I stayed in the League till around 1949."

Chalk Games, 1943

When Brooklyn-born Morris Engel was 18, in 1936, he noticed a Photo League advertisement in a newspaper. Learning photography sounded interesting; he decided to join and enrolled in the six-dollar course, a bargain even in that Depression year.

Once he had learned some of the basics of picture-taking, Engel joined several other young photographers in the Photo League Feature Group. Headed by Aaron Siskind [pages 102-103], the group first turned its attention to Harlem and produced what came to be called the Harlem Document. Engel recalls that at the time he had a job in a bank and was able to do photography only on weekends. He tramped around Harlem on Sundays, shooting roll after roll of film with his Rolleiflex. The picture at right of a Harlem candy and newspaper vendor staring out of a cluttered street-corner stand became part of the completed Document.

Engel also worked on another project known as "Park Avenue North and South." Park Avenue was sharply divided at 96th Street; to the north were slums, to the south an elegant residential area. The picture at left, taken well south of this dividing line, shows not only the nature of that well-to-do part of New York, but also captures a subtle relationship of individuals.

Park Avenue, South, 1938

Harlem Merchant, 1937

Street Procession, 1947

"These are photographs I feel I must do," Dan Weiner once said. "I'm interested in . . . how people live and in finding out how they are adjusting to the whole question of urbanization and industrialization."

The pictures on these pages were taken in New York City's Little Italy during the street festival held each September to mark the feast day of San Gennaro, patron saint of Naples. Weiner showed the people of the area celebrating in a manner that had withstood not only the pressures of the urban and industrial society they lived in, but also the drive for "Americanization" that has caused many Old World customs to die out among immigrant groups. At left, members of a fraternal society march beside a float bearing a figure of the saint; dollar bills for charity, passed up by the crowd, have been pinned to the figure. In the light-festooned street *(right),* throngs listening to a singer reflect a never-satisfied longing for the Old Country.

Weiner joined the Photo League before World War II as a self-taught photographer, and for several years taught a course for advanced students. On a magazine assignment in Kentucky in 1959, he was killed in a plane crash.

Street Festival, 1947

Man and Wife, 1941

Shortly after Lou Bernstein took up photography as a hobby he joined a camera club, but "their outlook was too pedagogical," he says, "so I tried the Photo League instead. I thought of photography as a means of self-expression and the League's philosophy suited me because it emphasized the expression of personal viewpoints, even in the photographs we took of social conditions. I think that's an attitude that is missing in almost all of the photography schools today; there should be an institution that encourages young photographers to express themselves."

The picture at left is of a Brooklyn building superintendent and his wife, who were acquaintances of Bernstein. He says of it, "I think the man's attitude tells something about how we cherish a person who is close to us, but at the same time I had the feeling he was flaunting himself." The picture at right was taken at Coney Island. Bernstein had been "watching how this baby was playing with her father, showing respect for him one moment and taking advantage of him the next, the way babies sometimes do. Here she's taken him by surprise, and gotten the upper hand for a second. I think pictures often reveal motives we don't even know about ourselves in our relationships with people—but exactly what they are is not for me to say; it's for each viewer to decide for himself."

Coney Island, 1943

115

Rose Laible, 1947

Around 1940, when Bill Witt was working as a photographer in a New York City studio, one of his coworkers, Dan Weiner *(pages 112-113),* brought him into the League. "Except for my four years in the service," says Witt, "I stayed in the League until 1949. I even taught a course in advanced technique for one semester after the war. The League meant different things to different people. For me, it was the only photographic group at the time that was producing meaningful pictures. I liked the FSA photographers *[Chapter 2],* and I felt that the League was trying to document the East as the FSA had documented the Dust Bowl.

"But I liked to photograph all aspects of life around me, and I was always more interested in esthetics than were many of the people in the League. I remember at the time of a big Photo League show in 1949 I had become interested in nature and abstract photography. I had some pictures of that type in the show, and they raised eyebrows.

"I used a Rollei to take this picture of my grandmother poring over the evening news when she was in her seventies. Since she lived downstairs from us in my house in Newark, I was in and out of her apartment—I was interested in recording the surroundings that old people manage to keep around them, like the old-fashioned lamps and tables she had. And she herself was a very interesting, strong person—she had been brought over from Germany as a child in a sailing ship, she married and had two children, and she lived to be 102."

Skipping Rope, 1950

"On my way home from work, I was attracted by the warm, natural joy of this child skipping rope. I sat down in a doorway, which shielded the lens from the sun, and got this shot," says Lester Talkington of the picture at left, taken on a block in Manhattan that borders East Harlem. His camera was a pocket-sized Kodak Vollenda, which he liked because he could carry it around, ready to slip out of his jacket and unfold for candid shots like this one, for which a shutter speed of 1/250 at an aperture of f/8 froze the little girl in mid-air.

A native of Fort Worth, Texas, Talkington began doing photography early, "playing with the family Kodak as a kid." He joined the League in 1947, after his wife, the daughter of a photographer, urged him to develop his craft. In the League he was exposed to "a real wonderful education. Their emphasis was on the documentary, but they didn't *make* you be a documentary photographer. They made you think about what you were doing. I still do documentary work occasionally, but what I get the greatest pleasure out of now is details of nature—like Edward Weston, only I use a 35mm camera and I get something quite different.

"I left the League around 1950 when I moved out of the neighborhood where the meetings were held. By then I had become good enough so that I had to decide whether to give up my job as an ad writer and go into photography full time. Babies were coming, so I stayed with my writing. But the League—they were really great people."

Honoring Humanity 4

A Commitment to Inspire 122

André Kertész 124

Paul Strand 132

Henri Cartier-Bresson 138

Dorothea Lange 146

W. Eugene Smith 154

ANDRÉ KERTÉSZ: *Blind Musician*, 1921

A Commitment to Inspire

To one elite group of documentary photographers, neither the literal reporting of the 19th Century nor the social criticism of the early 20th has sufficed to comment upon the world around them. Their careers extend over some six decades—nearly half the life span of photography itself. They have shared with the photographers in previous chapters the belief that a photograph can convey information accurately and provoke an active response. Yet their goals have been much more ambitious than those of even the most dedicated among their predecessors. Not content to mirror life's passing parade or to lobby through pictures for new laws to relieve poverty and oppression, these documentarians have striven to influence people's basic attitudes. They have hoped that their photographs might end the desire to oppress and exploit, that they might instill tolerance, respect, even love among men.

Five photographers—André Kertész, Paul Strand, Dorothea Lange, Henri Cartier-Bresson and W. Eugene Smith—represent this group on the following pages. All five share lofty human aims, yet each follows a unique approach to documentary photography. Kertész is now recognized as the father of an informal, personal style. It evolved naturally, while he was a very young man, out of his desire to keep a journal of his life. But instead of a pencil and notebook, he used a camera. Every scene he encountered was a subject: people he knew well and people he saw only once, the views he saw daily and the ones he would never see again. The blind violin player on the preceding page is a good example. While visiting a friend outside Budapest, Kertész chanced upon the itinerant musician, who was being led from place to place by his son. Another child, the friend's little boy, approached the pair with childish curiosity, and Kertész recognized the superficially ordinary scene as an extraordinary moment of human confrontation. He never saw the fiddler again, but his instantaneous response provided an inspiring record of gentleness and respect.

In the hands of Paul Strand, the photographing of ordinary people and scenes took on a more aggressive purpose and a stricter discipline. He shares Kertész's view that the world's ordinary people must not be forgotten, but he holds the conviction that they will be destroyed unless they fight those who would exploit them. He uses his camera to aid their cause, whether they be Mexicans, Egyptians, Frenchmen or Hebrideans. With documents of their faces and their works, he seeks to convince the viewer of their dignity and nobility. People in Strand's photographs seem to stare out in defiance of those who would crush them.

Henri Cartier-Bresson acknowledges Kertész as his teacher, and the work of the two men bears a similarity in its concern with every phase of human activity—whether play or work, love or war. But Cartier-Bresson imbues his pictures with a unique sense of time. They record what he calls the decisive moment, the instant when a mood is best expressed. Those shown here are not action pictures, although they may stop some movement of body or hand. What they freeze is attitude, the glance of an eye, the tilt of a head, the twist of a torso—of one person or several in one picture. His genius is to sense when a combination of expressions and postures communicates his message, and in that instant, to record the reality, refined and concentrated, of the pleasures and pains of ordinary experience.

Dorothea Lange, on the other hand, spent little time documenting the ordinary. One day early in the Depression, when she was working as a portrait photographer, she was drawn out of her studio by the realization that "outside the world was just in smithereens." From that day onward, her place was "outside." She used her camera for nearly 30 years to try to pick up the pieces of a shattered world. She deplored the miseries wrought by both men and nature, and her early FSA photographs *(pages 78-81)* were an attempt to combat them. She was most comfortable photographing her fellow Americans, although she seemed to record them most ably when their circumstances were painful. It was mainly in her later years, particularly when chance took her to the Middle and Far East, that she turned her camera on tranquil subjects *(pages 148-149),* but when she did, she extracted the very essence of what was right in the world.

W. Eugene Smith's work combines the elements of the other four photographers. Like Kertész and Cartier-Bresson he is intrigued by every facet of daily life. Like Strand he honors the strength of working people and like Miss Lange he makes documents both to expose ills and to record examples of perfection. But the special factor that marks Smith's photography is its fervent, gripping emotionalism. His pictures always contain (and arouse) powerful—sometimes violent—feelings. In a war scene, the viewer shares Smith's hatred of death and destruction; in a photograph of a doctor, his admiration; in a picture of a young animal, his love of its tenderness and vulnerability. If he could, Smith would expel pain from the life of every creature.

Despite the apparent disparities between these photographers, they are linked by their common belief that documentary photographs can help to bring out the best in people. They may have been the last generation to feel this hope; the photographers who came after them *(Chapter 5)* have chronicled the world from a less sanguine viewpoint. ☐

André Kertész

Quiet Day on the Polish Lines, 1915

As an infantryman in the Hungarian army, Kertész chronicled World War I. Lulls in the fighting, like the one depicted above, spoke most poignantly of the bleakness of soldiers' lives.

As a small boy in Budapest, André Kertész longed to own a camera. Finally, when he was 18, he was able to buy a small box ICA 4.5 x 6cm and with it he kept what he called an "optical diary," a portrait of his world intended for no one's eyes but his own.

This diary is simply a record of scenes—both ordinary and extraordi-nary—that gave character to life in Hungary in the years between 1912 and 1925. Kertész brought to it no train-ing in photography. But perception, cu-riosity, a keen eye for composition and his deep affection for the people and places around him equipped Ker-tész to create a series of documents that are at once vivid and appealing.

Paris Scene, 1929

Without consciously trying, he captured all the sensory elements that make a mood. In his Hungarian photographs the viewer can almost sense the dampness and earthy smell of the air, or the feel of mud rutted by wagon wheels and cobbles made slick by rain.

The basic character of Kertész's early work persisted more or less unchanged after he went to live in Paris in 1925. Places and people, whether famous artist friends or nameless passersby, were still his favorite subjects, and he portrayed them with the same affection that he had his native Hungary. One rule still guided his work—to photograph only what he loved: "If I do not have the contact, I do not touch."

For days the photographer watched this woman feeding stray cats and dogs. She was outraged when she caught him stalking her with his clumsy box camera. Changing tactics, he pursued her again for this picture only when he had a little Leica that escaped her suspicious eye.

Village near Budapest, 1919

Eugene, 1914

The bold light-and-shadow patterns (above) cast
by a street lamp over an empty square at night
caught Kertész's eye. But he felt the picture
needed a dark figure for balance, so he enlisted
his brother Eugene, who held perfectly still for the
three-to-four-minute exposure. The resulting
picture of a man and his shadow as he approaches
the menacing darkness records the essence of
night and solitude in the sleeping city of Budapest.

◄ From atop a steep hill, the photographer studied
the village of Budafok and its means of livelihood.
Softly rounded expanses of turf, covering wine
cellars, seem to cushion the sharp-peaked
houses, while in the distance, parallel cultivated
and fallow fields make stripes down a hillside.

Heading for Esztergom, 1916

*Total grayness deepens the mood of pathos
recorded in this glimpse of a peasant man and his
wife urging their fallen horse to its feet. The
buildings of the medieval town of Esztergom
appear as a faint curtain in the distance.*

Peasant Woman, 1924

In this picture of a peasant woman amid a family of
ducks, the photographer noted a moment of
pastoral peace in the Hungarian countryside. The
sun is warm and the woman, dappled in shade,
smiles with an evident sense of well-being.

Sunday Afternoon, 1916

To fill his optical diary, the photographer cultivated the habit of exploring the villages around Budapest, traveling by slow train. That is how he came to record these farmers in their holiday best, relaxing and swapping stories on a Sunday afternoon as they watch their cattle drinking from a trough in the town square.

"April—that is the fool month, isn't it?" says the photographer of this April day more than a half century ago. Spring had begun and the ground had thawed, when a blizzard flashed out of nowhere. He likens the resulting memento of the storm to an abstract painting because of the interplay of stark-white and deep-black patches.

April 13, 1913

A Woman of Gurna, Egypt, 1959

132

"It is one thing to photograph people," Paul Strand once wrote, "it is another to make others care about them by revealing the core of their humanness." Strand himself is one who cares. He has spent his career documenting the working people of many nations—and revealing in them the nobility that endures despite oppression.

His photographs gain their power from a simplicity as unadorned as the subjects he chooses. It is the product of slow, meticulous working methods; Strand has often been known to take months getting acquainted with a town and its inhabitants even before unpacking his gear. The gear includes large-format cameras and prisms he can attach to their lenses, allowing him to face a subject at right angles, thus going unnoticed as he works. And after his negatives are made, he often works for days on the prints. By experimenting he achieves the balance of richness and delicacy that he deems worthy of the people whose lives he records.

◄ *A nomad woman of stern beauty faces the camera with dignity, conveying by her steady gaze and serene composure the innate strength that Strand finds in human beings everywhere. Photographing such a woman was in itself an achievement, for her Muslim faith not only discourages social exchange between women and strangers but generally disapproves of posing for pictures.*

A tomb boldly painted with a symbolic mosque, which signifies that the deceased completed a pilgrimage to Mecca during his lifetime, documents an aspect of life in Upper Egypt, where people in the simplest village find esthetic expression in paying homage to their dead.

Tomb at Faiyum, Egypt, 1959

Charkieh, Delta Region, 1959

Galia Aitah, Woman of the Delta, 1959

◄ Spindly eucalyptus trees tower above a cluster of sun-dried brick houses at Charkieh, built in the same way that Egyptians have constructed their dwellings since ancient times. It was not history that attracted the photographer, but rather remnants of the past that could be revealed in the life style of present-day Egyptian villagers.

With glistening eyes ringed in kohl—a cosmetic older than Cleopatra—a young woman wears a traditional print dress with her glass earrings and bead necklace. Although the 1952 revolution gave Egyptian women considerable freedom to follow modern styles, most peasants, or fellahin, continue to dress as they have for centuries.

135

A retired fisherman, deprived by old age and failing vision of the dignity of his work, casts a vacant gaze beyond the camera toward the harbor from which he used to sail. The photographer returned to the site two years after recording this poignant scene—and found the grizzled sailor again seated on the same seaside bench, a living monument to the lassitude of old age.

A vineyard laborer in the Cognac district of ▶ France stands up to the camera with the serene gaze that comes from pride of workmanship —seemingly unconscious of the ironic contrast between his threadbare suit and the expensive liqueur his strong hands toil to help make.

Old Sailor, Brittany, France, 1950

Vineyard Laborer, Gondeville, France, 1951

View from Lenin Hills, 1954

138

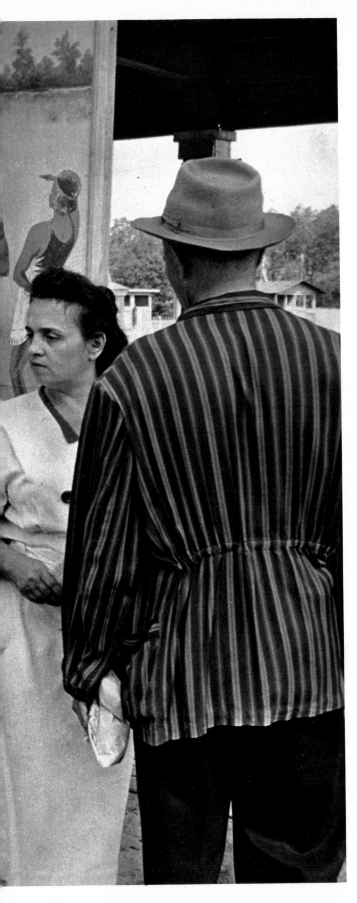

The beach at Silver Forest, in a Moscow suburb, is permeated in this picture by a mood of restrained relaxation—a restraint concentrated in the instant when hard furniture, hat angles, body postures and unsmiling faces combine to convey a certain stiffness. The photographer, who is known for his pictures of the more ebullient relaxation of his fellow Frenchmen, noted that the mood here "always remains quiet and decent."

Lunch Break, 1954

144

In an apartment building still under construction, the lively sound of accordion music led the photographer to an unfinished flat that the construction workers—male and female—had converted into a temporary clubhouse. On its walls were the standard Soviet décor: portraits of Lenin and Stalin, an honor roll of the best workers, messages exhorting increased production. But the workers seemed to take little note of these official encouragements; their lunch hour provided time for an impromptu dance, savored by participants and onlookers alike.

Dorothea Lange

Egyptian Villagers, 1963

Until she accompanied her husband, economist Paul S. Taylor, on a trip throughout Asia in 1958 when he was a government consultant on community development, Dorothea Lange had devoted most of her career to documenting America *(pages 78-81)*. She was fearful of entering, let alone photographing, an unknown land so remote from her own. But the photographs she brought home show that the Orient did not confound her. She found in Asian faces and attitudes a reflection of some of the human qualities she had always prized the most, and these were what she documented. A child's face became a symbol of inner peace, a dancer's hand the essence of grace.

Yet when another trip abroad came up four years later, in 1962, and she prepared to go to Egypt with her husband, Miss Lange again felt the same reluctance. She wrote to a friend, "I go because Paul's work takes him there. For my own work I would choose to remain in my own country." She was ill when they departed (she died two years later of cancer), but modern, Muslim Egypt captivated her, as the world around her always had, and it raised her above her fears. The people she saw were no antiques but were active, living in the present. And she photographed them that way: not as relics from the past, but as proud bearers of ancient tradition.

Miss Lange walked through villages seeking to photograph individual people close up, but her American features and her camera made such an unfamiliar sight that villagers jostled and crowded around her. So she often took pictures of groups like this trio, recording the warm curiosity that welcomed her wherever she went.

Classroom, Egypt, 1963

Fascinated by the newness of a foreigner—and a photographer, at that—these schoolchildren erupted with delight when Miss Lange entered their classroom. Cropped hair and choirboy uniforms could not disguise their impish ebullience. Like kids anywhere, they wanted to be in on the action—and to get in the picture.

147

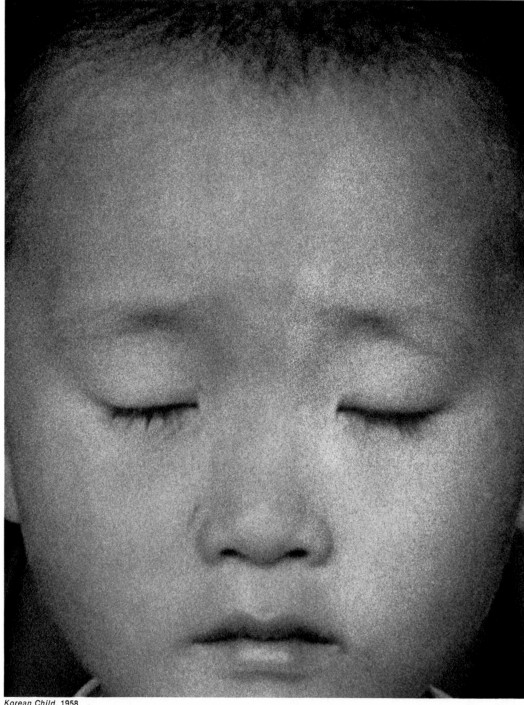

The expression of repose on the delicate features of a Korean child reflects a contemplative aspect of the Asian spirit. The photographer, by filling the frame with just nose, mouth and closed eyes, seems to have adopted the economy of style that is characteristic of much Oriental art.

Korean Child, 1958

A close-up of a tensely stretched hand says all there is to say about the exquisite grace of the Indonesian dance. The fluent gestures that are the rich symbolic vocabulary of this ancient ritual art form take years to learn. The picture reflects the discipline of this long apprenticeship.

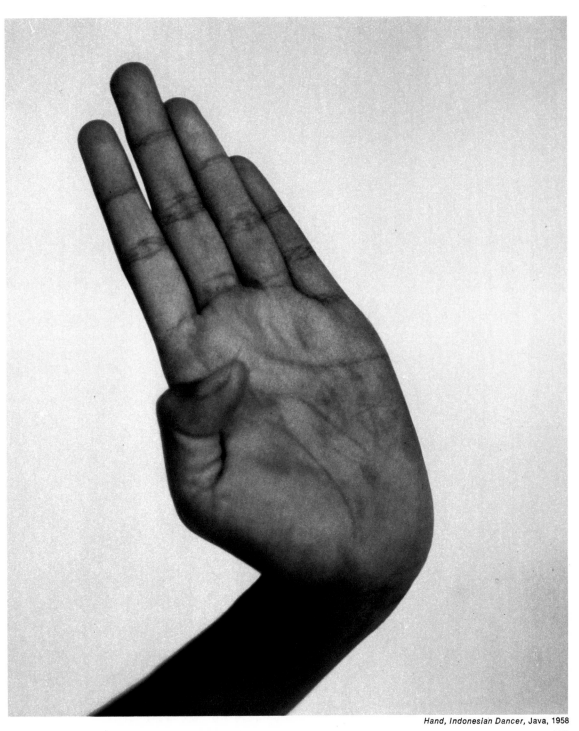

Hand, Indonesian Dancer, Java, 1958

149

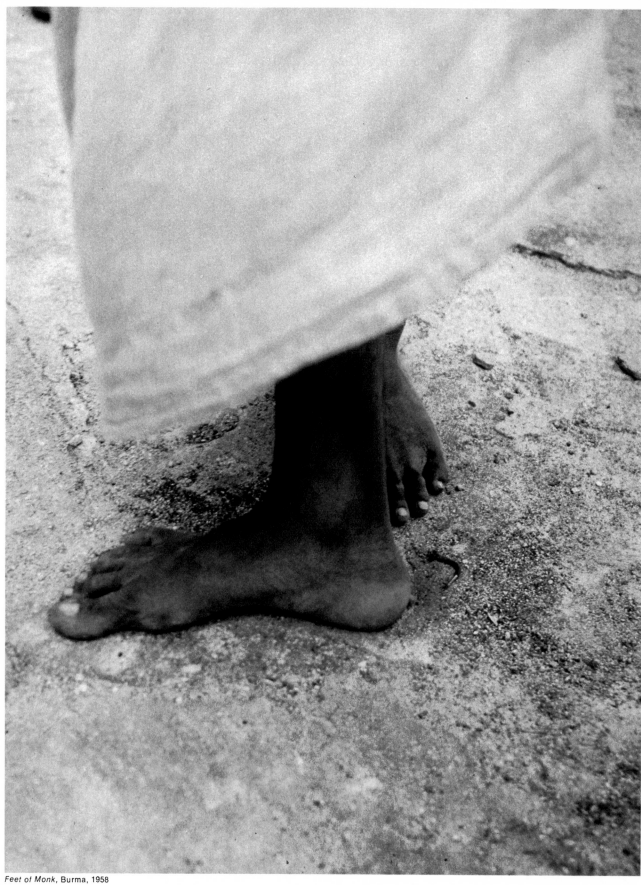

Feet of Monk, Burma, 1958

150

◄ *The stance of a Buddhist monk conveys the grace that, to many Westerners, is a notable trait of Orientals. This natural elegance is shown not with a full portrait of the holy man and his face but simply with a study of his feet.*

The wiry figure of this Egyptian farmer was emphasized by outlining him against the stark, cloudless sky. His well-worn workbasket and sinewy legs help to document the hard life of the fellahin in the Nile River region.

Nile Delta, Egypt, 1963

Woman in Purdah, Upper Egypt, 1963

An Egyptian woman, behind a traditional Muslim's veil, presents a shadowy, mysterious visage to the camera. Her hidden expression reflects the photographer's own quandary: Egypt was a strange land where an unknown language was spoken and unfamiliar traditions observed. The veil represents the obscurity through which the face of modern Egypt had to be perceived.

Led by a gay, dancing child, a procession of village women and children carry baskets of food to graves in honor of the dead. The ritual, which has survived 5,000 years of history, dramatizes the continuity between modern, Muslim Egypt and the enduring traditions of ancient times.

Bearing Food to the Dead, Upper Egypt, 1963

W. Eugene Smith

Dance of the Flaming Coke, 1956

Fawn, Africa, 1954

◄ *A steelworker gracefully coaxes flaming coal into an underground furnace, where temperatures up to 2,000° will convert it into the coke used to process iron ore. This photograph was part of an exhaustive picture story that documented every aspect of life and work in Pittsburgh.*

Smith once remarked that visitors to Albert Schweitzer's medical colony in Lambaréné were never sure "whether it is an African village, a game preserve or a medical hospital." He surmised that "it is the sum of all three," and showed that sum in his pictures. The gentle-eyed fawn was a respected member of the community as were its human citizens, including the missionary German doctor who headed it.

Twenty-five years after the close of World War II, W. Eugene Smith regards his shattering photographs of that global conflict as a failure: they did not cause war to be abolished for all time. His bitter feeling of defeat in an impossible task indicates the high goals this emotional documentarian has always set for himself. Throughout his career, Smith has poured his soul into his work, hoping to persuade those who viewed his pictures that wars and cruelty must

end, that respect and tenderness are due all living creatures.

Few viewers share Smith's conviction that he failed. The depth of feeling his photographs evoke is expressed in a letter he got after the war from a Japanese who had recently seen a Smith picture: "Please kindly accept pleasure I find of photograph. I see it first time. I hold it and see it until tears are make in my eyes. It was very beautiful photograph. I sorry, which we did."

155

Lambaréné, 1954

*On a balcony at Dr. Schweitzer's hospital in
Africa, a young chimpanzee, protectively nestling
a kitten, gazes trustingly at the camera. A
commonplace scene, it summed up the mood at
Lambaréné, where all life was cherished.*

Pont Bedeau Hospital, 1958

Patients at a Haitian mental hospital languish,
unclothed, in a bare shed with dirt floors. It seems
that society has simply penned them up where
they will be out of sight. But this revelation
of their misery, once seen, cannot be dismissed.

157

A sailor, casualty of a raid on Kwajalein atoll in World War II, is sent to his final rest in the Pacific off the deck of the aircraft carrier Bunker Hill. With such emotion-charged pictures, Smith eloquently pleaded for an end to the evils of war. He got his photographs at great personal risk. He spent most of the war covering the fighting—and two years recuperating from a severe shell wound he received on Okinawa.

Burial at Sea, 1944

For days, the photographer followed Dr. Ernest Guy Ceriani on his rounds in Kremmling, Colorado, for the famous Country Doctor essay that appeared in LIFE. The story reaches a climax with the poignant picture at right of Dr. Ceriani, who has just stitched the forehead of a child injured by a kick from a horse. Weary and deep in thought, he is searching for a way of telling her parents that she probably will lose the sight of one eye. An amputation, a birth and a death were part of the doctor's day; his selflessness is captured in every picture of the essay.

Country Doctor, 1948

A tiny kitten, barely able to open its eyes, mews in protest against the confinement of the hands that hold it. The kitten, called Mieko, was photographer Smith's; his household is never without cats, and he always gives them Japanese names. To him, this small squirming creature represented the most positive, joyful thing there is: a new life, bursting with promise.

Mieko, date unknown

Critics of Complacency 5

Uncovering the Wasteland of Affluence 164

Robert Frank 166

Lee Friedlander 178

Garry Winogrand 190

Diane Arbus 202

"I got into the Democratic Convention by stealing ▶ a badge from a jacket hanging in the men's room," the photographer confesses. "I liked Adlai Stevenson that year—but I was much more impressed by the spectacle than by who they would nominate." Here Frank shows a fragment of the spectacle, an intense discussion between members of the New York delegation. Caught up in argument, they are too absorbed in the politics of the moment to be aware of the camera.

ROBERT FRANK: *Convention Hall, Chicago,* 1956

Uncovering the Wasteland of Affluence

In a landmark book on economics in 1958, Harvard professor John Kenneth Galbraith reported on a radical change in income among Americans. In the wartime and postwar decade ending in 1950, the poorest fifth of United States families had increased their real income by 42 per cent. The income of the next-to-bottom fifth had grown by 37 per cent. Families in the middle fifth of the population were making 24 per cent more money. Some of the gains, but not many, had been won at the expense of those at the top of the heap of American society. Except for pockets of "insular poverty" in areas like Appalachia and among minorities, said Galbraith's *The Affluent Society,* Americans in general had become—without anybody realizing it—well off.

This revolution on the economic landscape doubtless helped to account for a revolutionary change in the viewpoint of photographers documenting the country's social landscape. From the time of Jacob Riis, concerned photographers had used their cameras as trumpets to sound a call for action against society's ills. Their pictures, realistically grimy, had first rallied the public to war on poverty and all its ugly consequences—slums, child labor, sharecropping, sweatshops. Later photographers had an even more ambitious goal: to combat through their pictures deficiencies in the ethical as well as the physical condition of mankind, not only in the United States but all over the world. In the view of John Szarkowski, director of photography at The Museum of Modern Art, all these documentarians aimed "to show what was wrong with the world and to persuade their fellows to take action to make it right." But by the 1950s a different attitude began to appear among documentary photographers: they looked at the fabric of the affluent society and although they found it full of holes they concluded that it was not up to them to mend it.

The Swiss-born Robert Frank, along with Lee Friedlander, Garry Winogrand and Diane Arbus, led this new generation of photographers that felt bound by no mission whatever except to see life clearly; they set out not to reform the world but merely to know and reflect it. Winogrand could have been speaking for the entire group when he said, "I don't have messages in my pictures. . . . The true business of photography is to capture a bit of reality (whatever that is) on film."

Explaining these people's refusal to act as reformers, critic Alan Trachtenberg wrote in *The Nation:* "These young photographers propose, with very rapid cameras, to present a view from within. There is no effort to judge but instead to express. The snapshot or the passing glimpse seems the appropriate vehicle for a society which has lost a sense of whole relationships. Many of the glimpses . . . show man-made but uninhabited landscapes; emptiness conveys the leading feeling of social desolation. The anatomy is exposed cold-heartedly. Apathy, loneliness, anomie are not simply reflected but ingrained in the chrome and Formica and plate glass surfaces which carry their distortions to the eye . . . mordant celebrations of a plastic environment. Glutted with artifacts, with artificialities, this social landscape suffocates. The word 'social' itself becomes a bitter joke. Many of these pictures leave the feelings paralyzed, gripped in fear and mystification.''

Along with intent, technique also changed. Though Diane Arbus worked slowly and deliberately, Frank, Winogrand and Friedlander are all fast shooters, snapping away without premeditation. It is not that they do not think as they work; rather they have speeded up their thought processes to make the act reflexive, shooting what they see before the conscious mind has time to analyze or rearrange it.

The pictures in this chapter—from Robert Frank's cynical look at some politicians on the previous page to Diane Arbus' peek into a living room all ready for Christmas *(page 203)*—simply argue that in the affluent society something is awry. If they have a hint of a prescription for curing social ills, it is no more than the straightforward notion that the solution to any problem begins with seeing it clearly. Such a coldly clear look is often disturbing, telling us things about ourselves we would rather not know, and these pictures are more likely to be provocative than pleasurable.

In defense of this kind of work Frank has said: "I have been frequently accused of deliberately twisting subject-matter to my point of view. Above all, I know that life for a photographer cannot be a matter of indifference. Opinion often consists of a kind of criticism. But criticism can come out of love. It is important to see what is invisible to others—perhaps the look of hope or the look of sadness. Also, it is always the instantaneous reaction to *oneself* that produces a photograph.'' ☐

Robert Frank

Robert Frank flared across the horizon of photography like a comet. He became something of a celebrity in 1959, and by 1962 had stopped making still pictures. But behind him he left what is generally regarded as the best single volume of contemporary United States documentary photography; his pictures still astonish his peers.

Frank turned to serious photography in Switzerland at the age of 18, and when he immigrated to America five years later he had already won some recognition for his work, which was basically European and sentimental. In the United States he did a stint of fashion work at *Harper's Bazaar,* and then in 1955 became the first European to win a Guggenheim Fellowship in photography. He promptly bought a secondhand Ford and set out to document his adopted nation.

After 10,000 miles of travel, Frank assembled 83 of his pictures in a book he called *The Americans*—and could find no publisher. "It was scrofulous stuff," says John Szarkowski of The Museum of Modern Art, "those lunch counters, those bus depots and those plastic booths and those nickelodeons! The book challenged the way Americans were supposed to look. . . . It was about whole segments of life that nobody had thought the proper concern of art."

Frank's pictures documented Americans as a remote, separated and alienated mass of human beings staring past each other. Frank was called a Communist—"a deliberate distortion," he says, "but you know how it was in the Fifties." He explains his dour documents by saying: "I had never traveled through the country. I saw something that was hidden and threatening. It is important to see what is invisible to others. You felt no tenderness."

Walker Evans was one of the few Americans to recognize the value of Frank's book. "It is a far cry from all the woolly, successful 'photo-sentiments' about human familyhood," he wrote. *The Americans* was finally published in 1958, not in the United States, however, but in Paris. "Only because the Paris publisher was a friend of mine," says Frank. A quantity of French-language copies was sold in the United States but that edition was soon remaindered.

Yet the word slowly spread, and the book, out of print, became much sought after. In 1959, Grove Press issued the first United States edition; in 1969, Grossman Press reissued it. Noting this 10th anniversary, *Creative Camera* of London said it "must be the most famous photoessay ever produced."

But by then Frank had finished with still photography. In 1961 or 1962, he thinks, he lost his Leica—and didn't mind at all. "Unless one becomes a commercial artist or a fashion photographer, making a living is almost impossible," he says. Today he makes his livelihood by teaching cinematography, some of which he does himself on a noncommercial basis. But as for the documentary photograph, he explains, "I had done it. I had made a book without interference. At best, to go on would have been a repetition."

Trolley, New Orleans, 1955

"A streetcar goes by on a main street, maybe
Bourbon Street, in New Orleans," Frank
remembers, "and there are people looking out at
something. I wasn't thinking about segregation
when I shot it. But I did feel that the black people
[in the back of the bus] were more dignified."

Parade, Hoboken, 1955

In 1955, when Hoboken, New Jersey, celebrated
its 100th anniversary, Frank happened to be there
visiting a friend. "This is a picture of two people
who were standing behind one of the flags, behind
glass and in shadows. They're sort of hiding." To
the photographer, it is "a threatening picture."

City Fathers, Hoboken, 1955

The day of the Hoboken centennial was cold, but most local political leaders, watching the end of the parade from a wooden reviewing stand, turned out in formal finery despite the weather. It was no accident, wrote photographer Walker Evans, "that Frank snapped just as those politicians in high silk hats were exuding the utmost fatuity. . . . Such strikes are not purely fortuitous. They happen consistently for expert practitioners."

169

St. Francis, Gas Station and City Hall, Los Angeles, 1956

*With cross held aloft, a statue of St. Francis
seems almost defiantly to confront the Los
Angeles City Hall. "What moved me," Frank
says, "was that, against the background of that
hideous city hall, there was the little vase
with a flower. The combination of that city hall,
that big gray block of cement and those recurring
images of gas stations and the flower. . . ."*

Charleston, South Carolina, 1955

"It was the first time I was in the South," the photographer remembers, "and the first time I really saw segregation. I found it extraordinary that whites would give their children to black women when they wouldn't allow the women to sit by them in the drugstore. I did very few pictures that made a political point like this."

171

Picnickers on Belle Isle, Detroit, 1955

"It is quite a strange, sad photo," says the
photographer about this riverfront scene. *"They
are pointless people—totally unimportant,
unglamorous, unnoticed."* The subjects are
presumably out for a good time in an island park,
but they do not even seem to notice one another.

Elevator, Miami Beach, 1956

An elevator is a small and intimate enclosure, yet
the people who ride it are generally anything but
intimate. In this impersonal record of an elevator
ride the operator, looking rather forlorn, seems
not so much human as a part of the machinery.
But where Frank kept "turning away after the click
of the shutter" when making most of the pictures
for his book, The Americans, something about this
girl made him linger awhile and talk to her.

173

Fourth of July, Jay, New York, 1955

Here is the Fourth of July pretty much as it is supposed to be: the Stars and Stripes bigger than life, floating over a busy scene of people walking about, children on the move, a whole community buzzing. But nobody is smiling, and the flag is patched. Behind the activity and decorations there is an emptiness of spirit.

In the isolation of the Arizona desert, bypassed ▶ by the mainstream of American life, these Indians from a Navajo reservation see and hear the transcontinental traffic that roars past them on Route 66—but rarely get more than a glimpse of the people in the speeding cars. Now sudden death on the highway has changed all that, depositing two of these remote people at their feet. Stolidly contemplating the two blanketed corpses from another world, the Indians are still as distant from that world as ever.

Accident on U.S. 66, Arizona, 1956

Ranch Market, Hollywood, 1956

Accident on U.S. 66, Arizona, 1956

Ranch Market, Hollywood, 1956

◄ *The countergirl under the Christmas decoration has walled herself off from Christmas and from the world. A young woman in a lively setting, face to face with hungry people, she has hardened her eyes and frozen her pleasant features into a mask that sets her apart—and makes the picture a chilling record of one soul lost among many.*

The girl in the foreground is a starlet come to a movie première, to be seen by the crowd. She is at a high point in her career, surrounded by fans yet a million miles away. Somehow she manages to look at once impregnable and defenseless.

Movie Première, Hollywood, 1956

Lee Friedlander

Lee Friedlander's pictures show a distraught and frantic America. A busy street alongside a gas station seems fractionated, its bits and pieces separated and stirred up—hurrying cars, rearview mirror, overhead lights, parts of people. A photograph of a quiet wedding party is disturbed and distorted by a passing automobile; a Manhattan singles bar is cold and grim, a place to size up the lonely.

There is a brooding message of disorientation, of something having gone askew in these pictures. Yet Friedlander, whose camera sees this, is puzzled when anyone suggests that he has documented a sense of 20th Century unease. A rather boyish man born in 1934, friendly and unpretentious, he shrugs his shoulders and says he just likes to take pictures; whatever the viewer sees in them is his own business. "It fascinates me that there is a variety of feeling about what I do. I'm not a premeditative photographer," he says. "I see a picture and I make it. If I had a chance, I'd be out shooting all the time. You don't have to go looking for pictures. The material is generous. You go out and the pictures are staring at you." Often they stare at him through car windows, for many of his photographs are scenes he spots as he drives on a trip or simply while doing errands near home.

Friedlander literally walked into photography one day in his native Aberdeen, Washington. His father had sent him to a portrait studio to pick up some proofs; when no one answered his ring, he recalls, "I walked through the curtain and there was this old man putting paper into dark water. He didn't see me. As he put the paper in, people's faces came out. It was the greatest trick." At 12, Friedlander got his first camera, an old folding model; and at 16, with high school finished, he went off to a Los Angeles photography school. By 1956 he was in New York doing record-album covers and other commercial work. A friend showed him books of photographs by the great documentarians Eugène Atget *(pages 36-42)* and Walker Evans *(pages 67-71).* "Wow, it knocked me out," he says. "It was a revelation. Seeing Evans' and Atget's work and meeting Evans was a breakthrough for me. From that time on that's the tradition I worked in."

Friedlander makes his living with commercial work, but in his characteristically easy-going way he melds it into his more personal photography. "Commercial work takes me, like teaching, to where I can do my own work. Wherever I work commercially it is not going to take me where I don't want to be; it won't take me into a vacuum."

Friedlander talks casually and openly about his craft, but in his pictures the smiling easiness vanishes. Here is a world that is cold, angular, bleak and dry of spirit. "Little poems of hate . . . bitterly funny observations," wrote his mentor Walker Evans of one collection of his pictures. "An atmosphere of disquieting fatality," says another critic. Even Friedlander's representations of people in physical contact with each other *(pages 187-188)* are hard, tough and stubbornly unromantic. Despite his disclaimers of intent, his work reveals a photographer who is intellectually perceptive, a man with a strong view of the world that emerges intuitively, like a reflex, in the 1/100 second that it takes to snap the scene.

Hillcrest, New York, 1970

One winter day the photographer stopped his
pickup truck for gasoline about five miles from
New City in Rockland County, New York, where he
lives. "It's a nothing, a couple of gas stations,
a shopping plaza, not many people, lots of cars.
I looked out and this is what I saw." What
he saw he caught in his camera: a crazy-quilt
pattern of cars, signs and suburban clutter.

179

Friedlander, his wife and two children stopped in this California town early one morning on a vacation trip. "I always walk around and look around when we hit some town or city," he says. He spied a window with some pictures in it; the bottom one was of Marilyn Monroe. He took a photograph that shows his lone shadow looming ominously over the ambiguous window.

This is a strange photo, the photographer says, ▶ "strange that it came out at all." He was driving by a village green when he noticed a group of people assembling to have a picture taken. It was a wedding party. Friedlander parked his car, rolled down the front window and started to take a photograph—when another car flashed past, imparting a startling sense of sudden, dramatic interruption to the easy ambiance of the wedding.

Monterey, California, 1970

Princeton, New Jersey, 1969

Seattle, Washington, 1970

*After a summer trip to Washington State, the
Friedlander family headed south to Los Angeles
where Lee was going to teach photography at the
University of California. Before leaving they put up
at a Seattle hotel. Early in the morning father and
son went into the street for a walk. In the
post-dawn light the boy stood on the street (left)
looking at himself in a window. His father's
picture, using the mirror image of himself, his son
and the nearly empty street, catches visually
the hush of a city before the morning rush.*

Somewhere in Mid-America, 1969

Told that this city scene appears desolate, the photographer said: "I didn't make the place. I take pictures where there are lots of people, too. I am always taking pictures of city landscapes." The air of mystery is enhanced by a glimpse of a soldier—part of a World War I memorial—peering out from the top of the shrubbery at right.

Madison, Wisconsin, 1966

*Friedlander believes that studio photographers'
windows tell a lot about a neighborhood. When he
looked at this window and saw his shadow on a
portrait he chuckled and snapped it. The result
memorializes a typical neighborhood portrait
studio—with the added intrusion of the visitor's
shadow. The picture is in a volume by Friedlander
called Self Portrait, containing 42 pictures,
each marked by his presence on the scene.*

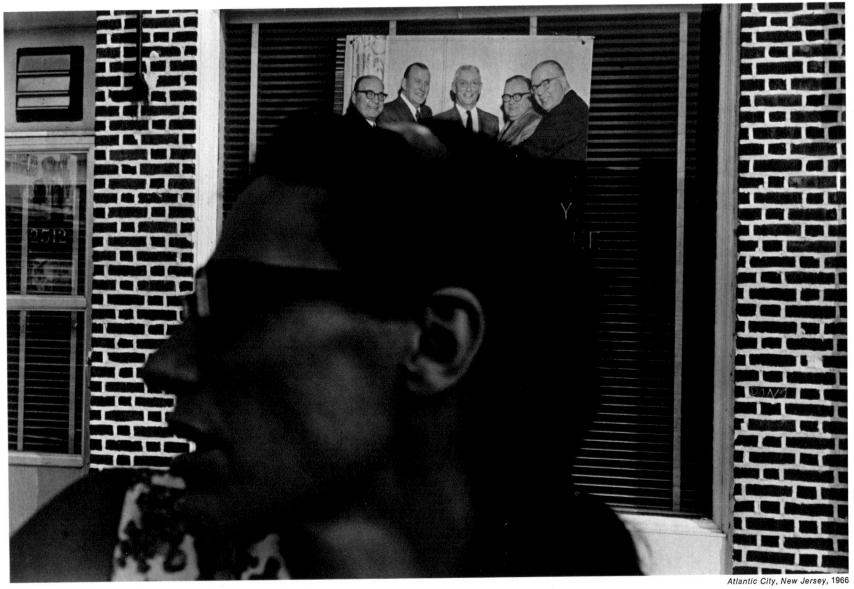

Atlantic City, New Jersey, 1966

The photographer was taking a picture of his wife
when something startled her. "The kids were
young then," he says, explaining her expression
to any parent; "maybe she was looking at them."
Mrs. Friedlander's taut face contrasts with the
joviality of the men in the blown-up picture in the
window behind her: in back, the self-conscious
smiles of men posing; in front, the unposed
look of a mother concerned about her children.

185

New York City, 1967

◄ *"This was made at a party following an old friend's wedding,"* the photographer explains (the friend was fellow photographer Garry Winogrand —pages 190-201). *"It was a small party at his apartment and it lasted a couple of hours. I don't know who the man is who was lying down."* But however unintentionally, Friedlander and his temporarily faceless subject document the tired frivolity into which parties often lapse.

"I went to a party with Ron Kitaj, the painter," says Friedlander. *"He was teaching classes at the University of California at Los Angeles at the same time I was. He was a much more social guy, and I asked if he could take me to any parties I could photograph. I think the party was for the young man in the picture; I don't really know. I didn't know anybody there except Ron."* Yet the photographer again recorded, through his nameless companions of the moment, the special quality of one kind of social gathering.

Los Angeles, 1970

187

New York City, 1968

Commissioned by a magazine to do a series of
photographs on Manhattan's singles bars, where
unattached people may become attached,
Friedlander went to four or five a night to get this
picture. He moved in on one packed crowd,
revealing in his close-up view the appraising eyes
behind the convivial, seemingly open-handed
gestures typical of these meeting places.

Glendale, California, 1970

While Friedlander was teaching at UCLA, he was invited to a wedding by a friend of the groom. "I took this picture while the wedding was going on," he says. "The people looked serious and thoughtful." In the split second recorded here, shooting over the shoulder of a spectator, he caught the solemnity that attends even an informal, highly casual California wedding.

189

Garry Winogrand

Garry Winogrand claims to deal in the banal and the commonplace. "I am a tourist," he says, and indeed, his photographs show ordinary people doing ordinary things. Yet somehow an unsettling element of strangeness appears. Many of his pictures document paradoxical groupings, momentary encounters between people *(right),* animals in unusual contexts—scenes that force the viewer to think twice about what kind of reality they show him.

Winogrand came to his unconventional style by a fairly conventional route. A native of New York City, he bought his first camera when he was a weather forecaster in the Army Air Forces of World War II, and afterward studied painting at New York's City College and Columbia University on the GI Bill. He turned permanently to photographing because "there wasn't a lot of torturous work with the brush." He quickly became a craftsman well able to achieve the results asked by clients, and made for himself a successful career as a commercial photographer.

But his private work turned to ordinary events and ordinary people.

These he records incessantly, his Leica clicking constantly—"the fastest gun in the East," as a contemporary remarks. "No one moment is most important," says Winogrand. "Any moment can be something." But he is very selective in the prints he makes from his rolls so that what the viewer gets to see is not a random moment of life but a view of humanity as Winogrand sees it. The pictures emerge taut, full of little twists and confrontations, telling brief stories, often mysterious: a mother, babe in arms and hair in curlers, watching a spit-and-polish military review; a walrus performing incongruously in a setting framed by apartment buildings; one dog leading another by a leash.

For such thought-provoking views of a world made up of dramas, confrontations and jokes, big and little, Winogrand adamantly refuses to supply any interpretations of his own. "The photo is a thing in itself," he says. "And that's what still photography is all about."

New York World's Fair, 1964

On a sunny afternoon at the New York World's
Fair, eight people rest on a bench: a white girl
talking to a young black; next to them a closely
linked trio of girls; then a pair of girls looking with
great interest at something outside the picture;
finally an older man, oblivious to them all,
reading his paper. The photographer is an
observer unobserved, noting the cryptic unfinished
stories that make up the reality of life.

Hollywood Boulevard, Los Angeles, 1969

Here is a typical Winogrand encounter—existing
not in the minds of its participants, but in the
eye of the photographer and his camera. Its
poignancy, as in the picture above, comes from
the deep gulf that lies between the close-together
people: in this case a helpless cripple shadowed
in his wheelchair and the three pretty, very
lively girls passing by in the bright sunlight.

Dallas, Texas, 1964

On a busy street corner during an American Legion convention, a legless man crawls across the pavement, begging alms. All around him are healthy, prosperous Legionnaires. They are aware of his presence, and they give him room, yet everyone carefully ignores him. The picture raises disturbing questions (did he and they share the same war?), and in leaving them unanswered it exposes some of the connections and separations that tangle the threads of American society.

Bronx Zoo, New York, 1959

*All this picture documents is the members of
two species cautiously investigating each
other—a boy with a handful of peanuts and a look
of wonder, and an elephant with an appetite. But
when it turned up on a contact sheet, the
photograph fascinated the photographer. He took
to frequenting zoos, and in the encounters
he witnessed there he found striking revelations,
like this one, of the funny and puzzling
relationships among the creatures of the world.*

Aquarium at Coney Island, 1963

An odd association between man and beast sets up a show within a show for the documentary camera. Spectators have crowded a gallery to watch a walrus perform, but the walrus has wandered offstage to look closely and quizzically at a keeper who is taking its picture; it seems almost to be confronting the keeper with a complaint: "Why are you stealing my act?"

Texas State Fair, 1964

A heroic, Texas-sized figure of a John Wayne-type cowboy dwarfs human visitors to the annual state fair in Dallas—and seems to cow them too.

At the Air Force Academy in Colorado Springs, ▶ two contradictory themes in American life collide. Informality, in the person of a mother in hair curlers and hair net, comes up against the embodiment of formality: cadets in ranks with rifles just so, arrayed on a manicured drill field that is framed by exactly placed buildings.

Dressed Up for the Parade, Air Force Academy, Colorado, 1964

Zoo, New York, 1962

*Many of Winogrand's pictures involve unusual
confrontations—often, but not always, between
people. This one depicts a three-way face-off
between humans and animals at the Bronx Zoo,
with all three couples apparently equally
intrigued by what goes on before their eyes.*

The Pet, 1962

The matter of relationships, which lies at the
core of so many Winogrand photographs, takes
on a different and humorous twist here as
applied to two dogs, one of which is inexplicably
but calmly leading the other by a leash.

Texas State Fair, 1964

*Roaming behind the scenes at a livestock show,
the photographer caught two trios juxtaposed as
though in a ballet. Three cowboys hunker in a row
while beyond them three Brahma bulls stand
upright, also in a row. Both groups manage to
ignore each other—and the picture comes
off as a satirical study in noncommunication.*

Albuquerque, New Mexico, 1958

*A child stands in blazing sunlight, limned against
the black void of a garage just off Route 66 in New
Mexico. This black-and-white contrast is repeated
by the ominous dark cloud looming out of the
Sandia Mountains; the tiny human figure
seems to set life against the blackness of death.*

Diane Arbus

In 1962 the late Diane Arbus, a 39-year-old New Yorker, applied to the Guggenheim Foundation for a fellowship in photography. She was no run-of-the-mill applicant: born to wealth in a department-store family, she grew up on Park Avenue, had a governess, was privately educated, married at 18, and afterward was an assistant to her husband, a fashion photographer. Neither was she a neophyte: her words and pictures, including portraits of people in the news, had appeared in *Harper's Bazaar* and other magazines. Now she wanted to strike out for herself in work of a more serious nature.

"I want," she wrote the Guggenheim committee, "to photograph the considerable ceremonies of our present." In that category of subject matter she included anything that went on in "Ceremonial Places" (the beauty parlor, the funeral parlor, even people's parlors), as well as "Ceremonies of Competition" (contests and sports events) and "Ceremonies of Celebration" (conventions and pageants).

The Guggenheim committee agreed. Diane Arbus, armed with camera and battery-powered strobe light, set out to document the commonplace, the taken-for-granted and the bypassed deviates or freaks of nature. To this human material, involved with ceremonies few thought ceremonial, she brought a wise child's eyes, a gentle manner and a steely persistence. Some of the remarkable pictures she took in the ensuing years appear on these pages. Time after time, the familiar looks unexpected and freakish when seen through her scathing eye, and the freakish looks unexpectedly familiar.

A short four years after getting the Guggenheim Fellowship—and a second one in 1966—she was an acknowledged artistic success, sharing a major show at New York's Museum of Modern Art with Lee Friedlander and Garry Winogrand *(preceding pages)*.

She usually worked in the manner of an old-fashioned portrait photographer, talking with her subjects earnestly and sympathetically, making pictures that were collaborations between the subjects and herself. For her camera no person was too ordinary—or too repugnant—to record. She painstakingly tracked down any subject that interested her—transvestites, suburbanites, dwarfs, prizewinners, twins, even nudists—working hard to document those aspects of mankind that most people overlook or look away from.

An immobile image of the lifeless quality of ▶ mechanically celebrated holidays, this acid photograph was taken at a suburban housing development on Long Island. The expensive furnishings and plentiful presents indicate the prosperity of the inhabitants, but the antiseptic arrangement suggests a spiritual coldness at odds with the open-hearted love and honor Christmas gifts should represent. For all the neatness of the room, the clocks do not agree.

Levittown, 1962

Veiled Woman, 1968

A low-angled close-up, harshly lit with a flash, this street shot shows the influence of news photography, which Diane Arbus greatly admired because she felt it was so factual. In her hands the journalistic technique achieved an honesty many levels higher than most news photographs attain, for the "reality" it discloses appears—as in this picture—to be put on, a mask for some deeper truth. "A photograph is a secret about a secret," she once wrote about such pictures. "The more it tells you the less you know."

An elegant coiffure and costume and a setting elaborately furnished with exotic objets d'art only accentuate the feeling that here something is awry. The appearance of a confident and well-ordered world is contradicted by the clutter at lower left—a contradiction reinforced by the subject's uneasy pose and strained expression.

At Home, 1965

*The 79-year-old king and 72-year-old queen
of a Seniorella Ball had never met before; their
names had been picked out of a hat at
a gathering of elderly people in New York City.
They face the camera with a grimness that belies
the festive nature of the affair they reign over.*

Senior Citizens, 1970

Bedecked with symbols of superpatriotism, a young man waits to take his place in a win-the-war-in-Vietnam parade in Manhattan. His expression and his trappings are so very ordinary the viewer senses that he—and the celebration he is about to join—are not ordinary at all but manifestations of most unusual times.

Parader, 1967

207

On the Dance Floor, 1968

This picture of a mismatched couple at a formal dance is another of Diane Arbus' documents of "ceremonies of our present." All uncover joylessness in what should be happy activities; here a man, peering over the shoulder of a partner half a head taller than he is, seems to be dancing not because he wants to but because it is a social duty. The question the photograph asks is, why in the world should it be required?

Two youngsters have the ballroom floor to themselves after disposing of all competition to win a dance contest and the trophies at their feet. It is an occasion that seems to call for congratulations. But the children's expressions, smug beyond their years, make this picture a savage comment on a world that encourages childish mimicry of adult sophistication.

Junior Interstate Ballroom Dance Champions, Yonkers, New York, 1962

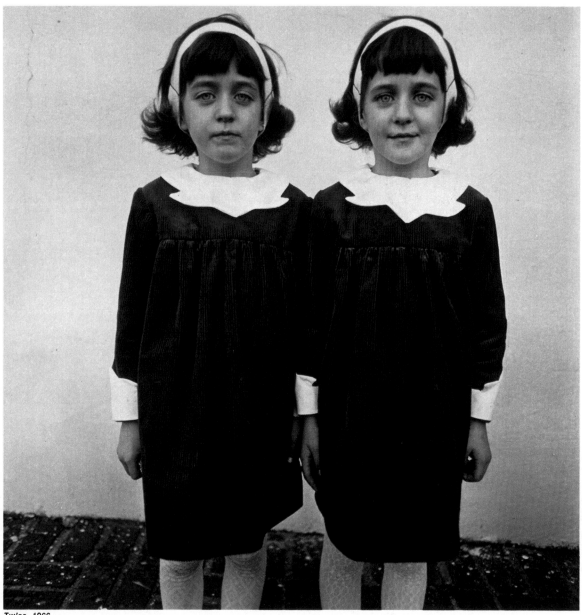

Twins, 1966

Cathleen (left) and Colleen were posed against a neutral background and placed within the frame so simply that the photograph resembles a snapshot. This casual treatment of what most people consider quite unusual—identical twins—was characteristic of the photographer's work: portraying the extraordinary as something perfectly ordinary and acceptable.

The Personal Document 6

Recording the Private World 214

Christian Sunde 216

Tom Zimmerman 224

Arthur Freed 230

CHRISTIAN SUNDE: *My Family on Avenue T, Brooklyn,* 1969

Recording the Private World

The generation of documentary photographers who matured in the 1960s had to find a new direction if they were to take their places alongside the masters of documentary photography who had preceded them. It seemed that man in society had now been looked at in every meaningful and unusual way. To be sure, there would always be new elements to document in the vastness and diversity of mankind, but those who had gone before—from Hine and Riis, campaigning for reform, to Friedlander and Arbus, commenting dispassionately—had been too comprehensive, all too penetrating, in their work. What could be left for the younger documentarians?

There was, really, only one way open. The young photographers turned their lenses away from the tumultuous world about them and attempted to find elemental truths in themselves and their own private moments. They documented their personal experiences, events that were judged not in relationship to life around them, but only in their effect on the photographer himself. This subjective approach was not totally new; Lartigue in particular had concentrated on his family and friends. But few in the field had consciously chosen to delve so deeply into themselves or been so ruthlessly honest and unflinching about displaying their private lives and emotions in public in their effort to communicate some aspect of reality to their audience. The photographers of the '60s adopted a confessional style, in which the camera served as therapist. The pictures often deliver insights—not only on subjects and photographers but on life itself—that verbal communication could never achieve. These photographers have to be bold in a special way; they do not blink at the moment when the frank picture has to be made; they do not turn away during episodes of psychological torment. Whether the subject is an innocent family portrait, such as the one on the preceding page by Christian Sunde, pictures brought back by the obsessive traveler Tom Zimmerman, or the relentless recording of the trials and hazards of lovers by Arthur Freed, these documentarians rely doggedly on personal experiences and observations as their source material.

Since they are not concerned directly with the historical surge and flow of our times, their pictures catch the piquant facets of existence—the ambiance of a place, the terror or joy of a given moment, the anger and tenderness that fill an everyday life. These are shifting moods, the common occurrences that most photographers—and people—tend to overlook. Yet these men, true to the traditions of documentary photography, find in the commonplace the large lessons of beauty and truth. By studying the apparently banal with their cameras they illuminate the world.

The concern of these photographers with emotional content makes esthetics seem almost unimportant. But their emphasis on visceral reaction gives their work a distinctive quality. The pictures appear random, more than

214

snapshots, less than conventionally accepted photographic art. They stand as documents of a state of mind. As such, they are often as difficult to make as they are to comprehend. A young father passing by his teen-age stepdaughter's room sees her in a warm embrace with her boyfriend. He is brought to a halt, his feelings mixed. But he takes the picture *(page 219),* a sensitive view of young people who are rapidly passing beyond the innocent games of puppy love. A disturbing scene for a father to witness, a difficult one to shoot, yet a truthful documentary picture.

Equally disquieting, these practitioners regularly find in their work more uncomplimentary insights into themselves than they wish they did. Arthur Freed, involved in a cross-country love story, unveiled the range of his feelings, from boyish compassion to open anger and aggressiveness. The trip caused some emotional hardships for both people involved, and they were recorded by Freed, his documents bearing testimony to the struggle humans must endure to achieve a balanced and meaningful relationship.

The three photographers whose work is displayed in this chapter are long-time friends, sharing photographic goals and difficulties. All three have worked at their art for years, building reputations but receiving little economic reward. Their private photographic visions are not made for, or aimed at, a mass audience. They have survived economically by taking an array of odd jobs, usually teaching photography or working in studios. Their concern for the revelation of the self on film drives them on. Their cameras are always ready wherever they are, whatever they are doing. They constantly watch for the time to press the shutter, to capture the scene that will provide more visual evidence of their special worlds. □

Christian Sunde

Liz in Montana, 1967

Christian Sunde once thought of his principal subjects—his wife and children—as obstacles to his development as a professional photographer. While he struggled to master the medium—he did not take up photography until he was 25 years old—the responsibility he felt for supporting his family made them seem a hindrance. But then he came under the influence of Tom Zimmerman *(pages 224-229),* who taught him to examine the personal in order to discover the universal. So Sunde trained his camera on his own family to capture their nuances of mood, personality and physical appearance. Through these studies he learned a great deal about his subjects, about himself—and about humanity. And such photographs, he feels, give him an important method of communicating with people and understanding them.

Sunde was born and raised in Brooklyn and did not leave the city until recently, long after he had committed himself to photography. He changed his way of life drastically, moving to northern Maine, there to build a house, grow his own vegetables and earn a subsistence wage however he could —currently by teaching English at a local public school. Even in the backwoods he continues to chart with his camera the innocence, the beauty and the frailties of those close to him.

Showing signs of fatigue after the climb up a 2,000-foot rise in front of Fort Peck Indian Reservation, Sunde's wife stands amid the rugged beauties of Montana. With her hair in a practical shingle cut, her simple, functional clothes and her weathered complexion, she looks thoughtful and relaxed, a down-to-earth woman who blends in with the elemental nature of the countryside.

Denise, Christian, Glenn and Luke, 1970

The way people can quickly become lost in their private reveries—even when crowded together—is shown in this picture of the children in Sunde's life: in the back of the family car, each looks his separate way. Denise, the photographer's teen-age stepdaughter, is at left, her gaze pensive. Christian, Sunde's son by his first marriage, sits in the rear looking at his fingers while Glenn, at right, lolls back dreamily. Little Luke, in the middle, has his attention caught by something outside.

Liz and Denise at the Beach, 1968

*In playful embrace Liz and her 14-year-old
daughter Denise display their affection during an
outing at a beach near New York City. The
closeness in age of mother and daughter—Liz was
only 18 years old when Denise was born—and
their resemblance to each other make them
appear to be sisters. This creates a charming but
complex confusion of personal relationships
whose difficulties are suggested here.*

Denise and Boyfriend, 1968

Sunde was walking down the hall past the room of
Denise, his stepdaughter, when he saw her
sharing a tender moment with her boyfriend. Her
hand rests idly on her face as she gazes up
through hooded eyes at the young man—two
adolescents learning the sensations of love. The
picture has always bothered Sunde—but he made
it deliberately, and considers it one of his best.

Denise at Gardner's Lake, 1968

*At a secluded spot in Maine where the family
often bathes in the nude, Denise giggles shyly
before the camera, her 14-year-old body draped
only with a towel. Her averted face and the
upward turn of her left hand detail her modesty,
while the clothes at right indicate her nudity. The
subject, composition and play of sunlight on
the leaves interact to transform the picture into
a charming, intimate view of a young girl.*

Tom Zimmerman

Tom Zimmerman is the documentarian of the road. Unlike most people on vacation trips who take pictures only when they reach the Grand Canyon or some other scenic destination, Zimmerman does not wait—he records all sorts of scenes along the way. He finds more documentary value in a picture of a truck parked off a highway leading to Chicago *(left)* than in a standard panoramic shot of that busy metropolis itself. The hypnotic effect of an empty highway *(page 226)*, the sense of being on a long car trip *(page 227)*, the fleeting glimpse of a passing town in a distant locale *(pages 228-229)* are the personal visual dispatches Zimmerman brings back from his wanderings.

An inveterate traveler, Zimmerman spends much of his life on the road. He crisscrosses the nation and dips down into Mexico, settling in one place only long enough to make money to finance his next trip. He sells an occasional photograph, teaches photography at such places as San Francisco's Art Institute, has worked as a photographic assistant and plays the tenor saxophone in a jazz combo. A shy, friendly man with flowing hair and a huge mustache, Zimmerman is a high-school dropout. His fascination with the road and the things he sees along the way are transformed into the documentation of a perpetual trip.

A tractor-trailer, its diesel idling in the snowy night, stands unattended at a truck stop along Interstate 35 in Kansas while the driver refuels himself at the nearby restaurant. The photographer took this picture, while driving his automobile from Mexico to Chicago, to show his feeling that the huge, modern trucks exert a dominating influence on the American highways.

Colima, Mexico, 1967

Pennsylvania Highway, 1966

The feeling of being on a long motor trip is
generated in the picture above, taken as the
Florida-bound photographer drove along a
Pennsylvania highway on a rainy afternoon. The
water-streaked windshield through which he shot
contributes the kind of hazy distortion that comes
with long hours behind the wheel. The car becomes
a world of its own; hints of the world outside—the
anonymous car that is being overtaken, the
gathering darkness, the approaching headlights
—re-create the incongruous mix of monotony
and anticipation that characterizes lengthy drives.

◄ Heading west toward the beaches of the Pacific
Ocean, Zimmerman stopped to make this picture
in Colima, Mexico. A long, hot, empty ribbon of
asphalt unrolls before the car, its ending lost in
the mass of mountains rising in the background.

Two men walk their bicycles down a dusty road
that leads into the central Mexican town of Xichú;
for a moment they are silhouetted in the light
filtering through the trees. The smallness of their
figures, the twin church spires that are the only
clue to the nearness of the town, the trees
towering over the scene—all combine to make an
unrepeatable, split-second record that testifies to
the ever-changing nature of life on the road.

Xichú, San Luis Potosí, Mexico, 1971

Arthur Freed

Just before leaving on his trip, the photographer made this picture of himself. While waiting for a traffic light to change, he set the self-timer and held the camera at arm's length until the shutter tripped. To him, the result is a candid confrontation with the camera that reveals his inner feelings: expectant, vulnerable, a little sad.

Since his student days, Arthur Freed has been using personal experience as the subject of his work. Through this detailed examination of his own actions he has tried to document the universality of all experience—believing that what one man can see clearly, all men can learn from.

Freed has a deferential attitude toward his photographs: he trusts them far more than he does his memory.

What he may remember as a moment of triumph his pictures may reveal as a time of vacillation and indecision. If so, Freed believes the pictures. Thus his work enables him to continually review his actions in order to gain insight, self-awareness and understanding.

Freed's preoccupation with photography started in high school in Buffalo, New York, when the piquant smell of the school photo lab drew him inside its

doors. At Rochester Institute of Technology he studied under the eminent photographer Minor White, who told his students that "all photographs are self-portraits," advice Freed never forgot. In time he became a teacher of photography and since 1963 has been on the faculty of Pratt Institute in Brooklyn.

The work on these pages is excerpted from a photographic diary he kept during an automobile trip from Denver to San Francisco in 1970. The pictures can be looked upon as a documentary series, a collection of candid and personal shots that reveal some of the complicated inter-relationships in the everyday life of a young couple. But each picture can also stand on its own as a record of a shared moment. Taken together or separately, the photographs unsparingly document the psychological states of two individuals.

In this unusual view of Leslie, the photographer shows her as a distant figure in a landscape, an ill-defined person resembling someone glimpsed in a dream. A deliberate sense of disorientation is created by the roof of the car, spreading before Leslie in a mysterious mass. The emptiness of the background isolates her, a human being in a mood of loneliness. The result is a picture exposing the strangeness and separateness that often disturbs two people who thought they knew each other well.

◄ Happy in each other's company, Arthur and Leslie walk arm in arm under a bright and cheerful sun at Rocky Mountain National Park in Colorado. His facility in taking pictures of himself even while engaged in a highly personal relationship gives an unusual quality to this picture: it is as if he stepped outside his body to document the mood of both subjects.

Leslie, in a moment of reflection, gazes idly at a kitten from the comfort of a bed. The informal quality of her kicked-off shoes and the soft way the kitten seems to blend into the wooden floor connote the quiet and casual tone of the scene, a relaxed time of serenity and ease.

With a road map unfolded before them, the couple argue over which road to take. Although such an argument might be considered trivial, there are signs that feelings are running deep. Arthur, his eyebrow seen arched in the rearview mirror, is irritated if not angry. Leslie is visible only as a hand held up as if to ward off the flow of the mood.

Bibliography

Chapter One

Atget, Eugène:
Abbott, Berenice, *The World of Atget*. Horizon Press, 1964.
and Marcel Proust, *A Vision of Paris*. Macmillan, 1963.
Lartigue, Jacques-Henri:
Boyhood Photos of J.-H. Lartigue. Ami Guichard, 1966.
Diary of a Century. Viking Press, 1970.
Stone, Benjamin:
Sir Benjamin Stone's Pictures: Records of National Life and History, 2 vols. Cassell and Company Ltd., 1906.
Thomson, John:
Illustrations of China and Its People, 4 vols. Sampson Low, Marston, Low and Searle, 1873-1874.
Newhall, Beaumont, *The History of Photography from 1839 to the Present Day*. The Museum of Modern Art, Doubleday, 1964.

Chapter Two

Farm Security Administration:
*Agee, James and Walker Evans, *Let Us Now Praise Famous Men*. Houghton Mifflin, 1941.
Anderson, Sherwood, *Home Town*. Alliance Book Corporation, 1940.
Baldwin, Sidney, *Poverty and Politics: The Rise and Decline of the Farm Security Administration*. University of North Carolina Press, 1968.
Evans, Walker, *American Photographs*. The Museum of Modern Art, Doubleday, 1938.
*Goldston, Robert, *The Great Depression: The United States in the Thirties*. Bobbs-Merrill, 1968.
Hurley, Forrest Jack, *To Document a Decade: Roy Stryker and the Development of Documentary Photography by the Farm Security Administration*. University Microfilms, Ann Arbor, Michigan, 1971.
*Lange, Dorothea, *Dorothea Lange Looks at the American Country Woman*. Amon Carter Museum of Western Art, Ward Ritchie Press, 1967.
*Lange, Dorothea and Paul Schuster Taylor, *An American Exodus*. Oakland Museum, Yale University Press, 1969.
MacLeish, Archibald, *Land of the Free*. Harcourt Brace, 1938.
Raper, Arthur F. and Ira De A. Reid, *Sharecroppers All*. University of North Carolina Press, 1941.
*Rothstein, Arthur, John Vachon and Roy Stryker, *Just Before the War: Urban America from 1935 to 1941 as seen by photographers of the Farm Security Administration*. October House, 1968.
†Steichen, Edward, ed., *The Bitter Years: 1935-1941*. The Museum of Modern Art, Doubleday, 1962.
Hine, Lewis W.:
Gutman, Judith Mara, *Lewis W. Hine and the American Social Conscience*. Walker and Co., 1967.

†Taylor, Florence I., *Child Labor Fact Book*. National Child Labor Committee, Publication No. 403, 1950.
Riis, Jacob A.:
*Cordasco, Francesco, ed., *Jacob Riis Revisited: Poverty and the Slum in Another Era*. Anchor, 1968.
Lubove, Roy, *The Progressives and the Slums: Tenement House Reform in New York City 1890-1917*. University of Pittsburgh Press, 1962.
How the Other Half Lives. Dover, 1971.
The Battle with the Slum. Macmillan, 1902.
The Making of an American. Macmillan, 1970.
Ware, Louise, *Jacob A. Riis: Police Reporter, Reformer, Useful Citizen*. D. Appleton-Century Company, 1938.

Chapter Three

Deschin, Jacob, *Say It With Your Camera: An Approach to Creative Photography*. Whittlesey House, First Edition, 1950.
†Grossman, Sid and Millard Lampell, *Journey to the Cape*. Grove Press, 1959.
†*Photo Notes*. The Photo League, published monthly in New York City, 1938-1951.

Chapter Four

Cartier-Bresson, Henri:
Cartier-Bresson's France. Viking Press, 1971.
The Decisive Moment. Simon and Schuster, 1952.
The Europeans. Simon and Schuster, 1955.
The People of Moscow. Simon and Schuster, 1955.
The World of Henri Cartier-Bresson. Viking Press, 1968.
*Kirstein, Lincoln and Beaumont Newhall, *Photographs by Cartier-Bresson*. Grossman, 1963.
Kertész, André:
*Capa, Cornell, ed., *The Concerned Photographer, The Photographs of Werner Bischof, Robert Capa, David Seymour, André Kertész, Leonard Freed, Dan Weiner*. Grossman, 1968.
†Fárová, Anna, ed., *André Kertész*. Grossman, 1966.
Lange, Dorothea:
Dorothea Lange. The Museum of Modern Art, Doubleday, 1966.
"The Making of a Documentary Photographer." Typed transcript of a tape-recorded interview conducted by Suzanne Riess, University of California Bancroft Library Regional Oral History Office, Berkeley, 1968.
Smith, W. Eugene:
W. Eugene Smith: His Photographs and Notes. Aperture Inc., 1969.
Strand, Paul:
Newhall, Nancy, *Paul Strand, Photographs 1915-1945*. The Museum of Modern Art, Simon and Schuster, 1945.

and James Aldridge. *Living Egypt*. Aperture Inc., Horizon Press, 1969.
and Basil Davidson, *Tir A'Mhurain*. Grossman, 1968.
and Claude Roy, *La France de Profil*. Éditions Clairefontaine, 1952.
and Cesare Zavattini, *Un Paese*. Giulio Einaudi editore S.P.A., 1955.

Chapter Five

Arbus, Diane, *A Box of Ten Photographs*, portfolio of original prints, 1971.
†*Five Photographers*. An international invitational exhibition shown at the Sheldon Memorial Art Gallery, University of Nebraska, 1968.
*Frank, Robert, *The Americans*. The Museum of Modern Art, Aperture Inc., Grossman, 1969.
*Friedlander, Lee, *Self Portrait*. Haywire Press, 1970.
*Friedlander, Lee and Jim Dine, *Work from the Same House*. Trigram Press, 1969.
Lyons, Nathan, ed., *Toward a Social Landscape: Bruce Davidson, Lee Friedlander, Garry Winogrand, Danny Lyon, Duane Michals*. George Eastman House, Horizon Press, 1966.
†Winogrand, Garry, *The Animals*. The Museum of Modern Art, New York Graphic Society Ltd., 1969.

Chapter Six

Freed, Arthur, *Eight Photographs*. Doubleday, 1971.

General

*Lyons, Nathan, ed., *Photographers on Photography*. Prentice-Hall, 1966.
†"The Photo Journalist: W. Eugene Smith, Dan Weiner." Transcript from The Fund for the Republic television series "The Press and the People," 1958.

Periodicals

Album, Aidan Ellis and Tristram Powell, London.
Art Forum, May 1971, Charles Cowles, New York City.
Art in America, No. 2, 1960, Art in America Co., New York City.
Camera, C. J. Bucher Ltd., Lucerne, Switzerland.
Creative Camera, International Federation of Amateur Photographers, London.
Infinity, American Society of Magazine Photographers, New York City.
The Nation, June 10, 1968, Nation Magazine Company, New York City.
Popular Photography, Ziff-Davis Publishing Co., New York City.
U.S. Camera World Annual, U.S. Camera Publishing Corp., New York City.

*Also available in paperback
†Available only in paperback

Acknowledgments

For help in the preparation of this volume, the editors would like to thank the following: Doon Arbus, New York City; Edward Bady, Hicksville, New York; Thomas F. Barrow, Associate Curator, Research Center, George Eastman House, Rochester, New York; Willa Baum, Director, Regional Oral History Office, The Bancroft Library, University of California, Berkeley, California; Peter C. Bunnell, Curator, Department of Photography, The Museum of Modern Art, New York City; Jerry Burchard, Chairman, Department of Photography, San Francisco Art Institute, San Francisco, California; John Collier, Associate Professor of Anthropology and Education, San Francisco State College, San Francisco, California; Arnold H. Crane, Chicago, Illinois; Jack Delano, Rio Piedras, Puerto Rico; Jacob Deschin, Contributing Editor, *Popular Photography*, New York City; Robert Doherty, Director, Allen R. Hite Art Institute, University of Louisville, Louisville, Kentucky; Robert M. Doty, Associate Curator, Whitney Museum of American Art, New York City; Walker Evans, Old Lyme, Connecticut; Alan Fern, Assistant Chief, Prints and Photographs Division, Library of Congress, Washington, D.C.; Robert Frank, New York City; Lee Friedlander, New City, New York; Terese Heyman, Curator of Photography, Oakland Museum, Oakland, California; Michael Hoffman, Publisher, *Aperture*, Millerton, New York; Forrest Jack Hurley, Assistant Professor of History, Memphis State University, Memphis, Tennessee; Marvin Israel, New York City; Jerry Kearns, Acting Head, Reference Section, Prints and Photographs Division, Library of Congress, Washington, D.C.; Russell Lee, Lecturer, Art Department, The University of Texas, Austin, Texas; Carl Mydans, Larchmont, New York; Charles Pratt, New York City; Johanna Robison, Curatorial Assistant, Oakland Museum, Oakland, California; Walter Rosenblum, Professor, Department of Art, Brooklyn College, Brooklyn, New York; Edwin Rosskam, Roosevelt, New Jersey; Arthur Rothstein, New Rochelle, New York; Bernarda B. Shahn, Roosevelt, New Jersey; Aaron Siskind, Providence, Rhode Island; Roy Stryker, Grand Junction, Colorado; John Szarkowski, Director, Department of Photography, The Museum of Modern Art, New York City; Paul S. Taylor, Professor of Economics Emeritus, University of California, Berkeley, California; David Vestal, Associate Editor, *Camera 35*, New York City; Garry Winogrand, New York City.

Picture Credits

Credits from left to right are separated by semicolons, from top to bottom by dashes.

COVER—Walker Evans, photograph taken for the Farm Security Administration, courtesy Library of Congress.

Chapter 1: 11—Robert Doisneau from Rapho Guillumette. 16 through 21—John Thomson, copied by Paulus Leeser, courtesy Arnold H. Crane Collection. 22 through 27—Reproduced by permission from the Sir Benjamin Stone Collection of Photographs in the Birmingham Reference Library. All photographs except page 27 copied by Derek Bayes. 28 through 35 —Jacques-Henri Lartigue from Rapho Guillumette. 36 through 42—Eugène Atget, courtesy The Museum of Modern Art, New York.

Chapter 2: 45—Lewis W. Hine, courtesy George Eastman House. 46—John Thomson, from *Street Life in London*, Sampson Low and Co., London, 1877, copied by Derek Bayes, courtesy Bill Jay. 48 —Jacob A. Riis, from *How the Other Half Lives*, Charles Scribner's Sons, copied by Paulus Leeser. 49 through 55—Jacob A. Riis, courtesy The Museum of the City of New York. 57 through 65—Lewis W. Hine, courtesy George Eastman House. 67—Walker Evans, courtesy The Museum of Modern Art, New York. 68—Walker Evans, copied by Paulus Leeser, courtesy The Museum of Modern Art, New York. 69—Walker Evans, courtesy The Museum of Modern Art, New York. All photographs on pages 70 through 84 except page 71 were taken for the Farm Security Administration, courtesy Library of Congress. 70 —Walker Evans. 71—Walker Evans, courtesy The Museum of Modern Art, New York. 72 through 77 —Ben Shahn. 78 through 81—Dorothea Lange. 82 through 84—Russell Lee.

Chapter 3: 87—Sid Grossman. 90,91—Sol Libsohn. 92,93—Walter Rosenblum. 94,95—Sid Grossman. 96,97—Jerome Liebling. 98,99—Jack Manning, courtesy George Eastman House. 100,101—Morris Huberland. 102,103—Aaron Siskind, courtesy George Eastman House. 104,105—Ruth Orkin. 106,107—Eliot Elisofon. 108,109—Arthur Leipzig. 110,111—Morris Engel. 112,113—Dan Weiner, courtesy Sandra Weiner. 114,115— Lou Bernstein. 116,117—William Witt. 118—Lester Talkington.

Chapter 4: 121,124 through 131—© André Kertész. 132 through 137—Paul Strand. 138 through 145—Henri Cartier-Bresson from Magnum. 146 through 153—Dorothea Lange, courtesy The Oakland Museum. 154 through 160 —W. Eugene Smith.

Chapter 5: 163,167 through 177—Robert Frank. 179 through 189—Lee Friedlander. 191 through 193 —Garry Winogrand. 194,195—Garry Winogrand, courtesy The Museum of Modern Art, New York. 196,197—Garry Winogrand. 198—Garry Winogrand, courtesy The Museum of Modern Art, New York. 199 through 201—Garry Winogrand. 203 through 210—Diane Arbus, courtesy Doon Arbus.

Chapter 6: 213,216 through 223—Christian Sunde. 224 through 229—Tom Zimmerman. 230 through 236—Arthur Freed.

Index
Numerals in italics indicate a photograph, painting or drawing of the subject mentioned.

Abbott, Berenice: and Photo League, 88
Adams, Ansel: and Photo League, 88
Americans, The (book), 15, *163*, 166, *166-177*
Arbus, Diane, 164, 165, 202; photographs by, *203, 204, 205, 206, 207, 208, 209, 210*
Atget, Eugène, 13, 36; photographs by, *36, 37, 38, 39, 40-41, 42*

Bernstein, Lou: and Photo League, 114; photographs by, *114, 115*
Bourke-White, Margaret: and Photo League, 88

Capa, Robert: and Photo League, 88
Cartier-Bresson, Henri, 122-123, 139; and Photo League, 88; photographs by, *138-139, 140, 141, 142-143, 144-145*
Ceriani, Ernest Guy, *159*
Child labor, 46-47, 51, 56, 58, 59, 60, 61, 63
Cox, Kenyon, drawing by, *48*

Decisive moment, 123
Documentary photography, 4, 7; definition, 12; as educator, 122-123, *124-160;* history of, 12-15; as personal record, 214-215, *216-236;* as persuader, 46-47, *48-84;* as record, *16-42;* as social document, 88-89, *90-118;* as social mirror, 164-165, *166-210*
Doisneau, Robert, photograph by, *11*

Elisofon, Eliot: and Photo League, 101, 106; photographs by, *106, 107*
Engel, Morris: and Photo League, 110; photographs by, *110, 111*
Evans, Walker, 4, 14, 69, 70, 71; photographs by, *cover, 67, 68, 69,*
70, 71; quoted on Robert Frank, 166; quoted on Lee Friedlander, 178

Farm Security Administration, 4, 47, 66; photographs, *67-84*
Film and Photo League, 88
Flashpowder, and documentary photography, 48
Frank, Robert, 14-15, 162, 164, 165, 166; *The Americans,* 15, *163,* 166, *167-177;* photographs by, *163, 167, 168, 169, 170, 171, 172, 173, 174, 175, 176, 177*
Freed, Arthur, 214, 215, *230, 232, 234-236;* photographs by, *230, 231, 232, 233, 234, 235, 236*
Friedlander, Lee, 164, 165, 178; photographs by, *179, 180, 181, 182, 183, 184, 185, 186, 187, 188, 189*

Galbraith, John Kenneth, 164
Grossman, Sid: and Photo League, 89, 92, 95; and Photo League School, 89, 95; photographs by, *87, 94, 95*

Hine, Lewis W., 14, 46-47, 56; and Photo League, 88; photographs by, *45, 57, 58, 59, 60, 61, 62, 63, 64, 65*
How the Other Half Lives (book), 46
Huberland, Morris: and Photo League, 111; photographs by, *110, 111*

Illustrations of China and Its People (book), *16-21*

Kertész, André, 14, 122, 124-125; photographs by, *121, 124, 125, 126-127, 128, 129, 130, 131*

Lange, Dorothea, 14, 122, 123, 146; and Farm Security Administration, 78; and Photo League, 88;
photographs by, *78, 79, 80, 81, 146, 147, 148, 149, 150, 151, 152-153*
Lartigue, Jacques-Henri, 12, 28; photographs by, *28-29, 30, 31, 32-33, 34, 35*
Lee, Russell, 83; photographs by, *82, 83, 84*
Leipzig, Arthur: and Photo League, 108; photographs by, *108, 109*
Libsohn, Sol: and Photo League, 90; photographs by, *90, 91*
Liebling, Jerome: and Photo League, 96; photographs by, *96, 97*

Manning, Jack: and Photo League, 98; photographs by, *98, 99*
Mydans, Carl, and Farm Security Administration, 66

National Child Labor Committee, 46, 56
Newhall, Beaumont, quoted on John Thomson, 16

Oistrakh, David, *140*
Orkin, Ruth: and Photo League, 105; photograph by, *104-105*

People of Moscow, The (book), *138-145*
Photo League: history of, 88-89; members' work, *87, 90-118*
"Photo Notes" (periodical), 88, 92

Red Cross, 56, 65
Resettlement Administration, 66
Riis, Jacob, 14, 46, 48; photographs by, *49, 50, 51, 52, 53, 54, 55*
Roosevelt, Franklin D., 66
Roosevelt, Theodore, 46
Rosenblum, Walter: and Photo League, 92, 96; photographs by, *92, 93*

Scribner's Magazine, 46, 48
Self Portrait (book), 184
photographs by, *78, 79, 80, 81, 146, 147, 148, 149, 150, 151, 152-153*

Shahn, Ben, 72; photographs by, *72, 73, 74, 75, 76, 77*
Siskind, Aaron: and Photo League, 98, 102, photographs by, *102, 103*
Smith, W. Eugene, 14, 122, 123, 155; photographs by, *154, 155, 156, 157, 158, 159, 160*
Stereoscope, 13
Stone, Sir Benjamin, 23; photographs by, *22, 23, 24-25, 26-27*
Strand, Paul, 122, 133; and Photo League, 88, 97; photographs by, *132, 133, 134, 135, 136, 137*
Stryker, Roy: and Farm Security Administration, 66; and Photo League, 88
Sunde, Christian, 214, 216; photographs by, *213, 216, 217, 218, 219, 220, 221, 222, 223*
Szarkowski, John, quoted, 164; quoted on Robert Frank, 166

Talkington, Lester: and Photo League, 118; photograph by, *118*
Thomson, John, 16, 46; photographs by, *16-17, 18, 19, 20, 21, 46*
Trachtenberg, Alan, quoted, 164-165
Tugwell, Rexford Guy, 66

Weiner, Dan: and Photo League, 112, 117; photographs by, *112, 113*
Weston, Edward: and Photo League, 88
White, Minor, and Arthur Freed, 231
Winogrand, Garry, 164, 165, 190; photographs by, *191, 192, 193, 194, 195, 196, 197, 198, 199, 200, 201*
Witt, Bill: and Photo League, 117; photograph by, *116-117*

Zimmerman, Tom, 215, 216, 225; photographs by, *224-225, 226-227, 228-229*

ROCKFORD
Public Library

presented by
Ron Fruin

in memory of

MICHAEL GRAVES

MICHAEL GRAVES

BUILDINGS AND PROJECTS
1995—2003

EDITED BY KAREN NICHOLS
ESSAY BY FRANCISCO SANIN

RIZZOLI
NEW YORK

Acknowledgments

First published in the United States of America in 2003 by
RIZZOLI INTERNATIONAL PUBLICATIONS, INC.
300 Park Avenue South
New York, NY 10010

Frontispiece: Archaic Landscape, painting by Michael Graves

Distributed to the United States trade by
St. Martin's Press, New York

2003 2004 2005 2006 2007 / 10 9 8 7 6 5 4 3 2 1

Printed and bound in China
Designed by Abigail Sturges

ISBN: 0-8478-2652-X (HC)
ISBN: 0-8478-2569-8 (PB)

Library of Congress Catalog Control Number: 2003104772

This monograph on the buildings and projects designed by
Michael Graves & Associates is the fourth volume in a series
documenting the chronology of our architectural practice. As
a principal of the firm and editor of this book, I would like to
acknowledge the collaborative efforts of many people.
Special thanks go to Stephen Case and David Morton of
Rizzoli for their continued support and guidance, and to
Abigail Sturges and her staff for graphic design services.
Francisco Sanin, a long-time colleague and friend, con-
tributed the essay.

Many staff members of Michael Graves & Associates played
essential roles in preparing and assembling the photographs,
drawings and text. Michael Graves and the four principals
who are studio heads—Patrick Burke, John Diebboll, Gary
Lapera and Tom Rowe—provided ongoing advice and guidance regarding the contents. Courtney Havran, the firm's
images librarian, took responsibility for organizing all of the
artwork. Marek Bulaj was responsible for in-house photography, and Caroline Hancock assisted with the text. Andrew
Merz contributed to the early organization of the book.

The considerable effort to track down and assemble hundreds
of project drawings was led by two associates, Craig Babe and
Mark Proicou. They were most recently assisted by numerous
staff members including, among others, Jacqueline Teo,
Ludwing Vaca, Stephanie Rigolot, Maria Ruiz, Brian
Ambroziak, Matt Ligas and Emily Estes.

Karen Nichols, FAIA
Princeton, New Jersey
2003

Contents

6   The Language of Michael Graves
           Francisco Sanin

12   List of Buildings and Projects

14   **Buildings and Projects**

344   Biographies

345   Associated Architects and Designers

345   Project Staff

347   Selected Honors and Awards

348   Selected Bibliography

352   Photography Credits

The Language of Michael Graves

Francisco Sanin

Archaic Landscape

Over the last three decades the work of Michael Graves has maintained a consistency and a commitment to an idea that very few architects have. In the face of changing movements, fashions and conditions, he has continued to pursue the idea of an architectural language and to explore its transformation and boundaries. In fact, the essay entitled "A Case for Figurative Architecture," which he wrote for his first Rizzoli monograph covering the years 1966–1981, could still be read as an introduction to the work published in this, the fourth volume in the series. A basic premise of that article is his statement that "it is crucial that we re-establish the thematic associations invented by our culture in order to allow the culture of architecture to represent the mythic and ritual aspirations of society." It was his contention then, as it is today, that only when architecture is engaged as a language and a figurative art can it maintain its relevance to society.

It is important to note that the argument developed in that article was framed not only in cultural terms but also, most interestingly, in terms of the potential for the figurative characteristics of architecture to be a source of invention and a stimulus for the architectural imagination. This it seems has been the force that has driven Graves' work: a commitment to an architecture that can communicate through its figurative qualities, and a corresponding commitment to explore the boundaries or limits of such a proposition. In the introduction to Graves' second monograph covering the years 1982–1989, Robert Maxwell discussed Graves' fascination with both rules and transgression, with the structures of language as a necessary foil for his own creativity: "Graves' dilemma is a tough one: in a time when all resolutions are considered provisional, he has to fight as hard to establish the rule system that will permit closure as he must fight to put the rules into question by transgressing them."

Graves' article on figurative architecture was a very influential text for a whole generation of architects who were looking for an alternative to what they saw as the limitations of modern architecture, specifically the incapacity to respond to new conditions of society and to convey meaning. Much has happened in architecture since the 1960s and 1970s when the debate focused on the need, and the potential, to explore the linguistic dimensions of architecture. As a professor at Princeton University (Graves recently retired after 39 years of teaching), he has been both a protagonist in and a witness to the major critical debates of the last four decades. It is well known that in the 1970s and 1980s Princeton was the center of some of the most intense debates about modernism and postmodernism, with the presence of theorists such as

Robert Maxwell, Alan Colquhoun and Anthony Vidler, among others. During that time, Graves' work at the university developed, if not in an atmosphere of complete agreement and theoretical alliances, at least in an atmosphere of common understanding of the basic references and boundaries of the discourse. By the late 1980s and early 1990s, the panorama had changed with the presence of theorists such as Mark Wigley and Beatriz Colomina. Princeton had become a center of debate on deconstructivist theory. Despite this changing context, Graves maintained his own line of work and inquiry. One may wonder if being in the middle of a debate that was quite distant from his own led him to become even more radicalized in his position. As described by Janet Abrams in her essay in Graves' third monograph dated 1990–1994, Graves saw himself becoming more of a radical by staying his course at a time when architectural debate was moving away from issues of language, meaning and representation.

His interest in an architecture that communicates and is thus accessible to the popular imagination led him further away from the debates not only in Princeton but also in the mainstream of academia. He seems to have focused instead on his architectural practice and his growing interest in product design, works that have brought him closer and closer to a mass audience. This desire to engage in a direct manner with popular culture has led to some of his most controversial designs, such as those for the Walt Disney Company, works that made some question how far one can go in this direction before the search for meaning becomes a rhetorical act. While admitting the challenges posed by the required "theming" of those projects, Graves saw the effect of his language another way: "It was like being a playwright who needed to master the difficulties of both tragedy and comedy."

Whatever the forum, Graves' work has maintained a lifelong commitment to the values of architecture as a language, a patient exploration of the potential and limits of that language. While he has not written much about his own architecture in recent times, his body of work itself reveals a continuous process of research and speculation.

Graves draws and paints. These are the tools of his trade and the methods of his research. Much has been written about his early experimentation with cubist themes and their relation to his building design strategies, both the organization of plans and the expression of building facades. His article, "The Necessity for Drawing: Tangible Speculation," published in *A.D. Magazine* in 1978, established drawing as the basis for

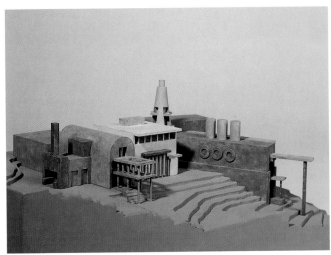

Pura-Williams Residence preliminary model

Topeka Library entrance

7

El Gouna hotels character studies

experimentation as well as documentation. Since then, painting has become not only his favorite form of expression but also the very site where he initially explores architectural and spatial ideas and, furthermore, the site where one can see them emerge in a more distilled form. Indeed, one can follow the development of his ideas from his early explorations in cubism, collage and transparency, to his subsequent fascination with Italian landscapes, and more recently to paintings in which one can see the emergence of new themes, themes that are more abstract and laconic, even enigmatic. These paintings are imaginary landscapes populated by objects that look familiar yet distant, shapes without specific scale or reference, strangely material and present and yet abstract. They remain within the language, and yet they do not convey a specific meaning other than their own presence.

One can see some of these qualities in several of his recent projects, a move away from his characteristic emphasis on the composition of plans and facades to a more objectlike, almost typological, approach. In a project such as the Pura-Williams

house of 1994, the composition is a collection (not really a collage) of architectural types; we recognize the vault, the cone, the cube in ways that remind one of Piero Ligorio's drawings of ancient Rome (which are among Graves' favorite references). However, the types have been transformed. Through shifts in scale and proportion and through the manipulation of elements such as windows and canopies, the forms are read in different and unexpected ways. Take for example, the canopies at the end of the office wing—one canopy on top of the other, too thin to be useful, and the column that supports them, too thick to be merely structural. Graves is playing a game with the language. At one moment the forms appear familiar, yet upon a closer look their condition is no longer so, creating a sort of delayed meaning that both puzzles and stimulates the imagination. One can say the same about the entrance "drum" of the library in Topeka and about the many pavilions of the resorts in El Gouna and Taba Heights, Egypt, in which the very nature of the program seems to have allowed Graves the space to explore all kinds of architectural inventions. Most of those buildings, which

El Gouna hotels details

are groups of guestrooms, utilize traditional local construction techniques featuring brick vaults, domes and arches. Graves uses these buildings as a point of departure to engage in a process of elaboration and invention that leads to some surprising results. While the individual pavilions offer a great variety of forms and transformations, the overall plan remains more in the tradition of previous projects in which the main concern is order and hierarchy, in which the plan provides a clarity that stabilizes the diversity of the three-dimensional compositions. The question remains as to what it means to use a local typology without making reference to the spatial fabric where it traditionally existed.

There are many other trends in Graves' current work, too numerous to mention here. Graves attributes this variety to his exploration of architectural character, and not to stylistic interest. Character, for him, is a way of creating and conveying meaning based on a figurative language. "Whether the architecture subliminally describes its function (for example, a civic building as opposed to a house) or explicitly responds

to its physical or cultural context, it relies on the use of familiar elements in the belief that people make natural associations with forms, colors and materials." Thus, the themes developed in the work demonstrate a broad range, from the vernacular to the neoclassical, from the figurative to the abstract. Compare for example, a library in the specific neo-Georgian context of Alexandria, Virginia to the more elaborate speculations in the Cotton Bay and Canary Islands resorts. In the Cotton Bay resort, the small pavilions seem to use the local vernacular as a point of departure. Given their relatively small scale, they are able to make reference to traditional construction methods and materials, something that is harder to do in the main hotel building given its size and scale. This exploration of the vernacular has limits when applied to a larger scale, since the specificity of the individual elements creates an uneasy tension when stretched over a more extensive composition.

In other projects such as St. Mary's Church in Florida, the simple and somewhat abstract forms possess a clarity and

9

Resort Hotel at Cotton Bay bar and restaurant

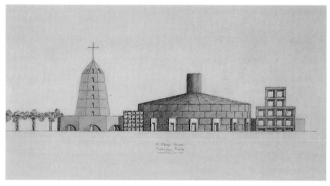

St. Mary's Church south elevation

power almost devoid of any tectonic or material quality—at least in the drawings and photographs—of scale. The themes are form, space, light and color. Compare this project to the student housing at Rice University, where the facades are conceived as a manipulation of the traditional and tangible elements of materials and construction—the frame, the horizontal banding, the brick infill and so on. The "expected" elements of the facade as construction are present but their proportions have been changed; the horizontal elements are so compressed that they become "too thin," and the bay windows are supported by one single column that gives them a strange figural condition. Graves seems to be concerned not with the tectonic but with the transformation of the elements of construction into a language that sets up a new system of relationships and proportions. Although he uses a traditional vocabulary of architectural elements, his interest is not to adopt the classical language of architecture in the strictest sense. Instead, he says, "I look at the root of the word 'classical' as it conveys the sense of classification, or hierarchical organization. My architectural language may classify the parts of a composition, such as the base, body and head of a tripartite facade or even a column, but it avoids the specific stylistic references." Thus, Graves continues to regard language itself as a source of invention and as a means to exercise his artistic imagination.

It is Graves' ability to continue to explore and expand the potential and the limits of the traditional language of architecture that sets his work apart from the rest. Most proponents of classical architecture seem to be interested in the canons and rules and in reducing the language to common denominators, reduced so it can be imitated. In contrast, Graves is constantly expanding his vocabulary. At a time when most architects have abandoned the idea of traditional architecture as a language, Graves has been left with the whole field to himself, and, like a child in an enormous playground, he is thoroughly enjoying the game.

Graves' interest in the figurative dimension of architecture has to do with its ability to communicate, to be understood by the "public," both in terms of the language and in terms of the space where architecture makes its presence. His projects continue to relate to ideas of public space based on known types: the square, the portico, the courtyard and the spatial sequence between inside and outside. In addition to exploring the figurative aspect of buildings, he continues to be interested in the potential figural quality of space defined by the building facades that surround it.

Of course, one can ask if it is still possible today to speak of common public space in a world wherein the logic is to reinvent—if not the languages—at least the systems of signification, so as to allow for a perpetual system of consumption. In these systems it is no longer possible to find consensus about what is good or bad, right or wrong. In a world of constant change and at a moment in history when information and communication tend to flow along non-material axes, is there still a role for a view that poses architecture as a cultural artifact capable of creating the conditions for public space? Clearly Graves thinks there should be. To put it another way, his position, if not a critique or a resistant stance, demonstrates his interest in exploring an alternative. A short anecdote may illustrate this point. Once, in a discussion with a colleague at Princeton, Graves questioned the fact that his colleague, a proponent of a different and completely non-traditional view of architecture, surrounded himself with traditional artifacts. I believe the example had to do with some English leather couches. The colleague's response was something like, "…but Michael, do you still believe in the continuity between life and art?" Graves responded, "Of course, an architect's art affects someone else's life." Whether one agrees with Graves' position or even shares his optimism, one has to respect the integrity and sincerity of his commitment.

Graves has been one of the major protagonists in the history of architecture in the last decades, as is attested by many publications and the significant awards he has received, including the American Institute of Architects Gold Medal and the National Medal of Arts, a presidential award. His work continues to evolve and change and to ask questions. Even at a time when some have declared what they call "the end of the semiotic nightmare," work like that of Graves argues that issues of representation are not so easily brushed aside. His work continues to ask questions about architecture in general and to test the limits of his own propositions in particular.

One may wish for Graves to write about his own work and ideas about architecture as he did in the early days when he would also talk about his design process, particularly the role of drawing as a form of speculation. His monographs are elegant and eloquent displays of his work, yet one still wishes there would be more of an attempt to make explicit both the ideas and the process that generates them. It may be just that in the current climate of critical debate about architecture, it is not enough to let the buildings speak for themselves. The cultural landscape has changed dramatically; it is now necessary to have a way to gain access to the development of ideas. Since Graves' work continues to be provocative and

Martel College student residence wing

rich in possibilities, a look inside the process can only help provoke a wider discussion. In the words of Robert Maxwell, in the essay mentioned above, "Viewed in this way, the work of Michael Graves takes on the character of play (as with any artist), a continual experimenting with his preferred materials and the opportunities that come to hand. That is not to deny its underlying seriousness. But it does enable us to assert its experimental nature and, in this sense to recognize that he is as much entitled to his space as any other artist, of whatever ideological color. And perhaps recognize also that he is doing useful work for the rest of us."

Graves' early decision to look for a direct engagement with popular culture has clearly paid off. By now he has become an established figure. His buildings are found in all corners of the world, from Europe to China, from Japan to Egypt, and in many cities across America, and his product designs have made him a household name throughout the world. It may be that recent changes in architectural debate are creating a climate in which it would be possible to examine his work in an objective way. At a time when the architectural landscape is going through major transformations, becoming more complex and fluid, it is time to drop the various "isms" that have been attached to Graves' work, and thus to have a more serious and critical discussion of the important contributions made to the discipline of architecture by the long career of this committed and very talented architect.

Syracuse–Seoul, July 2003

List of Building and Projects

Projects are catalogued by the primary year in which they were designed. This monograph illustrates projects that were either completed or commissioned during the years 1995–2003. Therefore, some of the projects shown here predate 1995.

1992

14 International Finance Corporation Headquarters, Washington, D.C.
20 Arts and Sciences Building, Richard Stockton College, Pomona, New Jersey
22 Indianapolis Art Center, Indianapolis, Indiana
24 Astrid Park Plaza Hotel, Antwerp, Belgium

1993

28 Castalia, The Hague, Netherlands
34 Nexus Momochi Residential Tower, Fukuoka, Japan
36 Taiwan National Museum of Pre-History, Taitung City, Taiwan
42 United States Post Office, Celebration, Florida

1994

43 Disney's Garden Pavilions, Orlando, Florida
44 1500 Ocean Drive, Miami Beach, Florida
48 One Port Center, Camden, New Jersey
50 House at Coolidge Point, Manchester-by-the-Sea, Massachusetts

1995

56 Miramar Resort Hotel, El Gouna, Egypt
64 Riverfront Sports Complex Master Plan, Cincinnati, Ohio
66 Laurel Hall, New Jersey Institute of Technology, Newark, New Jersey
68 Main Library of Topeka and Shawnee County, Topeka, Kansas

1996

72 O'Reilly Theater, Pittsburgh, Pennsylvania
80 Hyatt Regency Hotel, Taba Heights, Egypt
90 World Trade Exchange Center, Manila, Philippines
91 Ortigas Tycoon Twin Towers, Ortigas, Philippines
92 Miele Americas Headquarters, Princeton, New Jersey
96 Fujian Xingye Bank, Shanghai, China
98 Lake Hills Country Club, Seoul, Korea
102 Library of the French Institute/Alliance Française, New York, New York
104 LIFE Magazine Dream House
106 House at Indian Hill, Cincinnati, Ohio
114 Kolonihaven House, Copenhagen, Denmark
116 Charles E. Beatley, Jr. Central Library, Alexandria, Virginia

1997

120 Uffelman Country House, Reading, Connecticut
124 Rearrangement of the Florence Cathedral Choir, Florence, Italy
126 NCAA Headquarters and Hall of Champions, Indianapolis, Indiana
132 Fortis AG Headquarters, Brussels, Belgium
134 El Gouna Golf Hotel and Club, El Gouna, Egypt
146 Golf Villas, El Gouna, Egypt
150 De Luwte, On the River Vecht, Netherlands
152 InterContinental Hotel, Taba Heights, Egypt
154 Competition for Hotel Sofitel, New York, New York
156 North Hall, Drexel University, Philadelphia, Pennsylvania
160 Mixed-use Building, Fukuoka, Japan
162 United States Courthouse, Washington, D.C.
164 Ogoori Plaza, Ogoori, Japan
166 Hotel Makati, Manila, Philippines
167 Dongwha Hoiyun Mixed-use Building, Seoul, Korea
168 O'Grady Library, Saint Martin's College, Lacey, Washington
170 The Impala, New York, New York
174 Study for a Private Residence, Long Island, New York

1998

176 The Washington Monument Restoration, Washington, D.C.
180 Competition for Peek & Cloppenburg Department Store, Dusseldorf, Germany
184 Competition for the Main Library of Nashville and Davidson County, Nashville, Tennessee
188 St. Mary's Church, Rockledge, Florida
192 Private Residence, Livingston, New Jersey
194 Martel, Jones and Brown Colleges, Rice University, Houston, Texas
204 JAL Plaza Prototype, Japan
206 Resort Hotel at Cotton Bay, Eleuthera, Bahamas
208 Cedar Gables, Minnetonka, Minnesota
214 Lotus Hotel and Convention Center, Cairo, Egypt
216 Sharm Hills Resort Study, Sharm el Sheikh, Egypt
218 Competition for the National Bank of Abu Dhabi, Abu Dhabi, U.A.E.
220 The NovaCare Complex, Philadelphia Eagles Training Center, Philadelphia, Pennsylvania

1999

224 Philadelphia Eagles Football Stadium Study, Philadelphia, Pennsylvania
226 Target Stage at Harriet Island Park, St. Paul, Minnesota

227 Elephant Fountain at Target House,
    Memphis, Tennessee
228 Watch Technicum, Lancaster County, Pennsylvania
232 Competition for the Singapore National Library,
    Singapore
236 Private Residence, Lake Geneva, Switzerland
238 The Detroit Institute of Arts, Detroit, Michigan
242 Museum of the Shenandoah Valley,
    Winchester, Virginia
246 Cosmotoda Master Plan, Barcelona, Spain

2000

248 425 Fifth Avenue, New York, New York
250 Famille-Tsukishima, Tokyo, Japan
252 Hart Productions Studio, San Francisco, California
253 Tallahassee Community Hospital, Tallahassee, Florida
254 Private Offices, Washington, D.C.
258 Sportevo, North Charleston, South Carolina
260 Stoa Olympica, Maroussi (Athens), Greece
264 Piazza Duomo and Piazza Orsini, Benevento, Italy
266 Private Museum in the Middle East
268 Private Villa Compound in the Middle East
270 Houston Branch of the Federal Reserve Bank of Dallas,
    Houston, Texas
272 Discovery Square Master Plan, Erie, Pennsylvania
274 United States Embassy Compound, Seoul, Korea
278 Mahler 4, Amsterdam, Netherlands

2001

280 Competition for the West Palm Beach Library,
    West Palm Beach, Florida
282 Dameisha Resort Master Plan, Shenzhen, China
286 Competition for the United States Institute of Peace,
    Washington, D.C.
288 Minneapolis Institute of Arts, Minneapolis, Minnesota
292 Children's Theatre Company, Minneapolis, Minnesota
296 Study for St. Charles Porte d'Aix, Marseilles, France
298 Three on the Bund, Shanghai, China
302 House at Sagaponac, Southampton, New York

2002

304 St. Coletta's School, Washington, D.C.
308 Department of Transportation Headquarters,
    Washington, D.C.
312 New Jersey State Police Headquarters Master Plan,
    West Trenton, New Jersey
314 Competition for the Jacksonville Library,
    Jacksonville, Florida
318 Resort Master Plan, Canary Islands

326 Kennedy Center Expansion Study, Washington, D.C.
328 South Campus Master Plan, Rice University,
    Houston, Texas
330 Arts and Sciences Building, New Jersey City
    University, Jersey City, New Jersey
332 Expansion of the Kavli Institute for Theoretical
    Physics, University of California, Santa Barbara,
    California

2003

334 Kasteel Holterveste, Den Bosch, Netherlands
336 Club Wedd House
338 Pavilions
340 Campus Master Plan, Florida Tech, Melbourne, Florida
342 National Automobile Museum,
    The Hague, Netherlands

International Finance
Corporation Headquarters

Washington, D.C., 1992

Lobby

Reception

The headquarters of the World Bank Group's International Finance Corporation is located on a triangular site on Pennsylvania Avenue at Washington Circle. The architectural design of the 12-story building provides a fresh approach to classical organization and detailing within the context of traditional Washington. Several pavilions are pulled forward from the body of building along Pennsylvania Avenue, which helps break down the scale of the 600-foot-long facade and provides opportunities to plan numerous corner offices. A distinctive cylindrical belvedere marks the corner of the site at Washington Circle.

In addition to offices, the program for this 1.1-million-square-foot building includes common facilities such as a conference and training center, multipurpose auditorium, library, cafeteria and dining rooms. The full-height atrium with its expansive skylight allows natural light into the center of the building and serves as a focal point for orientation and circulation.

Facing page: Dining room

Auditorium

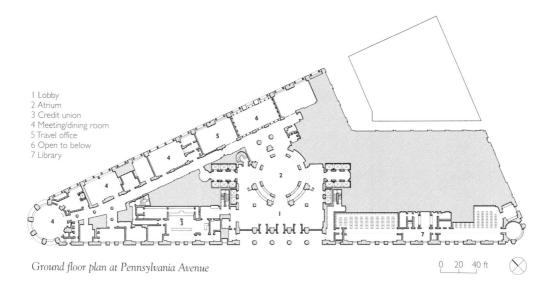

1 Lobby
2 Atrium
3 Credit union
4 Meeting/dining room
5 Travel office
6 Open to below
7 Library

Ground floor plan at Pennsylvania Avenue

0   20   40 ft

Arts and Sciences Building
Richard Stockton College

Pomona, New Jersey, 1992

The 37,000-square-foot Arts and Sciences Building at Richard Stockton College in the Pine Barrens of New Jersey establishes a gateway to the linked modern buildings of the campus developed in the 1970s. The entrance, a brick and cast stone portico, is located on axis with the concourse of the original buildings. A lecture hall with campus-wide usage is located on one side of the entrance. On the other side, a semi-detached art gallery was designed for future construction.

The building is arranged in a U-shaped configuration around a central, inward-facing courtyard. Faculty offices, study rooms and common areas face the courtyard, and classrooms, laboratories and studios face outward. The courtyard is articulated with closely spaced columns of green glazed brick reminiscent of the surrounding pine forests. The exterior of the building is clad in terra cotta, ochre and blue-green brick and cast stone, reflecting the colors of the sandy soil, indigenous vegetation and waterways of the Pine Barrens.

Courtyard

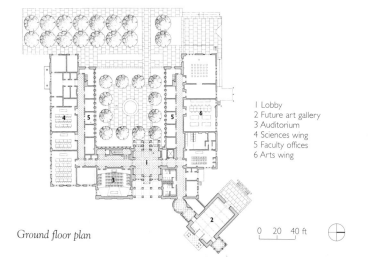

1 Lobby
2 Future art gallery
3 Auditorium
4 Sciences wing
5 Faculty offices
6 Arts wing

Ground floor plan

0   20   40 ft

Auditorium

Entrance facade

Indianapolis Art Center

Indianapolis, Indiana, 1992

Entrance facade

The Indianapolis Art Center contains studios for painting, sculpture, ceramics, photography and printmaking, an art gallery for changing exhibits, a 250-seat auditorium, a library, a gift shop and administrative offices. Site constraints limited the building's footprint to a long narrow bar of approximately 40,000 square feet and restricted the height to one story. Variations in window types help offset the effect of the length of the primary facades. The entrance and garden porticoes establish an axis through the building aligned with the termination of Ferguson Street, which links the Art Center with Broadripple Village five blocks away. The library is located in an octagonal pavilion facing the garden. The studios face north and open directly onto gardens along the White River, creating literal and figurative links between art and nature. Subsequent projects at the Indianapolis Art Center include the development of the gardens as a sensory art park for sculpture exhibitions and special events.

1 Gallery
2 Library
3 Auditorium
4 Studios

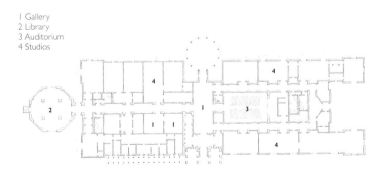

Ground floor plan

0   20   40 ft

Library

Astrid Park Plaza Hotel

Antwerp, Belgium, 1992

View from lounge toward train station

The mixed-use building in which the Astrid Park Plaza Hotel is located occupies an important urban site at the north end of Astrid Square facing Antwerp's monumental Beaux-Arts train station. In addition to the 240-room hotel, the building contains commercial office space, a conference center, a shopping center, restaurants and bars, underground parking and an entrance to the subterranean city-wide Metro system.

The massing, character and materials of the building reflect the eclectic nature of the immediate context and Antwerp in general. The architecture of this historic city is characterized by the richness of building facades that provide continuous streetwalls defining the public squares as outdoor rooms. Likewise, the frontal nature of the Astrid Park Plaza Hotel creates a sense of closure for Astrid Square and complements the massing of the train station. The main facade consists of a central section flanked by two narrow towers. A lower, cylindrical tower adjoining the west wall of the hotel contains retail shops and specialized hotel functions.

South facade facing Astrid Square

Ground floor plan

0 5 10 m

Second floor plan

1 Hotel lobby
2 Hotel lounge
3 Retail
4 Business center lobby
5 Metro entrance
6 Garage entrance
7 Restaurant
8 Prefunction
9 Meeting room
10 Banquet hall

Restaurant

Typical guestroom

Facing page: View from the west

Castalia
Ministries of Health, Welfare and Sport

The Hague, Netherlands, 1993

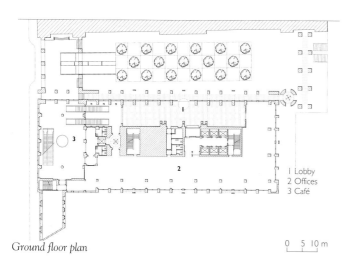

de Resident site with existing building to right of center

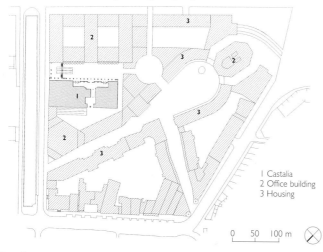

1 Castalia
2 Office building
3 Housing

0   50   100 m

Site plan

1 Lobby
2 Offices
3 Café

0   5   10 m

Ground floor plan

In the early 1990s, the architect Rob Krier prepared a mixed-use master plan for an area of The Hague called de Resident, which proposed a combination of new infill construction and renovation of existing buildings. Among the existing buildings was a 1950s jack-slab building that had been stripped of its failing facade and core and reduced to its structural system. Michael Graves & Associates was commissioned to redesign this building for the headquarters of the Ministries of Health, Welfare and Sport.

The building, known as Castalia, was expanded to 25 stories and 29,000 square meters in area. The design strategy reconciles the small scale of existing low-rise housing with the larger scale of surrounding medium- and high-rise office buildings. Its articulation as "twin towers" separated by protruding bay windows of glazed brick reinforces a new vertical reading. The dual towers also signified the initial intention that two ministries would occupy the building. The distinctive profile on the city skyline is reminiscent of the shape of typical Dutch steeply gabled roofs. While accommodating the constraints of the existing structure, the planar brick facades feature gridded window patterns characteristic of local traditional architecture although at a much larger scale.

City view

Lobby

Nexus Momochi
Residential Tower
Fukuoka, Japan, 1993

View from the bay

For the 1989 Asian-Pacific Exposition, the city of Fukuoka reclaimed a large portion of its bayside waterfront as a new residential district, which included a five-story apartment building designed by Michael Graves & Associates. Several years later, the firm was commissioned to design a 27-story luxury apartment tower at the end of the axis established by that first building. The tower, the tallest building in the area, occupies one of the most prestigious sites in this internationally acclaimed district. The building's exterior is composed as a slender, ochre-colored frame of precast concrete applied over a glass curtain wall. The layered yet transparent quality of the facade gives the tower a luminous presence when seen from the water, appearing as an abstract version of a lighthouse. The facade's generous fenestration also provides the apartments with spectacular waterfront views.

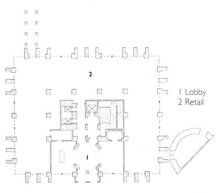

1 Lobby
2 Retail

Ground floor plan   0 2.5 5 m

Lobby

Taiwan National Museum
of Pre-History

Taitung City, Taiwan, 1993

Located near an important Neolithic archaeological site at Peinan on Taiwan's scenic Eastern coast, the National Museum of Pre-history is dedicated to the study, preservation and public exhibition of artifacts from the site, as well as materials from other prehistoric Austronesian cultures. The campus provides extensive indoor and outdoor visitor facilities, including interpretive exhibits that tell the story of man's evolving relationship with nature. The program for the 425,000-square-foot main building includes flexible exhibit galleries, a 200-seat theater, an international conference center, a research library, offices, curatorial laboratories and archival storage.

Major public programmatic elements are expressed as individual pavilions organized around a monumental courtyard. This outdoor space, the focal point of the complex, is designed for ceremonial performances and other public events. The campus is landscaped as a park, using the natural landforms and vegetation to evoke the feeling of prehistoric sites.

Northwest elevation

1 Visitor entrance
2 Mountain Square exhibit
3 Gallery
4 Administration entrance
5 Administrative offices
6 Academic research center

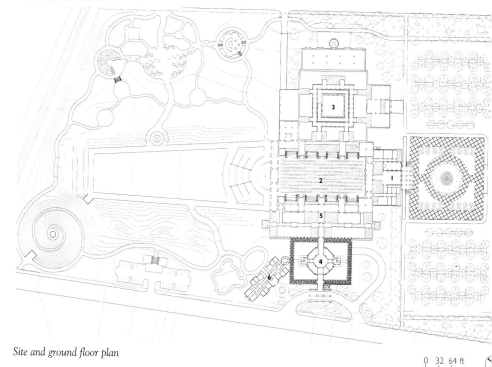

Site and ground floor plan

0 32 64 ft

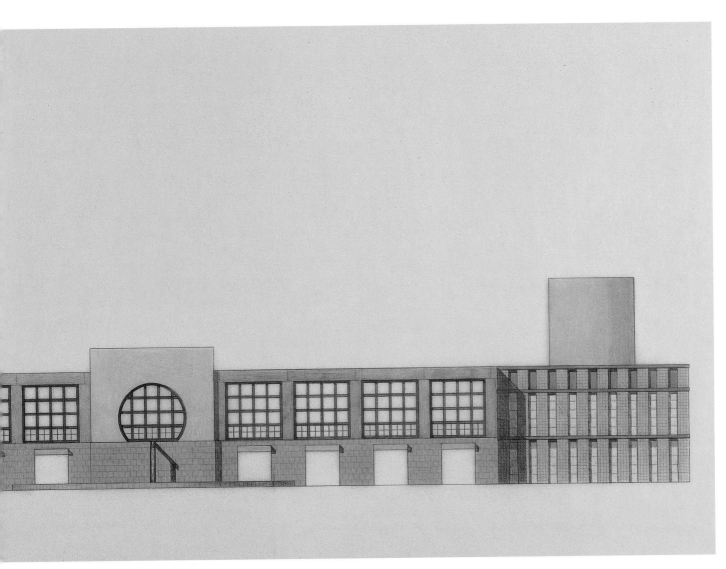

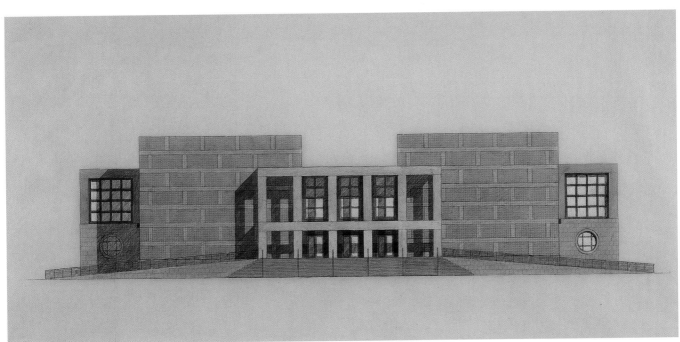

Entrance pavilion elevation

View from the north

Exhibit

United States Post Office

Celebration, Florida, 1993

View from the Town Square

The Post Office, located adjacent to Town Hall in the new community of Celebration, Florida, is composed in two simple parts: a rotunda that serves as the public entrance, and a rectangular block with an open-air loggia where mailboxes are located. The character of the Post Office respects the traditions of the building type as well as the prevailing architecture of the region. The rotunda announces this small building's public presence while the form of the loggia and the materials and colors of the building are typical of small-scale architecture found throughout Florida.

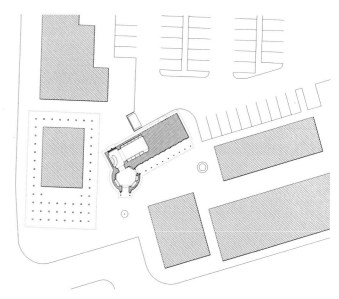

Site and ground floor plan

0 20 40 ft

Disney's Garden Pavilions

Orlando, Florida, 1994

View from the Walt Disney World® Dolphin Hotel

Two linked garden pavilions — the Sorcerer's Apprentice Pavilion and Dancing Hippos Pavilion — comprise a large-scale outdoor facility for special events, receptions and parties, located on the grounds of the Walt Disney World® Dolphin Hotel and Walt Disney World® Swan Hotel near Orlando, Florida. The covered but open-air spaces are supported by internal kitchen and restroom facilities. A large terrace with a stage adjoins them. Although the pavilions are permanent structures, the roofs have the character of tents so as to reinforce the temporary, festive nature of the activities taking place in the garden.

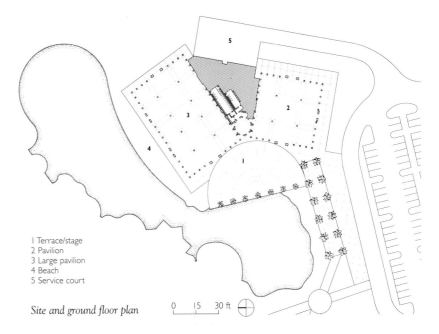

1 Terrace/stage
2 Pavilion
3 Large pavilion
4 Beach
5 Service court

Site and ground floor plan

0   15   30 ft

43

1500 Ocean Drive
Miami Beach, Florida, 1994

Cartoon for mural by Michael Graves

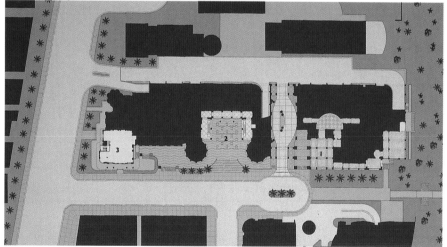

Site plan

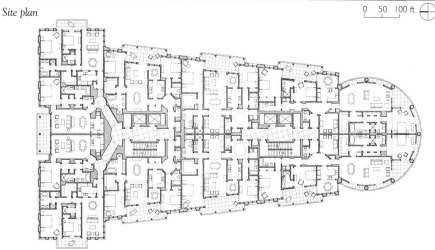

Typical condominium floor plan

Facing page: View of condominium building looking toward the ocean with retail center in foreground

The residential condominiums at 1500 Ocean Drive and the adjoining retail center, Ocean Steps, are located at the intersection of 15th Street and Ocean Drive in South Beach. The project's articulation, colors and detailing respect the scale and character of the context, which includes the adjacent famous Art Deco district and several contemporary apartment buildings.

The 15-story, 111-unit condominium building is oriented toward the ocean. Its beachfront cylindrical tower, evocative of a coastal beacon, offers panoramic views of the surroundings. Retail, restaurant and office spaces are contained in the former Bancroft Hotel, an adjacent historic Art Deco building which was renovated for retail and office use. A U-shaped retail courtyard at the visual terminus of Ocean Drive links the condominiums and the Bancroft Hotel.

1 Condominium building entrance
2 Ocean Steps retail center
3 Former Bancroft Hotel

0 50 100 ft

0 20 40 ft

One Port Center

Camden, New Jersey, 1994

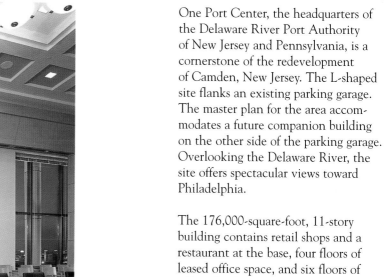

One Port Center, the headquarters of the Delaware River Port Authority of New Jersey and Pennsylvania, is a cornerstone of the redevelopment of Camden, New Jersey. The L-shaped site flanks an existing parking garage. The master plan for the area accommodates a future companion building on the other side of the parking garage. Overlooking the Delaware River, the site offers spectacular views toward Philadelphia.

The 176,000-square-foot, 11-story building contains retail shops and a restaurant at the base, four floors of leased office space, and six floors of offices for the Port Authority. The executive offices and boardroom are located on the top floor of the building behind three-story yellow aluminum composite columns. The blue and white glazed brick used at the lower level makes reference to the building's waterfront location.

Boardroom

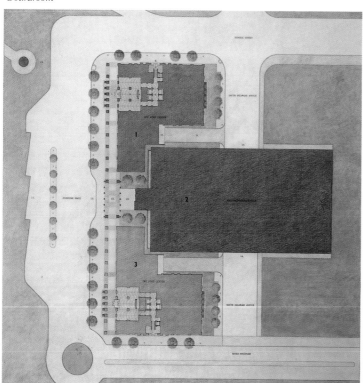

1 One Port Center
2 Parking garage
3 Future building

Site plan with current and future buildings

0   20   40 ft

House at Coolidge Point

Manchester-by-the-Sea,
Massachusetts, 1994

Porch overlooking the ocean

This single-family house is located on a bluff along the rocky New England coast, approximately 60 feet from the Atlantic Ocean. In response to both program and site, individual pavilions — a residence, an office, guest quarters, swimming pool, pool house and garden elements — are given their own identities. The casual nature of the composition in plan is reminiscent of New England compounds developed over time.

Each pavilion in the composition contains a separate function. The living and dining rooms anchor the composition, with other pavilions pinwheeling off this central block. The easternmost pavilion contains a library in a rotunda-like form. Internally, it acts as a hinge connecting the office, guest quarters, and the winter garden and pool. Externally, it acts as a marker, reminiscent of the lighthouses that characterize the region. Two courtyards, one forming the entry and the other facing the water, along with a variety of framed views, establish reciprocal relationships between the building and the landscape.

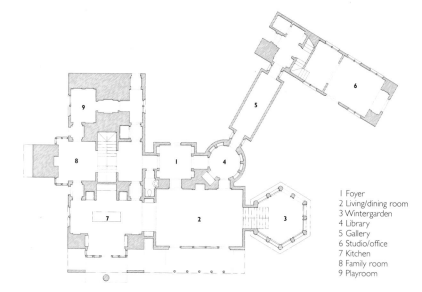

1 Foyer
2 Living/dining room
3 Wintergarden
4 Library
5 Gallery
6 Studio/office
7 Kitchen
8 Family room
9 Playroom

Ground floor plan

0   10   20 ft

Kitchen

Library

Miramar Resort Hotel

El Gouna, Egypt, 1995

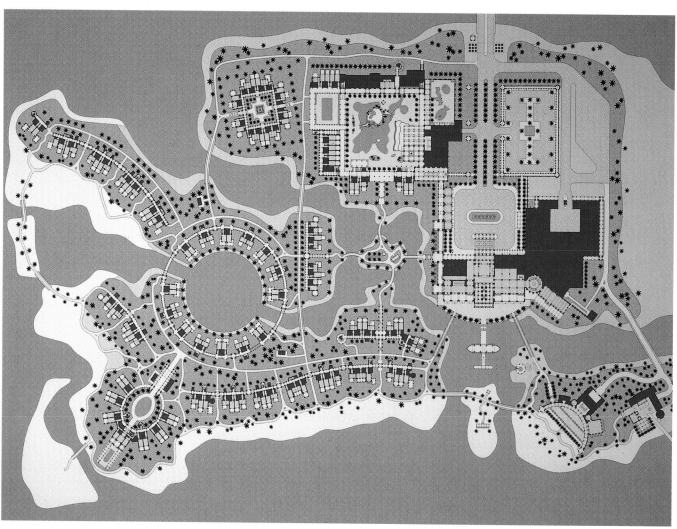

Site and ground floor plan

0   25   50 ft

The Sheraton hotel known as the Miramar is a five-star resort consisting of over 400 guestrooms and public spaces such as food and beverage facilities. Dramatically sited on the Red Sea, the project is bounded on all sides by water or shoreline. The landscaped grounds feature a myriad of canals and lagoons, providing each guestroom with a waterfront orientation. The elaborate swimming pool complex includes picturesque adult pools, an exercise pool and a pool for children. Built using traditional Egyptian vernacular construction methods and materials, the guestrooms feature brick vaulted and domed ceilings. The great variety in the forms and detailing of the hotel creates a unique resort that reflects its desert and waterfront context in an elegant and often surprising manner.

Character study

Main building entrance elevation

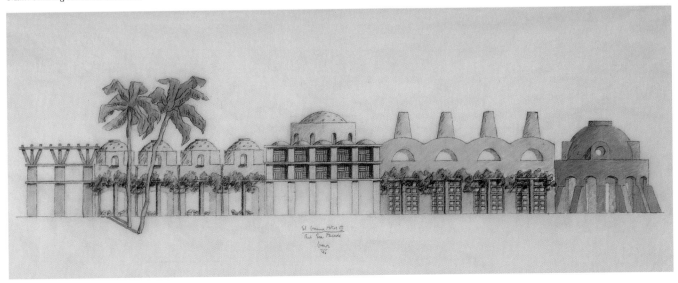

Main building beachfront elevation

59

View from the beach

Guestroom pavilions detail

Guestroom pavilions detail

Facing page: Lobby

Suite sitting room

Typical guestroom

Riverfront Sports Complex Master Plan

Cincinnati, Ohio, 1995

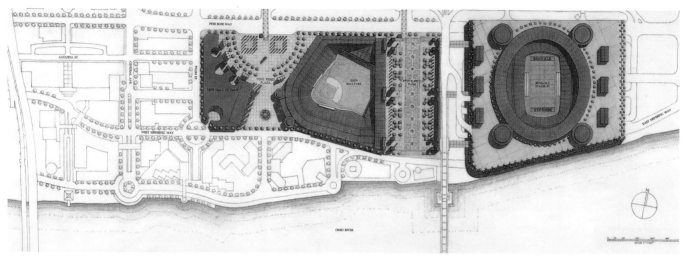

Site plan

0   125   250 ft

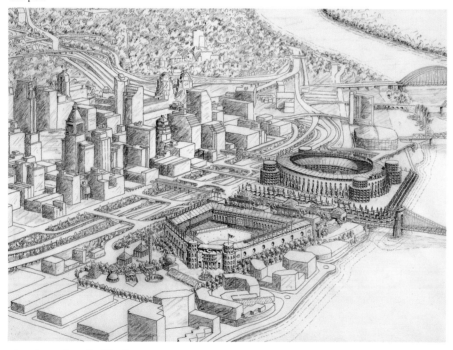

Aerial view from the Ohio River

The master plan for the Riverfront Sports Complex in Cincinnati was prepared to assist Hamilton County in its successful campaign to obtain public funding for the development. The master plan provides independent sports facilities for baseball and football, integrated into a complex of public places such as a park, a plaza and entertainment centers. The proposal to clad the buildings in brick is intended to reinforce continuity with the character of the urban surroundings.

The 45,000-seat ballpark for the Cincinnati Reds baseball team is sited so that it does not interfere with either the city fabric or views toward the Ohio River from neighboring streets. A public plaza adjacent to the ballpark also accommodates entertainment activities, restaurants, retail shops and a hall of fame. The master plan recommended replacement of the outmoded Riverfront Stadium with a new football stadium configured around the needs, traditions and rules of the game.

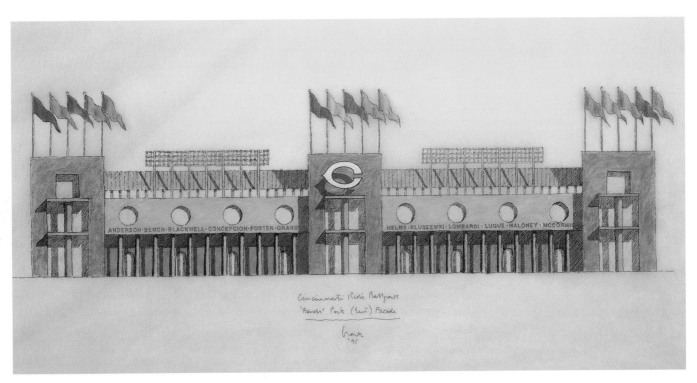

Cincinnati Reds ballpark

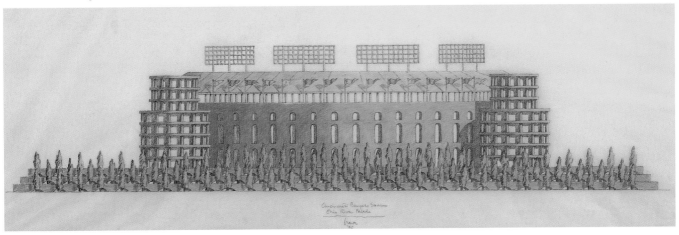

Cincinnati Bengals football stadium

Laurel Hall
New Jersey Institute of Technology

Newark, New Jersey, 1995 and 2000

In conjunction with a master plan prepared by Michael Graves & Associates for the New Jersey Institute of Technology, a series of projects establish a residential quadrangle for undergraduate students at the southeast edge of the urban campus. Laurel Hall, a 300-bed student residence that was the first project to be built, forms the longitudinal boundary of a new campus green opposite the school's parking deck. Oak Hall, a former industrial building previously converted to student housing, establishes the far boundary of the green. A new color scheme for Oak Hall's facades was created to complement Laurel Hall. These projects were followed several years later by an expansion of Laurel Hall, which approximately doubled its capacity. The expansion, extending along Warren Street perpendicular to the original building, completes the fourth side of the open space.

Laurel Hall's centralized entrance portico, with four-story aluminum columns supporting a thin flat roof, acts as a symbolic front porch. In order to lend a residential scale to the lengthy facades of the building, the single rooms and stairs are recessed from the plane of the facades and finished with dark gray-blue stucco as if in deep shadow.

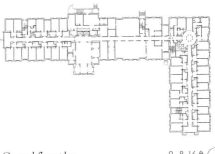

Ground floor plan　　　0　8　16 ft

67

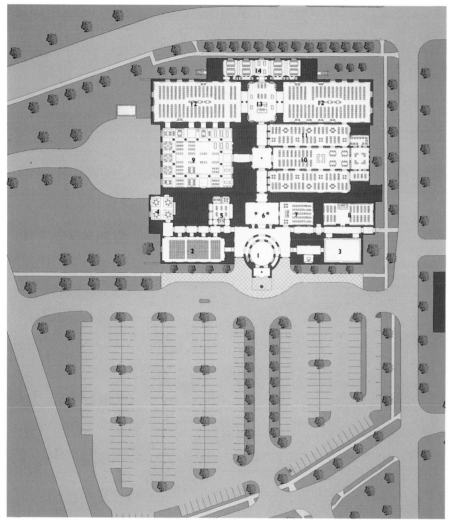

1 Rotunda foyer
2 Multipurpose room
3 Gallery
4 Café
5 Bookstore
6 Circulation desk
7 Red Carpet services
8 Audio-visual collection
9 Reference/Periodicals
10 Children's library
11 Young Adult Collection
12 Adult Collection
13 Service desk
14 Reading room

Site and ground floor plan

0 25 50 ft

Main Library of Topeka and Shawnee County

Topeka, Kansas, 1995

Upon the 125th anniversary of its founding, the Main Library of Topeka and Shawnee County commissioned the renovation of its 65,000-square-foot facility built in the 1950s and an expansion of 100,000 square feet. The expansion wraps around the existing structure, resulting in redesigned facades that establish a new identity for this important public institution.

A three-story rotunda on axis with Washburn Street creates a new public entrance facing adjacent parking. Flanking the entrance are several community facilities, including a 360-seat auditorium, a café, a bookstore and a 3,500-square-foot art gallery. The circular lobby reinforces the communality of these amenities and leads to the Topeka Room on the third level. Large circular skylights allow natural light to enter the building during the day and create a monumental beacon when lit from within at night. Internally, the intersection of the building's east-west and north-south axes is distinguished by an atrium lit from above by a skylight. The atrium allows users to orient themselves within the library and gain access to the surrounding Adult Collections, Periodicals and Youth Services Departments.

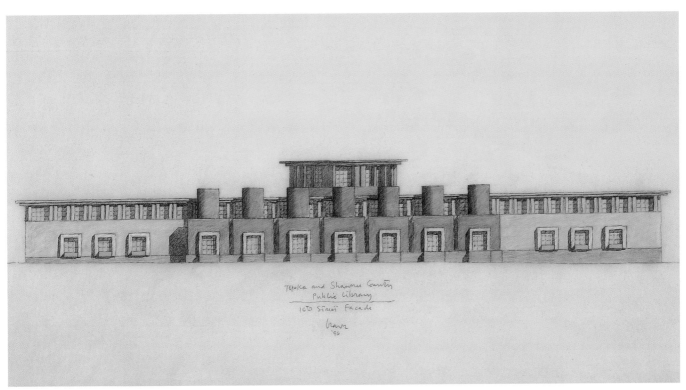

Preliminary 10th Street elevation

Model view from the south showing main entrance

69

Reading room

Atrium

O'Reilly Theater

Pittsburgh, Pennsylvania, 1996

Service center from Penn Avenue

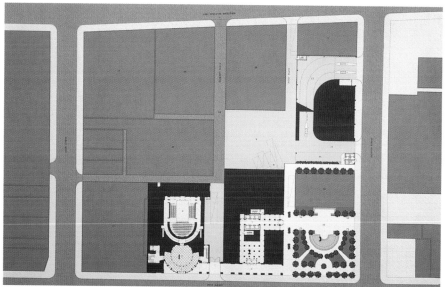

Site and ground floor plan

1 O'Reilly Theater
2 Service center
3 Park

0   30   60 ft

Lobby view from second floor.

The O'Reilly is a 650-seat legitimate theater located on Penn Avenue in Pittsburgh's Cultural District. The massing and composition of the building continue the existing streetwall while establishing a distinctive identity appropriate to a cultural institution. A curved overhanging copper roof and backlit building sign define the entrance and double-height lobby. The circular forms in plan and section foreshadow the shape of the auditorium and help define a unified experience for the theater audience.

The auditorium has a thrust stage around which the audience is seated on three levels, providing an intimate venue for repertory theater and chamber music. The differing acoustic needs of these two performance types were met through the shape of the space, the articulation of the surfaces and the choice of construction materials.

The project included the design of a public park in conjunction with landscape architect Dan Kiley and sculptor Louise Bourgeois. An adjacent service center, constructed in a subsequent phase, contains eight levels of parking above a ground floor with retail shops, a cabaret theater and a ticket office serving various venues within the Cultural District.

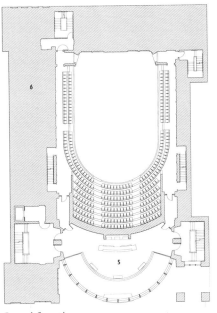

Second floor plan

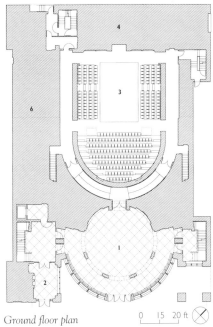

Ground floor plan

0 15 20 ft

1 Lobby
2 Tickets
3 Theater
4 Backstage
5 Intermission bar
6 Offices

Facing page: Theater balconies

Second floor intermission bar

Mural cartoon

Guestroom groups facing the lagoon

Site plan

0 20 40 m

The Hyatt Regency Hotel in Taba Heights is a five-star resort with 426 guestrooms, situated on the mountainous Sinai Peninsula facing the Bay of Aqaba. The main building, with its strong axial entrance and palm court, embraces a large terrace, where a restaurant, bar and other activities look out over manmade rock formations toward the sea. The outlying guestroom groups are sited in the hilly terrain so as to preserve views of the water from all quarters.

As with its companion project, the Sheraton Miramar Resort Hotel in El Gouna, which was designed for the same developer, the architecture is distinguished by the variety of building shapes and details. The character of the buildings, through massing, materials and facades, as well as through the custom-designed interior furnishings,

relates in an abstract way to the traditions of rural Egyptian architecture. Built using typical Egyptian construction methods and materials, many of the guestrooms feature brick vaulted or domed ceilings.

Pool snack bar

Pool court

View toward the Gulf of Aqaba

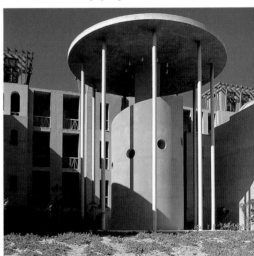

Stair tower

85

Bar

Guestroom

World Trade
Exchange Center

Manila, Philippines, 1996

The World Trade Exchange Center is a mixed-use building 35 stories high, located in Metro Manila's historic district near Manila Bay and the Pasig River. The massing, fenestration patterns and coloration articulate the various uses of the building. The base contains two floors of retail space. Above it are six floors of parking with openings in the facade shielded by awninglike metal louvers. The upper portion of the building, used principally for offices, is divided horizontally in two sections to help diminish the scale of the building in deference to its midrise neighbors. The cylindrical corner tower features expansive windows facing Manila Bay.

Calle Nimfa elevation

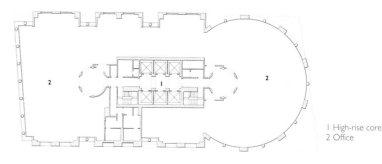

Typical office floor plan

1 High-rise core
2 Office

0   5   10 m

90

Southeast elevation

Ortigas Tycoon Twin Towers

Ortigas, Philippines, 1996

The Ortigas Tycoon Twin Towers is a mixed-use development consisting of two 38-story towers rising above a six-story plinth. The plinth contains retail and recreational facilities on the lowest levels and a parking garage above, characterized by awninglike metal louvers along the long horizontal facades. One of the towers contains office space and the other a condominium hotel.

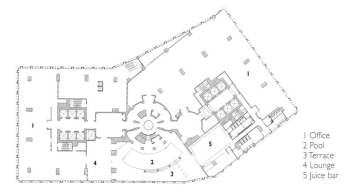

1 Office
2 Pool
3 Terrace
4 Lounge
5 Juice bar

Plinth plan at health club level

0 5 10 m

91

Miele Americas Headquarters

Princeton, New Jersey, 1996 and 1999

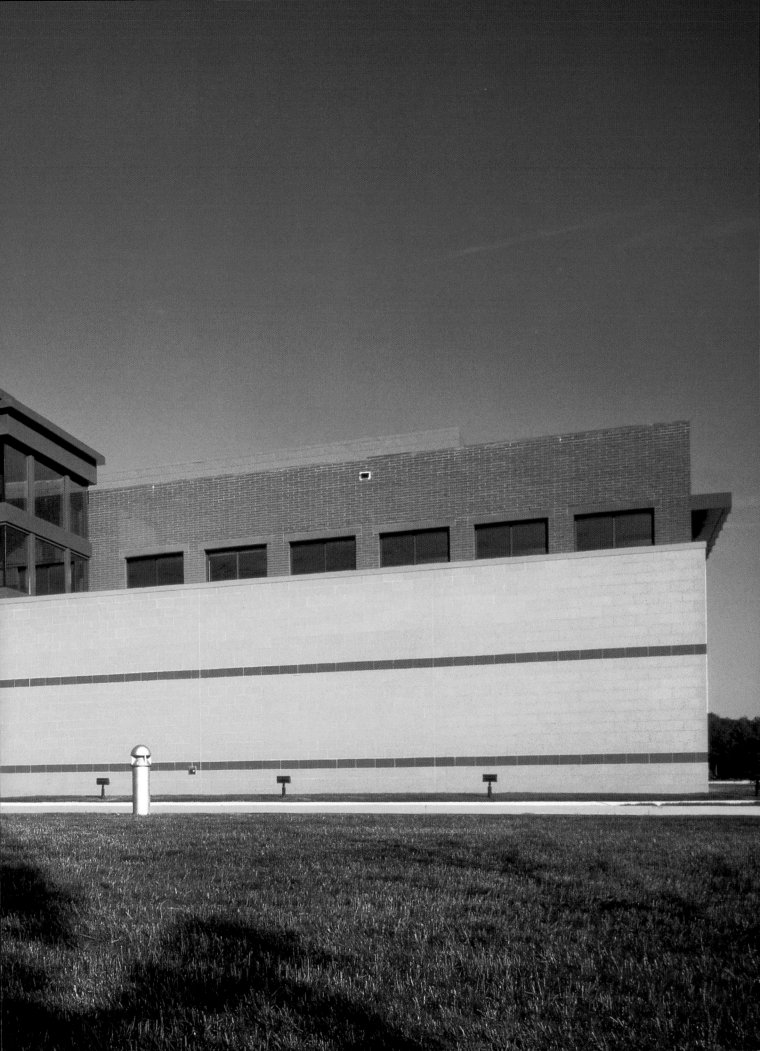

Lobby

The Americas headquarters of this international company specializing in high-quality household appliances is located on Route One near Princeton. Its brightly lit entrance pavilion topped by a large-scale sign allows the building to be easily identified from the highway.

The ground floor accommodates a large showroom to welcome visitors and provide display areas for various Miele products. A double-height portion of the showroom is enclosed in glass, allowing the space to be flooded with natural light during the day and become a glowing landmark at night. Surrounding the showroom are various spaces for the presentation of Miele products, including demonstration stations, a large training room and meeting rooms. The second floor is used for Miele's offices.

A planned expansion that doubled the size of the building was implemented soon after the completion of the first phase.

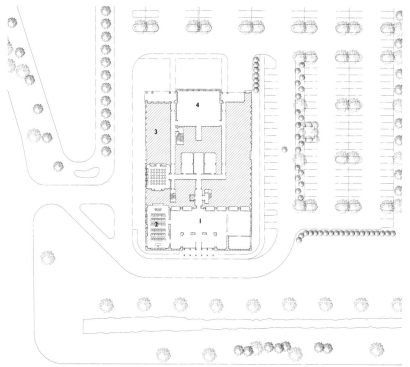

1 Showroom
2 Demonstration kitchen
3 Meeting room
4 Technical support

Site and ground floor plan

0 16 32 ft

Fujian Xingye Bank

Shanghai, China, 1996

The Fujian Xingye Bank, upon acquiring a site in the historic district of Shanghai near the Courthouse and Customs Building and facing the Bund, commissioned alternative conceptual designs for a 26-story mixed-use building. The lower 10 floors would contain banking facilities as well as retail and office space. The tower would contain tenant office space. These several functions of the building are expressed through massing, architectural design, materials and colors. The bank subsequently sold the site and the project designed by Michael Graves & Associates did not proceed.

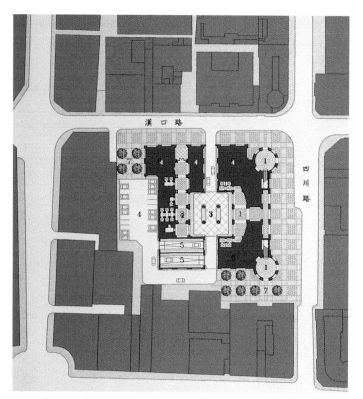

Site and ground floor plan

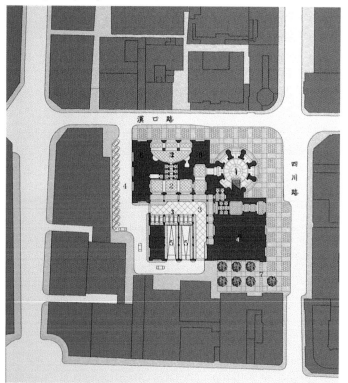

Preliminary site and ground floor plan

1 Bank lobby
2 Office tower lobby
3 Motor court
4 Retail

0   10   20 m

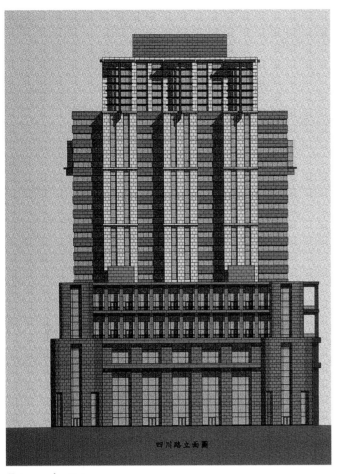

Entrance elevation

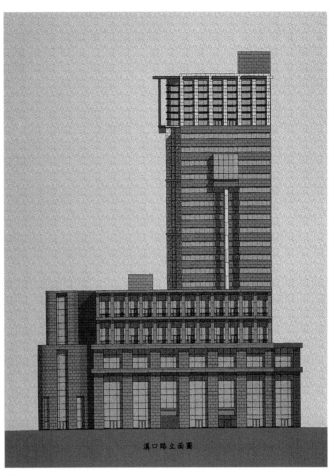

Side elevation

Preliminary entrance elevation

Preliminary side elevation

Lake Hills Country Club

Seoul, Korea, 1996

Lobby

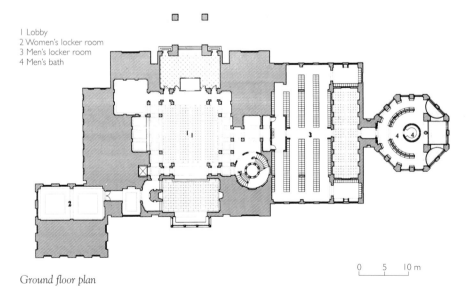

1 Lobby
2 Women's locker room
3 Men's locker room
4 Men's bath

Ground floor plan

0 5 10 m

Facing page: Golf course facade

The clubhouse for Lake Hills Country Club in Seoul overlooks the golf course and contains a restaurant, breakfast room, baths and changing rooms for men and women, as well as golf cart storage and other service spaces. The men's baths are located in the octagonal tower, and the women's baths are located in a pavilion at the opposite end of the building.

As a building type, a golf club embodies the spirit of sport, camaraderie and the pleasures of domestic comfort. At the client's request, the clubhouse was given an architectural character intended to recall a traditional manor house, an inviting and familiar place for members and their guests.

Library of the French Institute/Alliance Française

New York, New York, 1996

Reading room

The French Institute/Alliance Française is located in a historic townhouse at 22 East 60th Street in the Upper East Side of Manhattan. Its library is housed in approximately 5,800 square feet on the second and third floors. In this complete renovation of the library, the second floor accommodates public spaces, including the reception room and gallery, the main reading room, the reference room, a computer learning center and the children's collection. Openings in the ceiling provide visual connection to the stacks located on the third floor.

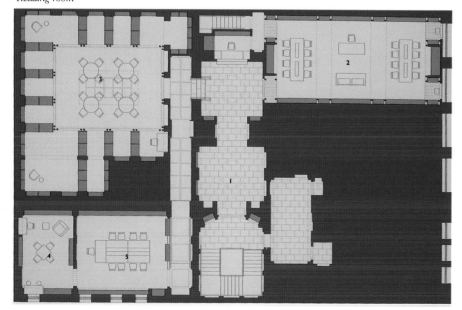

Second floor plan

1 Reception
2 Reference/Periodicals
3 Reading room
4 Children's collection
5 Computer workstations

0   8   16 ft

East 60th Street elevation

LIFE Magazine
Dream House

1996

LIFE Magazine commissioned Michael
Graves to design its third annual pro-
totypical "Dream House." LIFE's goal
was to show its readers that a well-
known architect could create a house
design comparable in size and cost to
the average new house being built
in the United States. The design
anticipates flexibility in its plans and
materials in order to be adaptable to
the requirements of various families
and sites.

The rotunda foyer is central to the
organization of the plan and sets up
the procession through the house. The
orderly nature of the architecture and
interiors allows the owners to achieve
a comfortable sense of well-being in
the house and to personalize it for
their lifestyles.

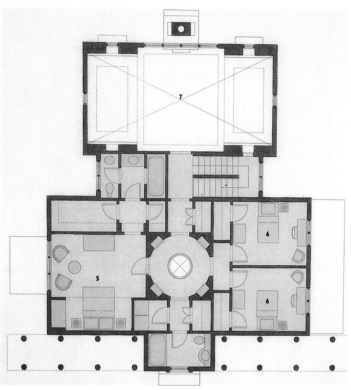

1 Foyer
2 Kitchen
3 Garage
4 Living/dining room
5 Master bedroom
6 Bedroom
7 Open to below

Second floor plan

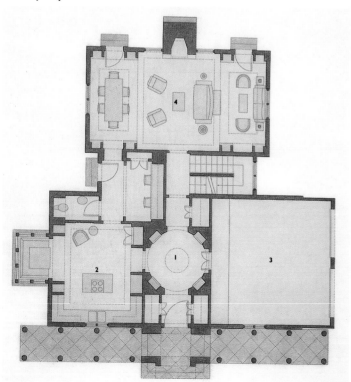

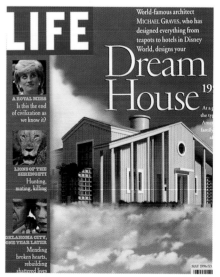

Ground floor plan

0   8   16 ft

LIFE Magazine cover

Street elevation

Kitchen

Living/dining room

105

House at Indian Hill

Cincinnati, Ohio, 1996

View toward house from studio and potting shed

Located on a 3.5-acre lot adjacent to heavily wooded public parkland, and overlooking the Little Miami River, this 6,000-square-foot house uses an L-shaped configuration to engage the surrounding landscape. The massing consists of 10 distinct pavilions carefully arranged within a building area constrained by zoning requirements. The pavilions evolved from different programmatic uses and are individualized through distinctive shapes, colors and materials.

A formal tripartite facade and a square paved forecourt mark the entry to the house. Views to the river are framed in a variety of ways from the vaulted living room, the study, the dining room, the solarium and the master bedroom's elevated covered terrace. A guest wing above the three-car garage is connected to the main house by a circular stair tower clad with fieldstone. A path from the sheltered court at the rear of the house leads past a pyramidal pool house and swimming pool and into the parkland beyond. At the far end of the site, set in a field near the river, a folly affectionately called the "potting shed" contains a greenhouse and a small studio.

Potting shed

View from the east

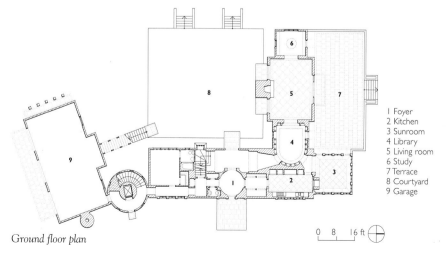

1 Foyer
2 Kitchen
3 Sunroom
4 Library
5 Living room
6 Study
7 Terrace
8 Courtyard
9 Garage

Ground floor plan

0   8   16 ft

Dining room

Kolonihaven House

Copenhagen, Denmark, 1996

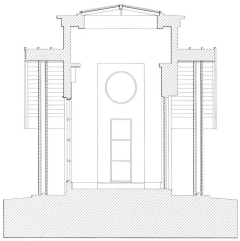

Section

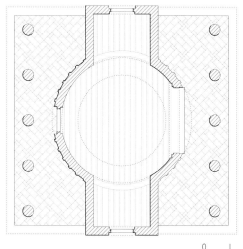

Plan

0   1   2 m

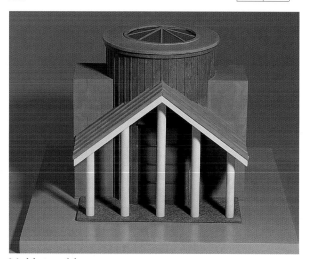

Model view of the entrance

To celebrate Copenhagen as the 1996 European Cultural Capital, 14 internationally known architects were commissioned to reinterpret the "Kolonihaven House," a traditional building type found in Danish garden colonies. These small structures of approximately 7.5 square meters range from simple farm buildings to colorfully decorated pleasure pavilions found in romantic gardens. In their simplest form, they invoke the pleasures of summer gardening to provide sustenance for the household as well as an idyllic escape from the hectic nature of urban life. Michael Graves & Associates' version of the Kolonihaven House consists of a simple rotunda flanked by porches that connect the house to the garden.

In addition to being exhibited through drawings and models, the Kolonihaven Houses are to be constructed in Denmark's first architecture park in Vallenbæk, south of Copenhagen.

Entrance elevation

Side elevation

Charles E. Beatley, Jr. Central Library

Alexandria, Virginia, 1996

Entrance elevation

The several programmatic functions of the 45,000-square-foot Charles E. Beatley, Jr. Central Library are composed as distinctive volumes around a semi-public courtyard, creating a massing strategy reminiscent of a village square. The library has two primary facades, one forming the entrance from Pickett Street, and the other providing a public presence along Duke Street. The building is topped by a dozen roofs that recall the community's roots in Old Town. The resulting silhouette symbolizes the first step toward the city's master plan goal of establishing a new civic center on the west side of Alexandria.

The interior of the library is open in plan. However, the various departments are distinguished by the configuration of the ceilings, which reflect the distinctive roof structures.

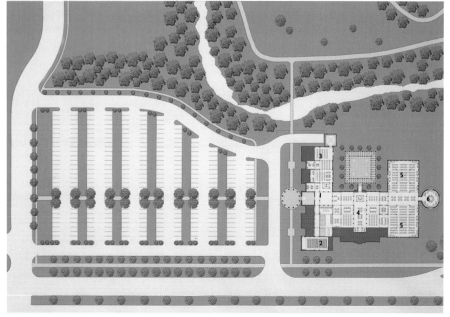

Site and ground floor plan

0   50   100 ft

1 Lobby
2 Community room
3 Children's library
4 Reference
5 Adult collection
6 Periodicals

Facing page: Reading room

View from Duke Street

East facade

FRANK AND BETTY WRIGHT
READING GARDEN
A GIFT OF THE FRANK AND BETTY WRIGHT FOUNDATION

Uffelman Country House

Reading, Connecticut, 1997

Garden elevation

At the client's request, this weekend house draws its inspiration from the tradition of decorative pavilions or follies found in romantic country gardens. As amusements that provide escape from the realities of everyday life, such buildings are often playful and picturesque.

This country house is sited at the top of a hill from where it overlooks a private golf, rolling wooded terrain and a pond. The four-story fieldstone stair tower in the center of the house leads to a study on the top floor. The tower is flanked by two multistory wings that are given the character of festive striped tents. One wing contains the living room and guest bedroom, and the other contains a family room, dining room, kitchen and bedrooms.

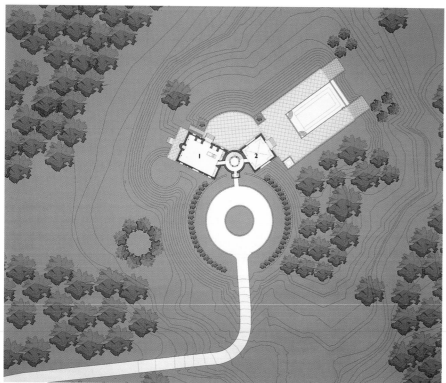

Site and ground floor plan

0   25   50 ft

1 Kitchen and
   dining/family room
2 Living room

Stair hall from above

Living room

Rearrangement of the Florence Cathedral Choir

Florence, Italy, 1997

Sectional model showing baldachin

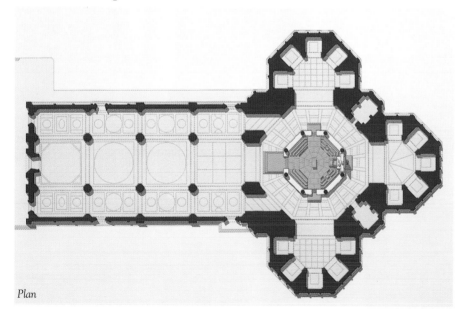

Plan

Several architects were invited to participate in an "international consultation" concerning the rearrangement of the choir of the Florence Cathedral. The choir, located beneath the magnificent Renaissance dome by Filippo Brunelleschi, culminates the nave and marks the crossing with an octagonal walled enclosure within which mass is celebrated. To contemporary ecclesiastic sensibilities, the choir enclosure is a barrier, separating clergy from the assembly area and limiting participation of the faithful in church rituals. Rearrangement of altar, pulpit, seating and the sculpture by Baccio Bandinelli were to meet current liturgical needs while respecting the original concept.

The proposal to center a new framelike baldachin beneath the dome takes into account centroidal and linear readings of the architecture. The form of the baldachin relates to the dome above, and its wooden structure is more open and ephemeral in comparison to the surrounding church. The platform below the baldachin is raised above floor level to resolve the current lack of visibility. From the platform, an apron extends toward the nave, acknowledging the linear progression of the basilican church plan and providing a functional setting for celebratory rituals.

Sketch of Bandinelli sculpture

Photo collage of baldachin in the cathedral

NCAA Headquarters and
Hall of Champions

Indianapolis, Indiana, 1997

Commemorative print by Michael Graves

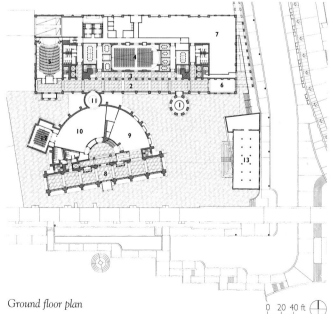

The headquarters office building, conference center, and Hall of Champions of the National Collegiate Athletic Association occupies a prominent site on the Central Canal in White River State Park in Indianapolis. The complex is composed as a series of interconnected structures that create a campuslike setting, which both reflects the character of the park and refers to the collegiate atmosphere of the NCAA's member institutions.

The 140,000-square-foot program for the offices and conference center is accommodated in a four-story block at the north side of the site. Upper floor offices look over a full-height internal atrium and the entrance plaza. The simple massing of the office building allows it to serve as a backdrop for the more specialized features of the project: the Hall of Champions and the historic Acme Evans Superintendent's Building, which houses a high school athletic organization.

The 40,000-square-foot program for the Hall of Champions includes a 90-seat theater and two floors of exhibitions featuring the history of the NCAA and the achievements of teams and individual scholar-athletes. It is entered through an arcade reminiscent of collegiate athletic facilities in which a 45-foot-high lobby gallery is open to the public without charge.

1 Office building entrance
2 Atrium
3 Prefunction
4 Multipurpose room
5 Auditorium
6 Boardroom
7 Library
8 Hall of Champions
  Great Hall
9 Gift shop
10 Exhibit
11 Champions room
12 Auditorium
13 High school federation
   offices

Ground floor plan

0 20 40 ft

Hall of Champions

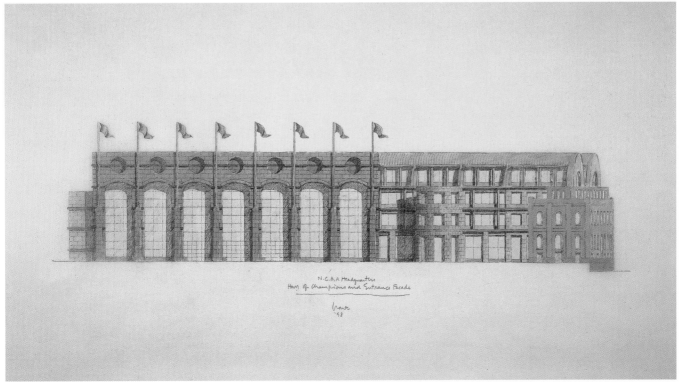

Entrance elevation

Facing page: Atrium

Upper floor offices

Fortis AG Headquarters

Brussels, Belgium, 1997

Lobby

The headquarters office building for the Belgian banking, insurance and real estate company Fortis AG is located at No. 53 Boulevard Emile Jacqmain in the heart of the historic old pentagon of Brussels. There was an existing building on the site that was extensively reworked inside and given new facades as part of this project. Michael Graves & Associates, working with two local architects, was responsible for the design of the facades and public lobby. In response to the traditional nature of the context, the exterior is reminiscent of characteristically Belgian facade rhythms, materials and detailing but at the same time presents a fresh and contemporary public image for the company.

El Gouna Golf Hotel and Club

El Gouna, Egypt, 1997

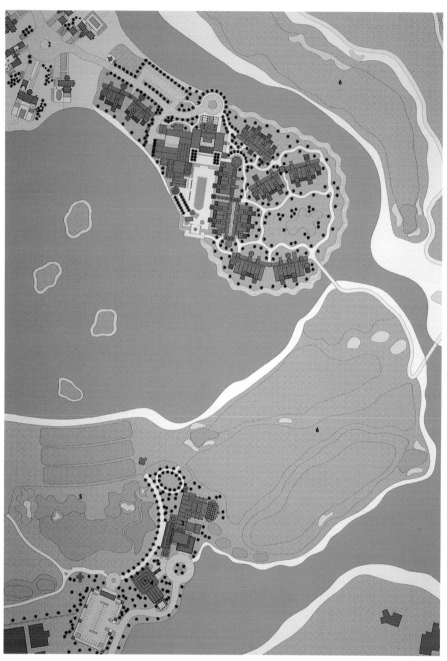

The El Gouna Golf Hotel and Club
are the centerpieces of a golf and villa
development on the Red Sea at the
end of a large peninsula among the
lagoons of the 18-hole El Gouna golf
course.

The Golf Hotel contains 208 guestrooms and serviced apartments. The
main building steps down towards a
long lap pool with wide terraces ori-
enting views over the lagoon to the
golf clubhouse and pyramid-shaped
restaurant. Clusters of guestroom
groups are built around the edge of the
peninsula, with the terraces of individual units overlooking the surrounding
golf course. Large putting greens and
golf cart parking bring golfers to the
public areas of the hotel. A bar and
game room is located on the upper
level with views over the roofs of the
guestrooms.

The clubhouse contains a pro shop,
golf pro offices, lockers, a health club
with Turkish baths and a long viewing
terrace that overlooks the practice
green and the golf course. A separate
restaurant and bar take the form of a
tall truncated pyramid atop a viewing
platform. The entire golf course and
the sea beyond can be seen from this
pyramid.

1 Golf hotel
2 Golf villas
3 Golf club
4 Restaurant
5 Golf practice area
6 Golf course

Site plan

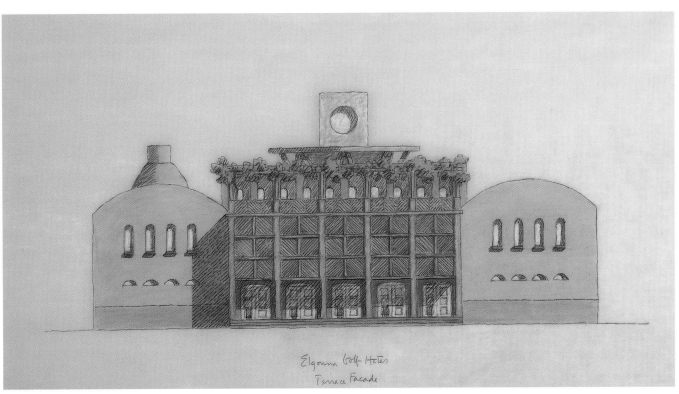

Main building entrance elevation

Main building terrace elevation

Pool court

Pool court

139

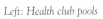
Left: Health club pools

Café terrace

Right: Lobby

Following pages: View of golf clubhouse and restaurant pavilion

Guestroom

Golf Villas

El Gouna, Egypt, 1997

Villa, construction photograph

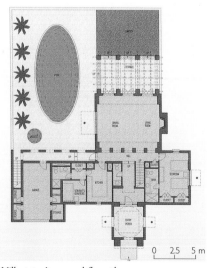

Villa type 1, ground floor plan

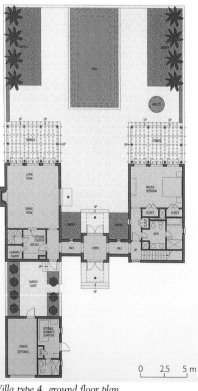

Villa type 4, ground floor plan

The golf villas, a golf hotel and a clubhouse comprise an extensive development sited on a large peninsula surrounded by seawater lagoons and oriented toward the 18-hole golf course in El Gouna. The character of the villas is related to the architecture of the nearby golf hotel and clubhouse, which recall traditional Egyptian rural architecture.

The villas are intended as casual vacation and weekend retreats. The organization of their living areas around an outdoor terrace, swimming pool and garden establishes an easy flow between indoors and outdoors. Six distinct villa designs were prepared, ranging in size from 200 to 300 square meters and including options for adding garages, servants quarters and more bedrooms.

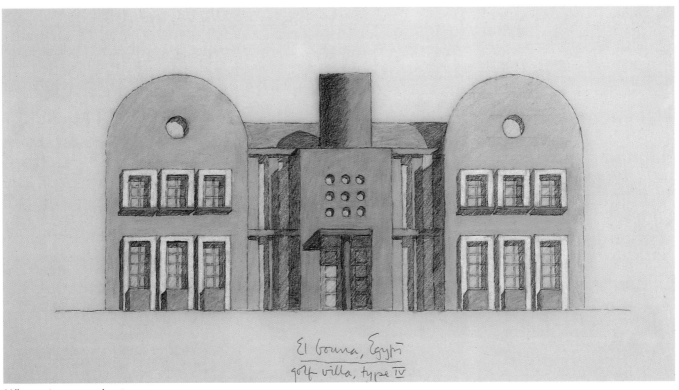

El bouna, Egypt
golf villa, type IV

Villa type 1, entrance elevation

Villa type 4, entrance elevation

De Luwte

On the River Vecht, Netherlands, 1997

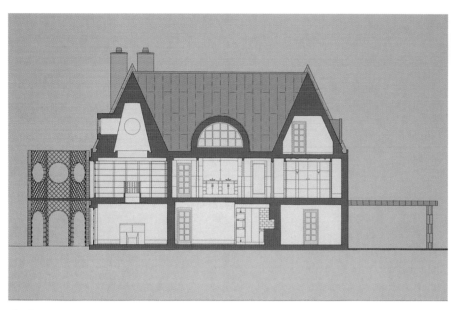

Section

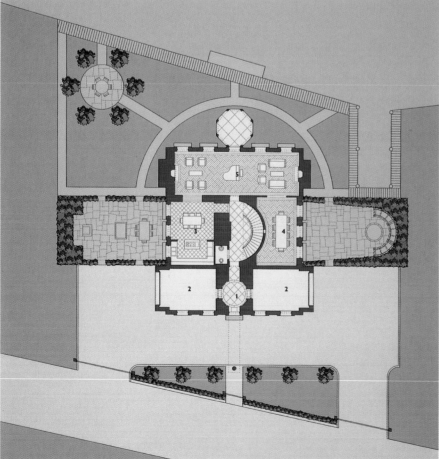

Site and ground floor plan

De Luwte is a single-family house located on the banks of the River Vecht near Amsterdam. In order to emphasize the importance of the relationship between the house and the river, the client named the house De Luwte, which translates as "The Lee," a shelter from wind and water. The living room, master bedroom and study look out to the water, while the kitchen and dining room open onto riverfront terraces. The outdoor spaces are designed as extensions of the interiors so that there is an easy transition between the house and the outdoors. The semicircular stair provides a graceful means of moving between floors and draws light into the center of the house.

The Dutch tradition of gabled roofs and brick construction is reinterpreted in the massing and materials used in the house.

1 Foyer
2 Garage
3 Kitchen
4 Dining room
5 Living room

0   4   8 m

Garden elevation study

Entrance elevation study

151

InterContinental Hotel

Taba Heights, Egypt, 1997

Construction photographs of guestroom group

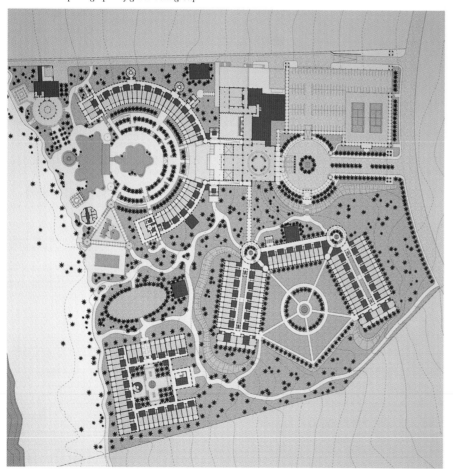

Site and ground floor plan

The InterContinental beach resort hotel located on the Aqaba Bay is a 500-room, international five-star hotel. The three-story main building is entered on the upper floor and, following the rather steep slope of the land, steps down to the restaurant and the health club levels. The guestrooms are organized in three large clusters, each with its own shape and character. Throughout the resort, there are surprising views to the bay, with a foreground of lively beach restaurants and bars surrounding generous swimming pools.

0   25   50 m

Courtyard elevation of guestroom group

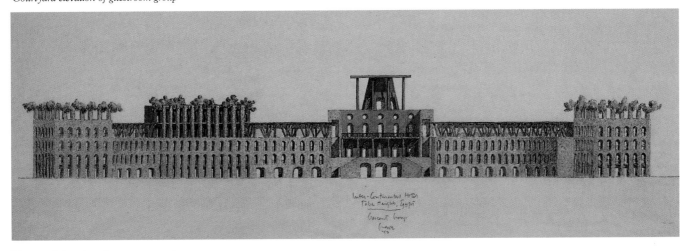

Courtyard elevation of guestroom group

45th Street elevation

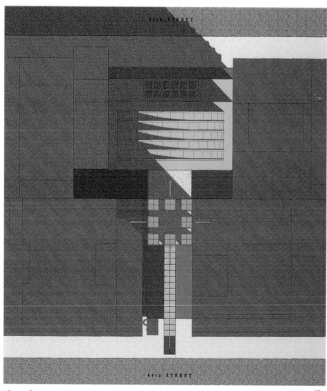

Site plan

Competition for Hotel Sofitel

New York, New York, 1997

Hotel Sofitel occupies a through-block site between West 44th and 45th Street Streets near Fifth Avenue in New York City. The site measures the width of a typical brownstone on West 44th Street, where the developer wanted the entrance to be located, and widens to approximately 100 feet on West 45th Street. The entrance pavilion, with a marquee featuring a new logotype for the hotel, is four stories tall and conforms to the prevailing context. The midblock contains a thin tower with additional projecting logotypes, connected to the main body of the hotel facing 45th Street. This scheme was not selected for further development.

Model view from 45th Street

North Hall
Drexel University

Philadelphia, Pennsylvania, 1997

View from the southeast

North Hall is a 171,300-square-foot student residence that occupies an entire city block between Race and Cherry Streets at the edge of the Drexel University campus adjacent to the Powellton Village residential neighborhood. The building is organized in two six-story wings connected at each floor by a circular stair tower that serves as the main public space. The residence hall accommodates 500 students in a combination of four- and six-person apartment-style suites.

The building is urban in character, but rather than establishing a streetwall along the property line, the design reserves the corner of the site at Cherry and 33rd Streets as open green space, creating a transition from the city to the adjacent neighborhood. The organization of the building in two wings helps to break down the scale in deference to the residential scale of the neighborhood. The top floor of each wing is expressed as an attic story reminiscent of traditional Philadelphia-area architecture.

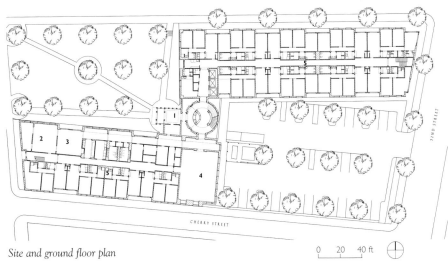

Site and ground floor plan

1 Entrance
2 Game room
3 Lounge
4 Meeting room
5 Suites

0   20   40 ft

South facade detail

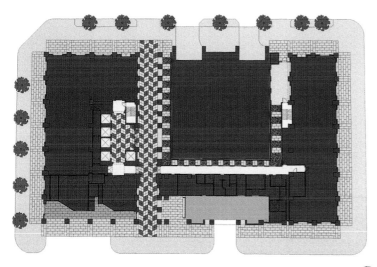

Facade detail

Mixed-use Building

Fukuoka, Japan, 1997

This 10-story, 24,000-square-meter speculative development is located near Hakata Station in the most prominent office district in Fukuoka. The program includes retail shops at the base of the building and high-quality rental offices above. The U-shaped site wraps around an existing structure in the middle of the block. The composition of the new building creates pavilion-like projections on the building's facades, which create a continuous context surrounding the existing building.

Site and ground floor plan

0   5   10 m

United States Courthouse
Washington, D.C., 1997

Courtroom

This project for the United States Federal District Courts involves renovation of the existing 576,500-square-foot Prettyman Courthouse and new construction of a 351,000-square-foot Annex. The Annex contains courtsets for the U.S. District and Appellate Courts, chambersets for the District and the Court of Appeals and offices. The program also includes extensive ancillary functions such as a food service complex, library, health unit, press room, fitness center, credit union and other support facilities.

Located at Constitution and Pennsylvania Avenues and within sight of the Capitol, the Annex defines a pivotal point in the city. Its massing and organization respond to contextual challenges while addressing the institutional values and practical requirements of a courthouse. Critical to the contextual response is the rotunda at the intersection of Pennsylvania and Constitution Avenues. Internally, a key feature of the Annex is the atrium, which links the existing and new structures and introduces natural light into adjacent interiors, particularly the courtrooms in the Annex.

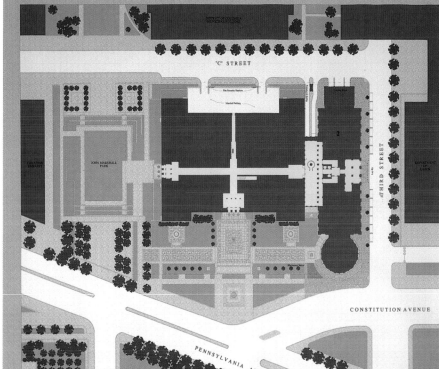

Site and ground floor plan

1 Existing courthouse
2 Annex

0 8 16 m

Third Street elevation

View from Pennsylvania and Constitution Avenues

Ogoori Plaza

Ogoori, Japan, 1997

A feasibility study for an extensive new development encompassed the renovation of the Ogoori Railroad Station and construction of an extensive mixed-use complex on a site to the north of the station. Among the functions planned for the development are a business hotel, a tour bus depot, a department store and other retail shops, a cultural hall accommodating approximately 3000 people, a multiplex cinema, residences and parking.

Train station and bus depot elevation

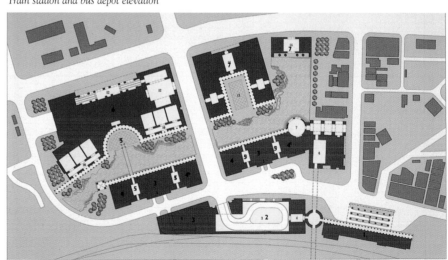

Site plan

1 Ogoori Railroad Station
2 Bus depot
3 Parking
4 Retail/restaurant, residential above
5 Riverwalk plaza
6 Cultural hall
7 Office building

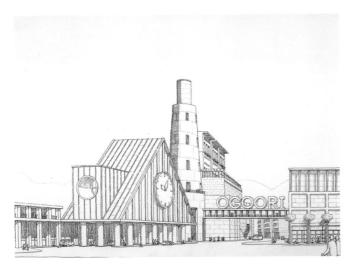

View of train station and hotel

View along Riverwalk

Hotel Makati

Manila, Philippines, 1997

Hotel Makati is a 27-story mixed-use development located between Kalayaan Avenue and Alfonso Street in Manila. It contains approximately 26,000 square meters of commercial, parking, recreational, hotel and residential uses. There are 300 rooms for hotel and service apartments.

Site and ground floor plan

0 10 20 m

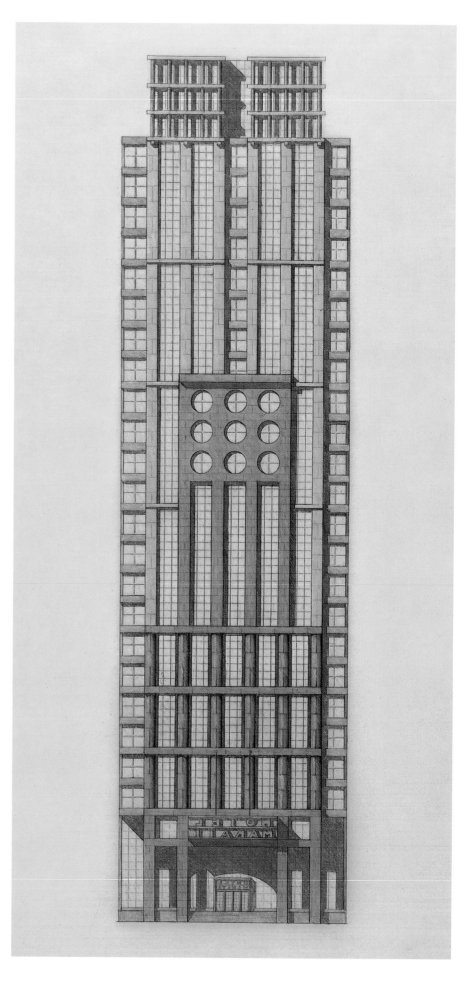

Dongwha Hoiyun Mixed-use Building

Seoul, Korea, 1997

The proposed mixed-use building located in the Hoiyhun Redevelopment Area in Seoul has 33 floors above grade and eight below. Included in the approximately 137,500-square-meter program are residential apartments, commercial offices, a discount department store, athletic facilities, and parking.

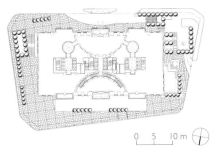

Site and ground floor plan

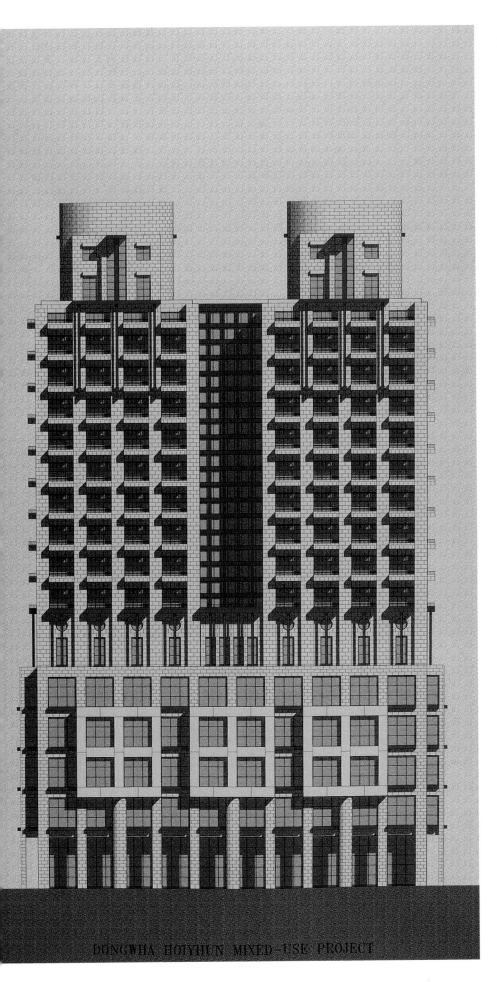

DONGWHA HOIYHUN MIXED-USE PROJECT

O'Grady Library
Saint Martin's College

Lacey, Washington, 1997

Saint Martin's College is a Benedictine institution that serves students living on campus as well as commuting from the surrounding area. The O'Grady Library, which houses collections of books and other media and provides instructional space, is central to the college's educational program and the students' academic pursuits while on campus. The site, located in a developing area of the campus, slopes steeply down from existing academic buildings toward the entrance road and thus offers the possibility of establishing a new, visible academic core distinct from the more private monastic zone of the other side of campus.

The building is organized around a central core of stacks and collection areas, lit from above by clerestory windows. Reading and study areas around the perimeter of the building provide natural light and views of the surrounding forest. The building's character relates to Saint Martin's Benedictine traditions and adjacent campus buildings through the use of pointed arch windows and other familiar detailing.

Entrance facade

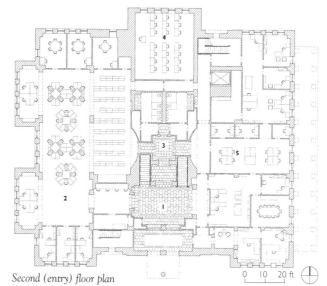

Second (entry) floor plan

1 Lobby
2 Reference
3 Stair hall
4 Computer
5 Media services

0 10 20 ft

Circulation desk

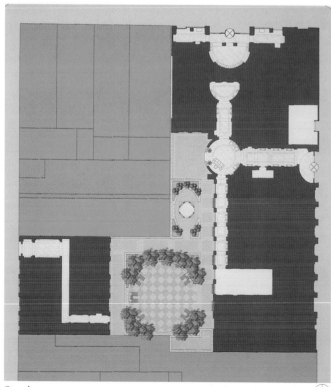

The Impala

New York, New York, 1997

This 268,000-square-foot rental apartment and condominium complex contains approximately 200 residential units in three buildings around a landscaped courtyard. Design challenges included the necessity of working within a narrow range of massing options dictated by zoning. Facing First Avenue, the building contains commercial and retail spaces. Medical offices are located on 76th Street side. Most of the housing is located in a 24-story tower above a seven-story base. The Impala's residential lobby faces the building's private courtyard garden, while the massing maintains the street edge that typifies local residential neighborhoods.

Aesthetically, the design takes as a starting point some of the traditional residential buildings of New York City, particularly those on the Upper East Side. The articulation surrounding the windows is expanded in scale to modulate the size of the apartment tower as a whole. Thus, two stories read as one through the double-height precast frames around the windows. The combination of red brick and white trim is reminiscent of materials and colors associated with neo-Georgian residential architecture, although expressed at the scale of the urban context.

View along East 76th Street

Site plan

0   12   24 ft

Facing page: Courtyard

Lobby looking toward reception desk

Model apartment living room

Study for a Private Residence

Long Island, New York, 1997

This residence for a family of six is designed like a rambling English manor house in which individually articulated pavilions house different internal functions. This strategy preserves a domestic scale while accommodating an expansive program, and allows the house to engage the surrounding landscape. The long drive into the site through an existing allée of trees terminates in a circular courtyard and a crescent-shaped library. The house is entered at the lower level, but the primary living spaces are located on the *piano nobile*. The crescent balances the living room on one side with the master bedroom suite on the other. A separate children's wing contains bedrooms on the upper level and a playroom and media room below.

Preliminary elevation with entrance courtyard in foreground

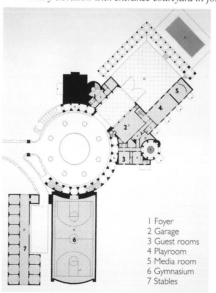

Preliminary ground floor plan

1 Foyer
2 Garage
3 Guest rooms
4 Playroom
5 Media room
6 Gymnasium
7 Stables

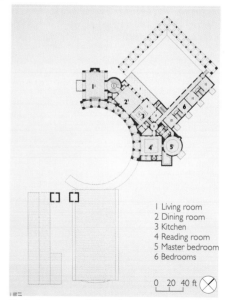

Preliminary second floor plan

1 Living room
2 Dining room
3 Kitchen
4 Reading room
5 Master bedroom
6 Bedrooms

0 20 40 ft

Model view of the entrance and courtyard

The Washington Monument
Restoration

Washington, D.C., 1998

Scaffolding detail

When the Washington Monument needed major restoration work to combat years of weathering and aging, a public-private partnership of the National Park Service and Target Stores commissioned the design of the scaffolding, which surrounded the monument for three years, as well as the redesign of the interior observation and interpretive areas. The scaffolding, which was engineered by the contractor, followed the profile of the monument. It was embellished with a blue semi-transparent architectural mesh fabric attached in a running bond masonry pattern that reflected the monument's stone mortar joints at a larger scale. At night, the scaffolding was lit from within by hundreds of lights.

By allowing a view of the restoration work being performed behind the scaffolding, the design appropriately allowed visitors to gain an appreciation for the importance of the task. In a sense, two monuments were presented to the public: the one being restored, and the one erected for the purpose of facilitating the restoration. The spirit of the project was captured in a simple yet elegant manner, without diminishing the Washington Monument's visibility or its importance as a cultural icon on the mall of the nation's capital.

Commemorative print by Michael Graves

Competition for Peek & Cloppenburg Department Store

Dusseldorf, Germany, 1998

The competition entry for a department store for one of Germany's largest clothing companies reflects its dynamic urban surroundings and makes the internal retail displays visible to the passerby. The site, located on Schadowstrasse, the city's most prominent shopping street, is influenced by an adjacent elevated highway, the landmark Berliner Allee. Two glass pylons, one developed at the most prominent corner of the building and the other located directly across the street, form a prominent gateway in the city and provide a well-lit showcase for general merchandise and special promotions. This competition entry was not chosen for implementation.

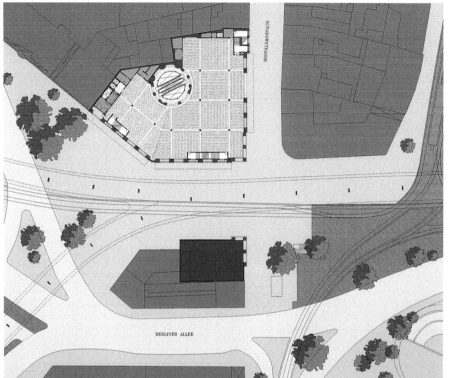

Site and ground floor plan

0 5 10 m

Preliminary model view from Schadowstrasse

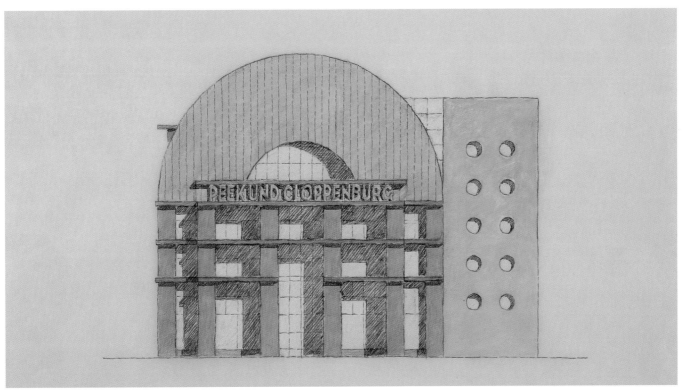

Preliminary Berliner Allee elevation

Preliminary Schadowstrasse elevation

Model view from Berliner Allee

Night view from Schadowstrasse

Competition for the Main Library of Nashville and Davidson County

Nashville, Tennessee, 1998

1 Young adult collection
2 Children's library
3 Storytelling pavilion

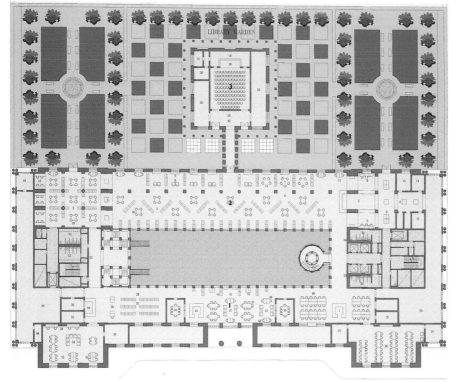

Second floor plan

The competition entry for Nashville's Main Library relates to its urban context, creates a dynamic and memorable public image, and provides special places for individual study and contemplation. The massing and entrance are organized symmetrically about the axis of Capitol Boulevard, which becomes an urban forecourt to the building, leading up to the Tennessee State Capitol.

Internally, the library is organized around two large public spaces, the Main Lobby and the Grand Reading Room, which are stacked above each other. Library-goers immediately encounter information and circulation desks in the lobby and gain views to the Children's Department on the second floor. The Children's Department opens onto the rooftop of an adjacent garage, developed as a garden containing a whimsical storytelling pavilion. The Grand Reading Room for the adult collections is organized around a two-story vaulted atrium connecting the fourth and fifth floors. The atrium's wooden columns and struts, along with warm wood detailing and paneling throughout the library, relate to the lore of this hilly, forested area of Tennessee, thus enhancing the public's identification with the region. This scheme was not selected for implementation.

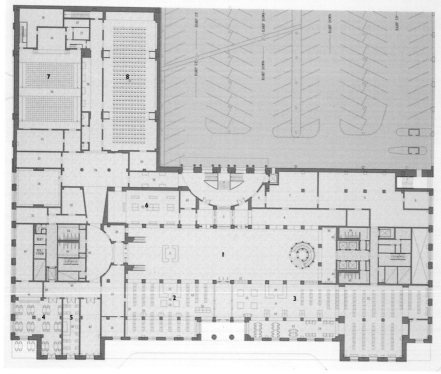

Ground floor plan

0 16 32 ft

1 Lobby
2 Audio-visual collection
3 Popular library
4 Café
5 Bookstore
6 Gallery
7 Auditorium
8 Multipurpose room

Church Street elevation study

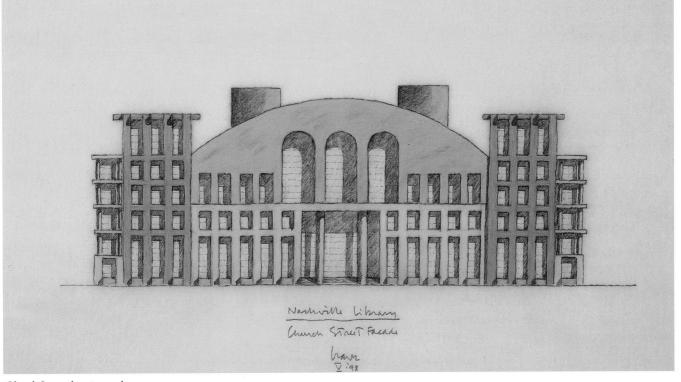

Church Street elevation study

Grand Reading Room

Lobby

Night view from Church Street

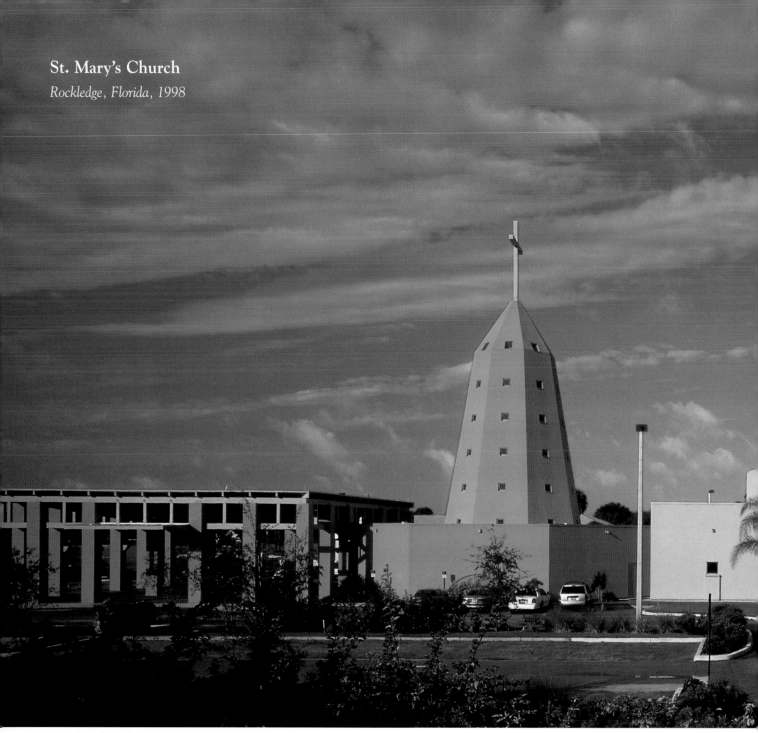

St. Mary's Church

Rockledge, Florida, 1998

View from the south

St. Mary's Church, the parish church for a large congregation in central Florida, is located on a 40-acre site adjacent to a small school and convent. The program includes a 1200-seat main assembly space and a 130-seat daily chapel.

The design of the church, which comprises a series of elements along a linear axis, symbolizes the pilgrimage, an important metaphor in Catholic teaching. The site design further emphasizes the linear axis of the church, extending it beyond the building through an open-roofed space and along a processional way — an outdoor walk lined by the depictions of the Stations of the Cross. The several elements of the building are articulated as geometrically distinct forms enhanced by variations in color.

The main assembly gathers both the congregation and clergy into a single, circular space where all participate in the celebration of the mass, embodying the theology that the church is created by the active participation of all.

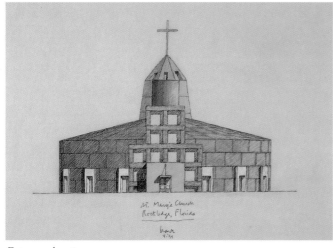

Entrance elevation

Garden elevation

Facing page: Entrance and gathering area

Main assembly

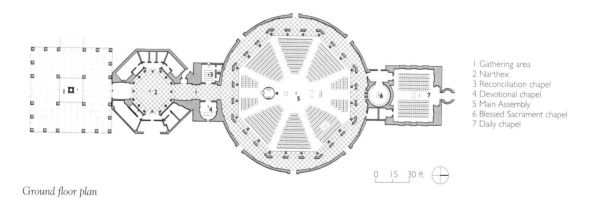

1 Gathering area
2 Narthex
3 Reconciliation chapel
4 Devotional chapel
5 Main Assembly
6 Blessed Sacrament chapel
7 Daily chapel

0   15   30 ft

Ground floor plan

Private Residence

Livingston, New Jersey, 1998

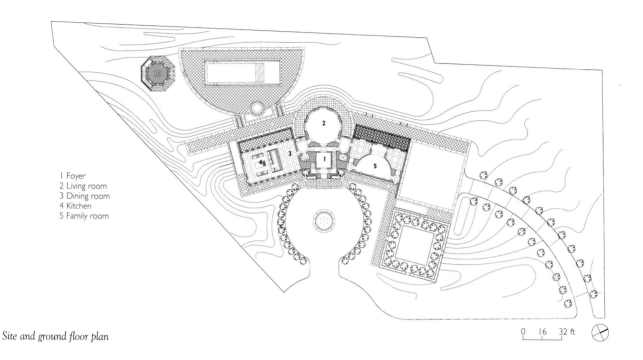

1 Foyer
2 Living room
3 Dining room
4 Kitchen
5 Family room

Site and ground floor plan

0   16   32 ft

This single-family house is sited on a hillside in northern New Jersey, which offers an expansive view of the landscape to the west. The extensive program is divided into three distinct sections connected horizontally and vertically by a three-story stair. The house is entered at the middle level on axis with a large rotunda containing the living room, a small gymnasium below and the master bedroom above.

The south wing, a light-filled pavilion distinguished by a row of two-story columns, contains the dining rooms and kitchen, bedrooms above and a small theater and family room below. The lower level opens onto stepped terraces, fountains and a swimming pool. In contrast, the north wing is more private, with offices and a second family room on the main floor, bedrooms upstairs, and guestrooms, storage and garages below.

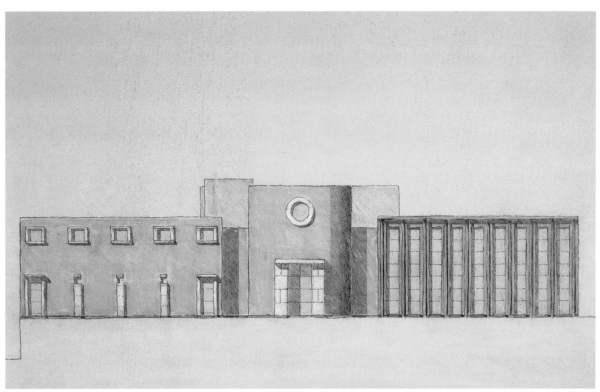

Entrance elevation

Garden elevation

193

Martel, Jones and Brown Colleges Rice University

Houston, Texas, 1998

The master plan for Rice University's north campus includes construction of a new residential college, Martel College, and expansion of two neighboring 1970s-era colleges, Jones and Brown. Martel College is a self-contained 106,000-square-foot complex containing a 234-bed dormitory, classrooms and study areas, a library, apartments for residential advisors and visiting faculty, a house for the College Master and family, lounges and dining commons, and a kitchen and servery that provide central food preparation for all three colleges. The expansions of the other two colleges contain new dining rooms, additional living quarters, classrooms, a library for Brown, and a Master's House for Jones.

The planning strategy provides a clear identity for this area of the campus, which recalls the open residential courtyards and axial planning of Rice University's historic main campus designed around 1913 by Ralph Adams Cram and Bertram Goodhue. Similarly, the building facades and use of materials, especially the brickwork with its large horizontal joints, are compatible with the original campus buildings, yet also establish a fresh architectural character for the colleges.

Martel College student residence wing

194

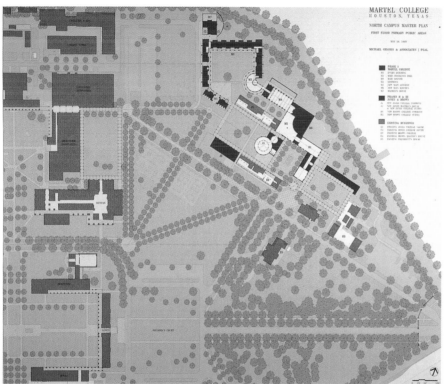

Preliminary site plan

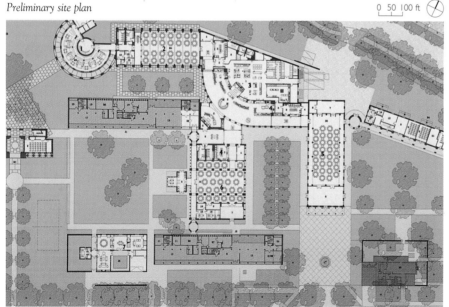

Preliminary ground floor plan of new dining facilities

1 Martel College lounge
2 Martel College commons
3 Central kitchen/servery
4 Satellite servery
5 Brown College commons and lounge
6 Jones College commons and lounge
7 Jones College master's house

*Preceding pages: Martel College lounge
and stair tower*

Jones College expansion

Master's house

Jones College dining room

JAL Plaza Prototype

Japan, 1998

Scheme B entrance elevation

JAL Plaza is a prototype intended for development in various suburban locations throughout Japan. A large-scale shopping mall is organized around a public galleria at the center of the building. Located to one side of the mall is a 200-room wedding hotel with extensive banquet facilities. An entertainment center anchors the other end of the building and includes movie theaters, bowling alleys, pachinko parlors and a spa. The massing and facades of the three parts of the program are given distinctive identities in order to create an image that would be recognizable from location to location.

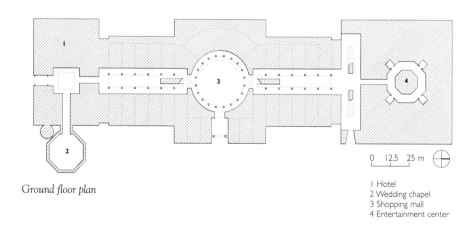

Ground floor plan

0   12.5   25 m

1 Hotel
2 Wedding chapel
3 Shopping mall
4 Entertainment center

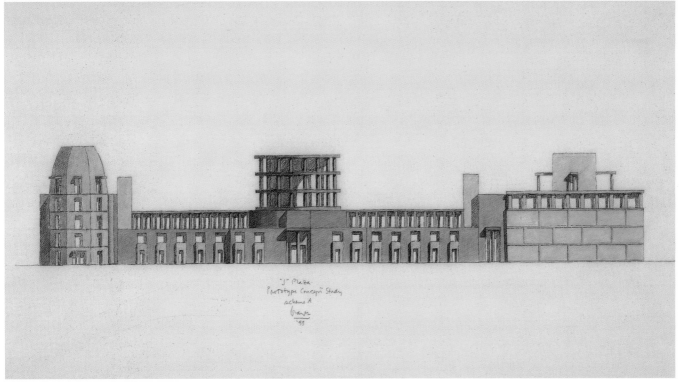

Scheme A entrance elevation

Resort Hotel at Cotton Bay

Eleuthera, Bahamas, 1998

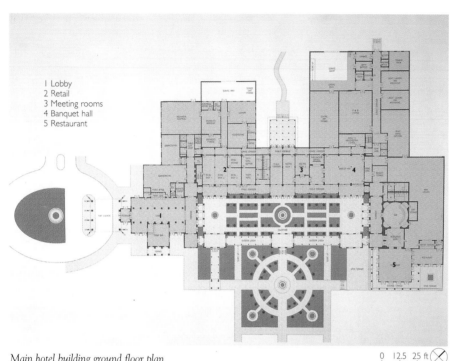

1 Lobby
2 Retail
3 Meeting rooms
4 Banquet hall
5 Restaurant

Main hotel building ground floor plan

0 12.5 25 ft

Site plan

0 50 100 ft

The design of the resort hotel at Cotton Bay emphasizes the relationship between buildings and the landscape, including the bay and the adjacent golf course. The hotel is composed as a series of individual buildings oriented toward the bay, and incorporates numerous landscape features such as pools and gardens. The 64-room U-shaped main building is organized around a formal landscaped courtyard onto which face various public facilities such as the bar, restaurants and banquet hall. Seven stories of guest rooms are organized in a single-loaded corridor configuration that allows water views from every room. The remaining guestrooms are accommodated in two arc-shaped buildings centered on a landscaped swimming pool and the beach.

Throughout the resort, the buildings are given a quiet elegance resulting from a combination of traditional architectural character and vernacular associations. The facades are clad in whitewashed rough stone accented with wood treillage, shutters and louvers. To complement the simple nature of the buildings, the landscaping creates an informal, natural tropical environment of indigenous vegetation such as palm trees, climbing vines and flowers.

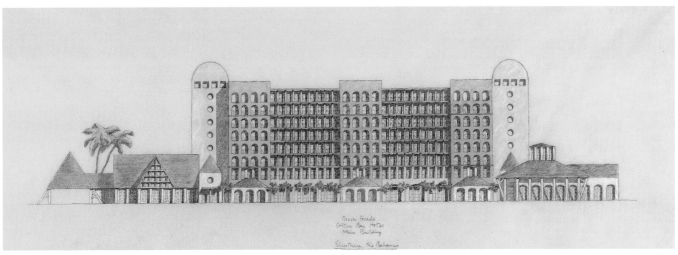

Main hotel building elevation

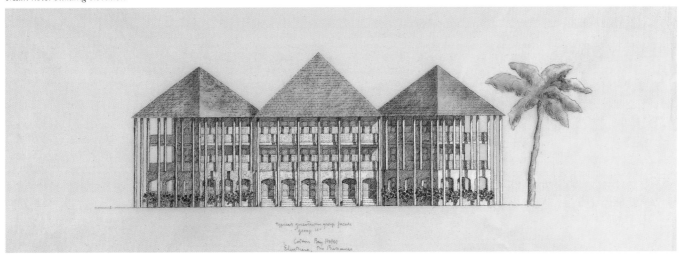

Guestroom group beachfront elevation

Bar and restaurant beachfront elevation

207

Cedar Gables

Minnetonka, Minnesota, 1998

Street facade

Cedar Gables is a house designed for the 1999 Parade of Homes show house tour in the Minneapolis area. Its name refers to the distinctive symmetrical three-gabled cedar-shingled roof forms. The windows are framed with deep trim, and the roof and second floor overhang the main level, creating shadows and strong forms and massing that distinguish this house within its suburban neighborhood.

Cedar Gables has 4,300 square feet of living space on two levels, a three-car garage and a walk-out basement. The plan features a centrally located double-height stair hall that opens up the middle of the house. A two-story, maple-paneled Great Room adjoins an eat-in kitchen with a deck overlooking a pond.

The interiors of the house incorporate many elements designed by Graves, including lighting fixtures, plumbing fixtures and fittings, carpets and door and drapery hardware. The house was furnished with numerous items of indoor and outdoor furniture, framed art, housewares and decorative accessories designed for Target Stores.

Right: Dining room

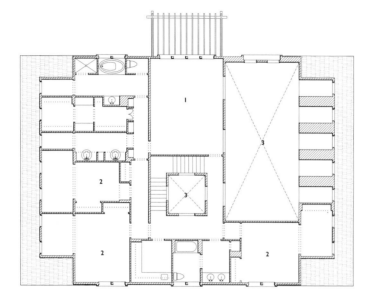

1 Master bedroom
2 Bedroom
3 Open to below

Second floor plan

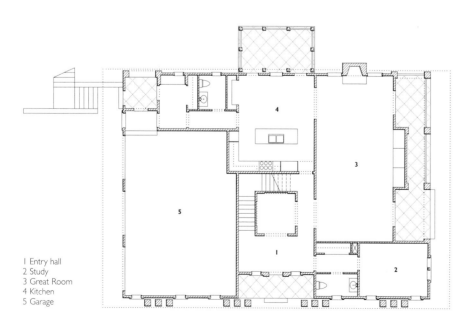

1 Entry hall
2 Study
3 Great Room
4 Kitchen
5 Garage

Ground floor plan

0   5   10 ft

Master bedroom

Lotus Hotel and Convention Center

26th of October City (Cairo), Egypt, 1998

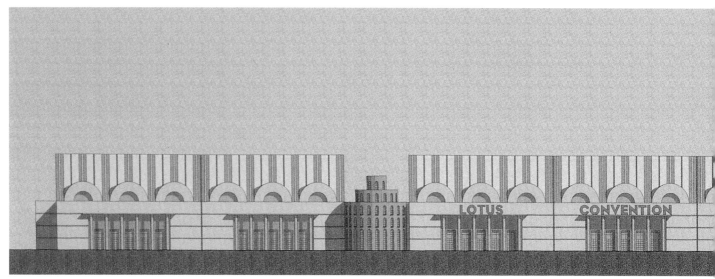

Convention center and hotel street elevation

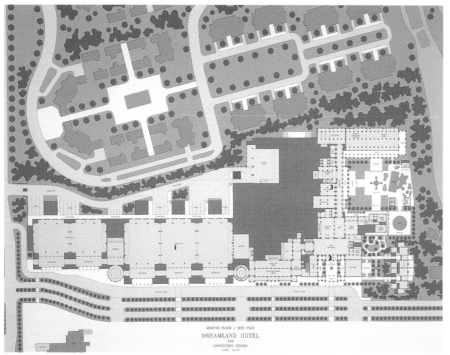

Site and ground floor plan

0 12.5 25 m

1 Convention Center
2 Conference Hall
3 Hotel

The Lotus Hotel and Convention Center is sited in a larger development in 26th of October City, a new city outside Cairo. The project is planned for phased construction, necessitating organizing the major components on separate footprints adjacent to each other. One phase, facing the golf course, consists of a 550-room business hotel and a series of multi-unit condominium villas. In subsequent phases, a convention center is planned to extend along a major public street. Included in the program are two banquet halls, a 15,000-square-meter exhibition hall and meetings rooms. The project is intended to be international and urban in character but still make reference to its Egyptian location through facade details, materials and colors.

214

Hotel courtyard elevation

Sharm Hills Resort Study

Sharm el Sheikh, Egypt, 1998

Beachfront elevation

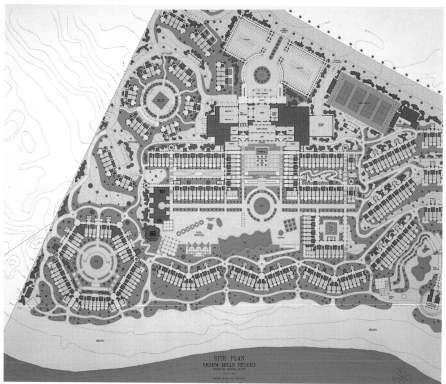

Site and ground floor plan

0 12.5 25 m

216

The Sharm Hills Resort, located on the waterfront in Sharm el Sheikh at the southernmost point of the Sinai Peninsula, is a 48,000-square-meter hotel development with approximately 400 conventional and time-share guest rooms and 54 individual cottages. Supporting facilities include restaurants, retail shops, a health club and an aquatic center.

The site's rocky, arid landscape slopes steeply to the water's edge. The main hotel building is sited at the top of the slope and smaller scale guestroom clusters are developed close to the beach, taking advantage of the terrain to maximize views toward the water. The character of the resort in form, materials and coloration was intended to reflect local vernacular architecture and building techniques.

Aerial view of the resort

Competition for the National Bank of Abu Dhabi

Abu Dhabi, U.A.E., 1998

The proposed headquarters of the National Bank of Abu Dhabi occupies a prominent site that anchors a line of modern commercial buildings on both sides of Sheikh Khalifa Bin Zahed Street at the intersection of Lulu Street. The site has views to both the Al Asima Public Gardens to the east across Lulu Street and the Arabian Gulf approximately 500 meters to the north beyond the Corniche Road.

This competition entry, which was not chosen for development, combines contemporary tall building technology with the aesthetic sense of traditional Islamic masonry architecture. The 25-story tower contains the main branch of the National Bank on five floors within the base of the building, and offices for the bank and tenants on the upper floors. The bank's executive offices are located in the penthouse. A multipurpose reception hall is located at the top of the building, adjacent to which a double-height exterior court with an open-air oculus and palm trees provides an unexpected gardenlike space with a spectacular view of the Arabian Gulf.

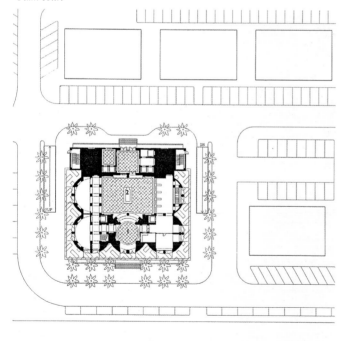

Palm court

1 Lobby
2 Banking hall

Site and ground floor plan

0   5   10 m

218

The NovaCare Complex Philadelphia Eagles Training Center

Philadelphia, Pennsylvania, 1998

The NovaCare Complex, a training center for the Philadelphia Eagles football team, is located on the site of a former Naval Hospital near the stadium in Philadelphia. The L-shaped building contains a two-story office wing and a one-story athletic wing. The entrance to the office wing is flanked by large-scale team emblems. The athletic wing contains high-end locker rooms, a dining hall for the players, an executive dining room, a video room and a television and radio production facility. This wing, with its vaulted roof reminiscent of traditional athletic field houses, faces outdoor practice fields located on the site. The project also includes an indoor practice field in a separate structure.

View from the practice field

1 Lobby
2 Cafeteria
3 Executive dining room
4 Auditorium
5 Locker room
6 Weight room

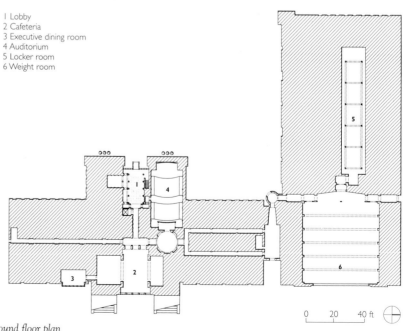

Ground floor plan

0   20   40 ft

Entrance facade

Boardroom

Weight room

Auditorium

Locker room

Philadelphia Eagles Football Stadium Study

Philadelphia, Pennsylvania, 1999

Located on Broad and Pattison Streets in Philadelphia, this open-bowl 60,000-seat stadium is designed primarily for football. The scheme creates an important public space in front of the stadium, as the beginning of a procession through the concourse to the seating. By locating the various program elements at one end of the stadium and organizing them in section, the concourse is opened up to the field. Spectators walking along the concourse thus always have a view of the field.

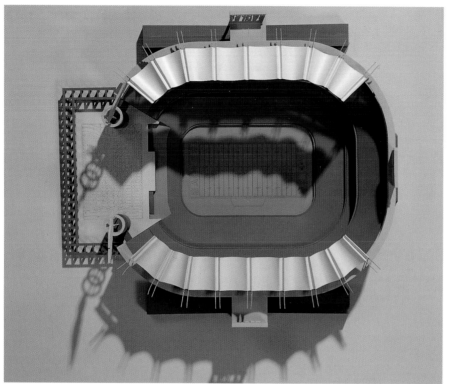

Overhead view of stadium model

Model view of stadium entrance facade

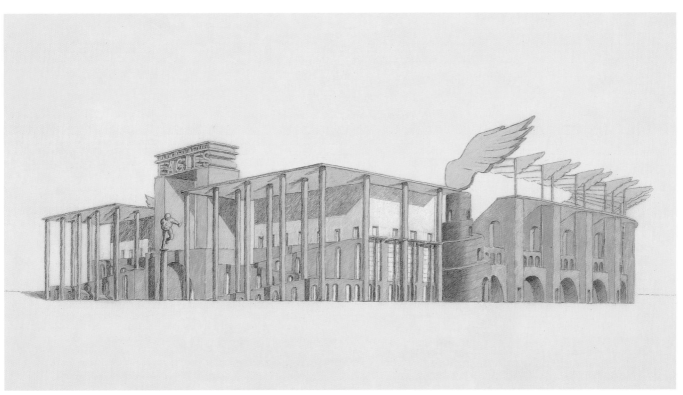

Perspective view of entrance and stadium

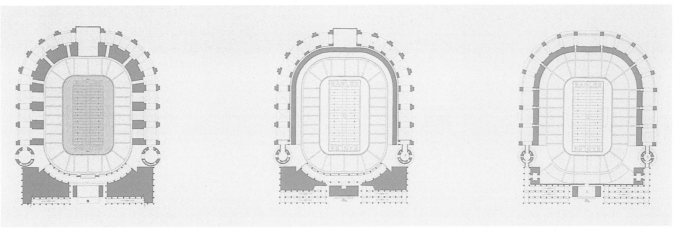

Lower concourse plan

Box and suite level plan

Upper concourse plan

Target Stage
at Harriet Island Park

St. Paul, Minnesota, 1999

Target Stage

Target Stage is located in a public park on Harriet Island and accommodates a variety of events, including graduations and various other seasonal community events, weddings, dance recitals, school plays, readings and concerts. It was also designed to be suitable for use by the Minnesota Orchestra and other major regional performance groups.

The park commission wanted the stage structure to be whimsical, transparent and ephemeral. The resulting design is a lacy, open steel structure that refers to the truss work of the bridges crossing the river and the industrial landscape that is part of the history of Saint Paul's riverfront.

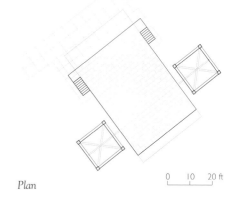

Plan

0   10   20 ft

Elephant Fountain
at Target House

Memphis, Tennessee, 1999

Elephant fountain

Elephant fountain study

Target House is a residential building at St. Jude Children's Research Hospital where families, whose terminally ill children are undergoing long-term treatment, can assume as normal a family life as possible. In 1999, various personalities affiliated with Target either sponsored or designed facilities for Target House. The Michael Graves project is a large fountain located in a forecourt at the building entrance.

The fountain features four families of elephants made of copper and hammered to resemble topiary designed in collaboration with the sculptor Charlie Smith. Elephants were chosen as a theme since they are a symbol of luck and stand for the healing power of families. The fountain, designed by Hobbs Architectural Fountains is elaborately programmed with variations in water activity from multiple perimeter and central jets and from the elephants themselves. There is also a disk at child height that can be pushed to initiate a water sequence, creating an interactive environment.

Watch Technicum

Lancaster County, Pennsylvania, 1999

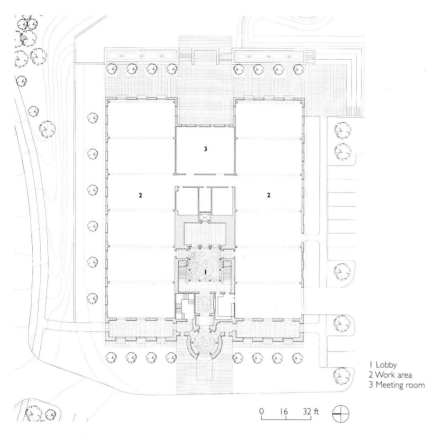

1 Lobby
2 Work area
3 Meeting room

0   16   32 ft

Site and ground floor plan

This 45,000-square-foot watch-making and service center is occupied by one of the most prestigious watch companies in the world. The fieldstone building complex with its barn motif provides a contextual interpretation of its Pennsylvania Dutch setting.

The dramatic entrance lobby features exposed timber truss work that is also reminiscent of the agricultural locale and Amish presence. Extensive site landscaping is accented by natural stone and completed by an outdoor seating area and pond with fountain.

Competition for the
Singapore National Library

Singapore, 1999

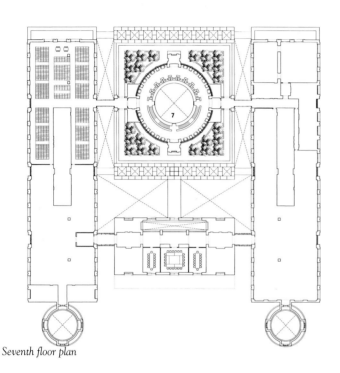

Seventh floor plan

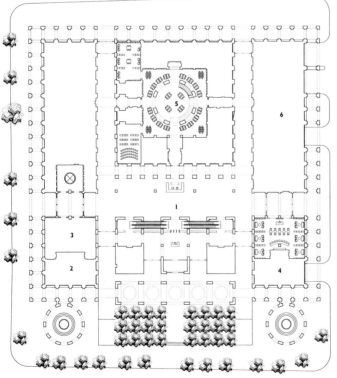

Ground floor plan

The program for the Singapore National Library comprises four discrete library departments separated by skylit internal "streets" connected above ground level by bridges. These passages visually and physically connect the departments and recall Singapore's traditional arcade-lined streets. The passages also help break up the potentially large floor plates and provide identity to the individual departments.

The plan and massing attempt to be as clear as possible so that the building can be readily understood by the public and easily administered by the staff. The two largest and most heavily used departments, the Lending Library and the Heritage Library, are centrally positioned to facilitate access and, in the case of the Heritage Reading Room, to offer views of the city.

The library's primary public entrance is located on Victoria Street adjacent to a tree-lined plaza defined by corner turrets and a covered arcade. Local materials such as limestone or sandstone used for the facades and flooring identify the library as specific to Singapore while the copper-clad parabolic roofs and rotundas effectively mark the building on the skyline. This competition entry was not selected for further development.

1 Lobby
2 Multipurpose room
3 Gallery
4 Gift shop and café
5 Reference library
6 Service
7 Heritage Library
   reading room

0 4   8 m

Heritage Reading Room

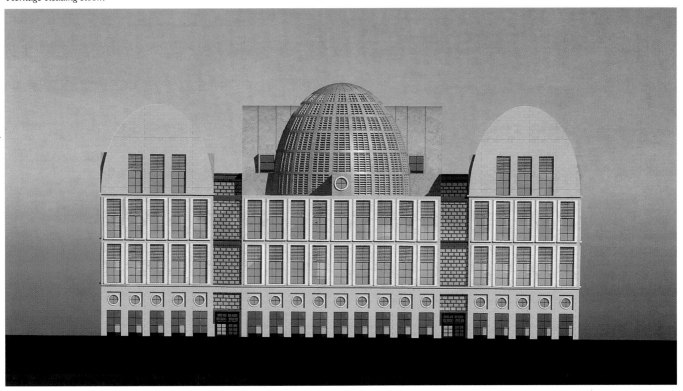

Victoria Street elevation

Private Residence

Lake Geneva, Switzerland, 1999

The site for this private residence slopes steeply from the road to Lake Geneva. The entrance driveway creates a forecourt to a formal public facade facing the road; whereas, the water side of the house is informal and picturesque. Two wings that flank a central rotunda in the main body of the house and a parallel barrel-vaulted garden pavilion form a rear courtyard. Attached to the house, the kitchen occupies its own single-story wing with a rooftop terrace surrounded by a pergola.

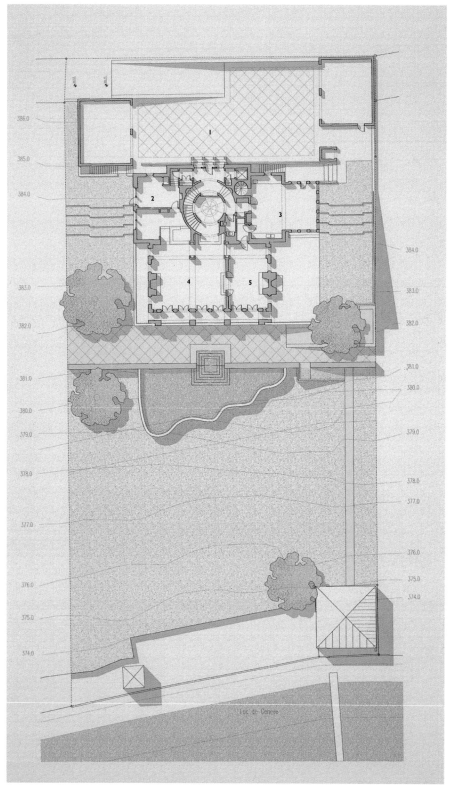

1 Entry court
2 Study
3 Kitchen
4 Living room
5 Dining room

Site and ground floor plan

0   2   4 m

Entrance elevation

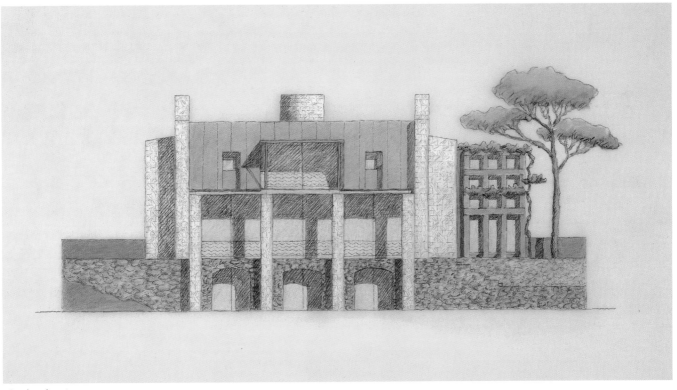

Garden elevation

The Detroit Institute of Arts

Detroit, Michigan, 1999

The approximately 600,000-square-foot building complex of the Detroit Institute of Arts encompasses a historic building designed by Paul Cret and completed in 1927, and two modern additions completed in 1966 and 1971.

The main architectural goals of the renovation and expansion project depicted here are to improve the vertical and horizontal public circulation and thus make the visitor experience more legible, to increase the size and flexibility of the permanent and temporary exhibit galleries, to expand the educational center and museum shop, and to consolidate and upgrade food service facilities.

Circulation and orientation in the museum are greatly improved by the introduction of a significant new north-south passageway on the Woodward Avenue edge of the museum, punctuated with new public stairways that allow natural light into the passageway at both ends. As part of the renovation, the deteriorating facades of the modern wings are replaced in a manner compatible with Cret's design in composition, materials and color. A 40,000-square-foot addition for future galleries on the east side of the south wing provides temporary swing space for phasing construction in order to keep the museum operating and open to the public.

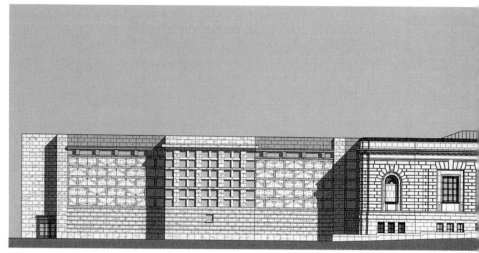

Woodward Avenue elevation

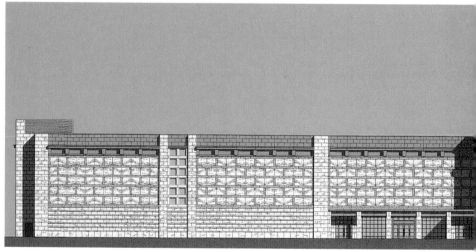

John R. Street elevation

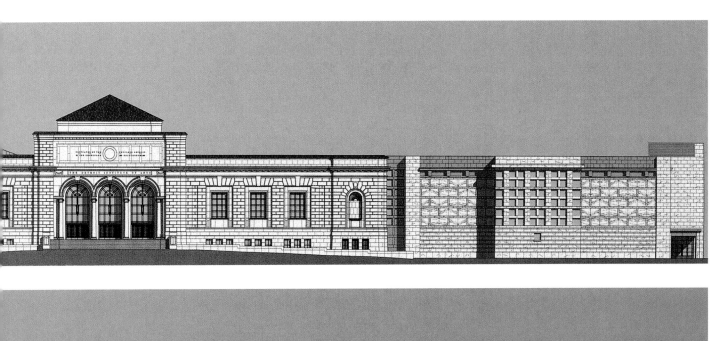

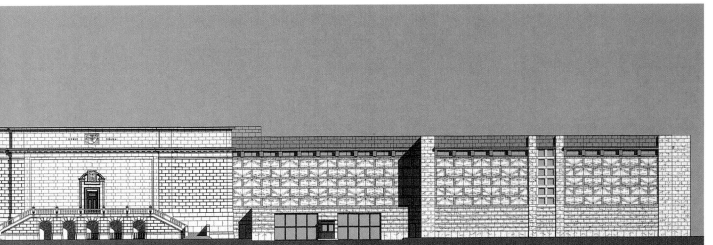

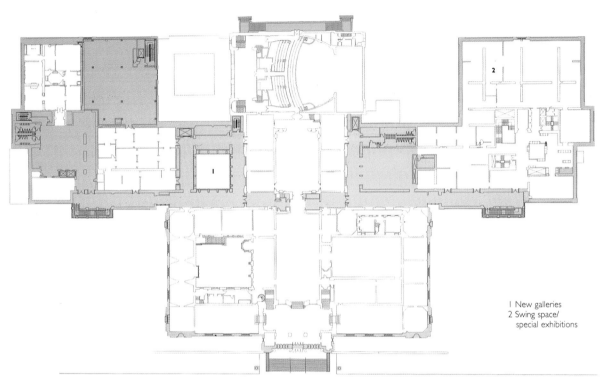

Main floor plan with alterations shaded

1 New galleries
2 Swing space/
   special exhibitions

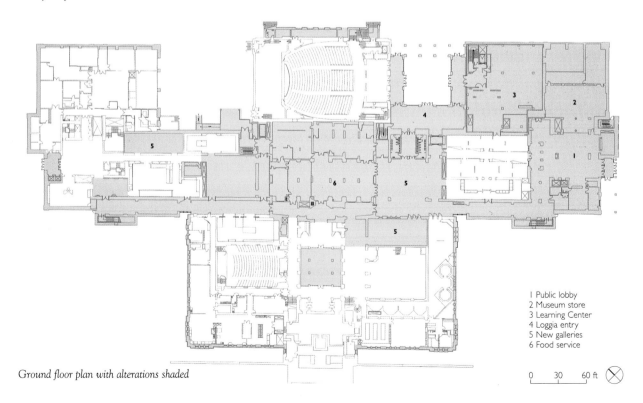

Ground floor plan with alterations shaded

1 Public lobby
2 Museum store
3 Learning Center
4 Loggia entry
5 New galleries
6 Food service

0   30   60 ft

Dining room

Museum of the Shenandoah Valley

Winchester, Virginia, 1999

The Museum of the Shenandoah Valley is a new institution located on the grounds of the historic Glen Burnie estate in Winchester, Virginia, which contains 25 acres of gardens and the house of Winchester's founder, James Wood. The house is furnished with the decorative and fine arts collections of Wood's descendant, Julian Wood Glass, Jr., and is open to the public.

The design of the museum establishes its own identity within its historic context, reflecting the character of traditional local architecture, ranging from manor houses to farm buildings. The overall theme of the museum is "making a home in the Shenandoah Valley." The exhibits focus on furniture and decorative arts of the Shenandoah Valley, providing a rich context for visitors to see Glen Burnie's historic house, collections and gardens.

Entrance elevation

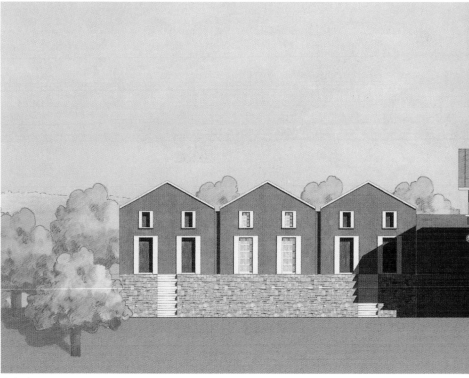

Side elevation

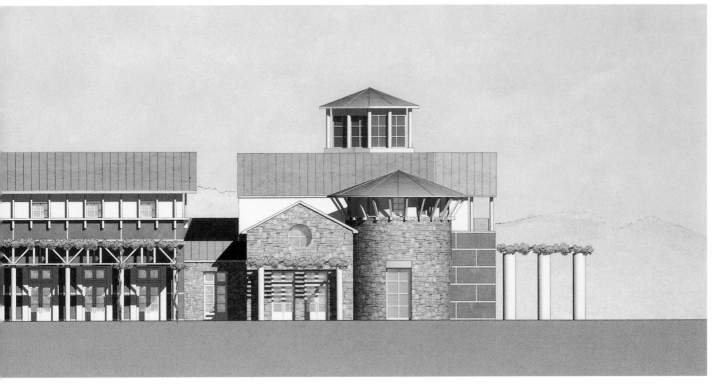

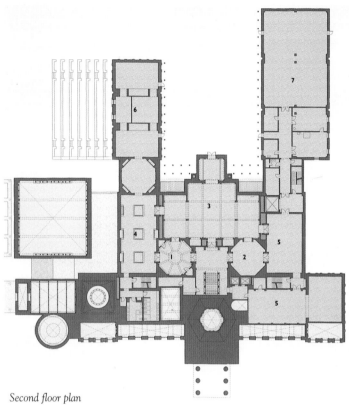

Second floor plan

1 Lobby
2 Learning Center
3 Research center
4 Museum store
5 Tearoom
6 Prefunction
7 Reception all

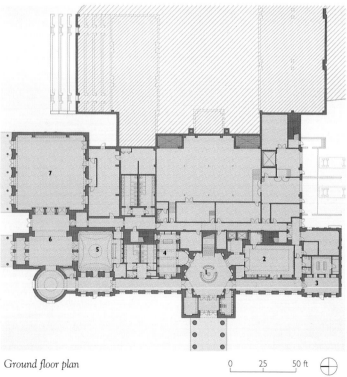

Ground floor plan

1 Orientation gallery
2 Miniatures gallery
3 Shenandoah Valley gallery
4 Decorative Arts gallery
5 Changing exhibitions gallery
6 Julian Wood Glass, Jr. galleries
7 Collections storage

0   25   50 ft

Model view looking toward the entrance

Glen Burnie historic house

Cosmotoda Master Plan

Barcelona, Spain, 1999

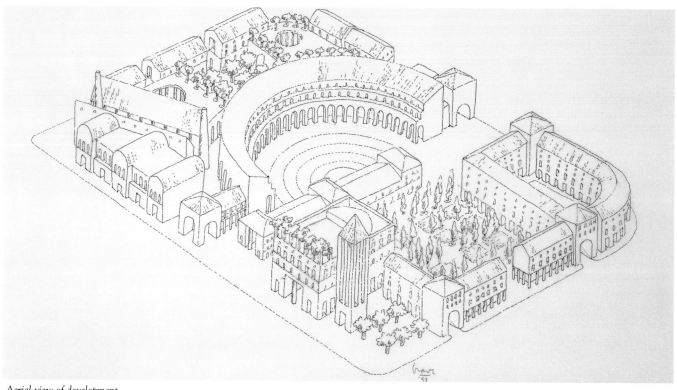

Aerial view of development

The Master Plan for the block in l'Hospitalet bounded by Avenida Enric Prat de la Riba, Josep Tarradellas i Joan, Carrer Canigo and Carrer Batllori proposes an exciting new residential and retail project that is intended to be a catalyst for neighboring developments.

The plan for new construction accommodates several existing structures, including a seven-story automobile dealership and a four-story former factory. The urban planning approach is characteristic of the city's traditional land-use patterns, in that the new buildings are positioned both to reinforce the edges of the surrounding streets and to define a series of figural, axially connected outdoor spaces in the center. Typical of Barcelona, entries to the block occur at the street intersections and also along the length of surrounding streets.

The existing factory building, located in the approximate center of the block, is proposed for future conversion to a cultural facility serving the community. To the east and west of the factory, two large-scaled landscaped garden plazas integrate this building with adjacent structures. Programmatically, the new buildings comprise two floors of retail and three floors of housing. The retail levels are articulated with pedestrian-scaled entrances and arcades, which provide vitality at the street level. Variety in the massing of the upper levels and roofs of the buildings create opportunities for creating roof terraces for the residences. The range of forms and articulation of small-scale details impart a sense of domestic life to this project in keeping with the character of the traditional sections of l'Hospitalet and Barcelona.

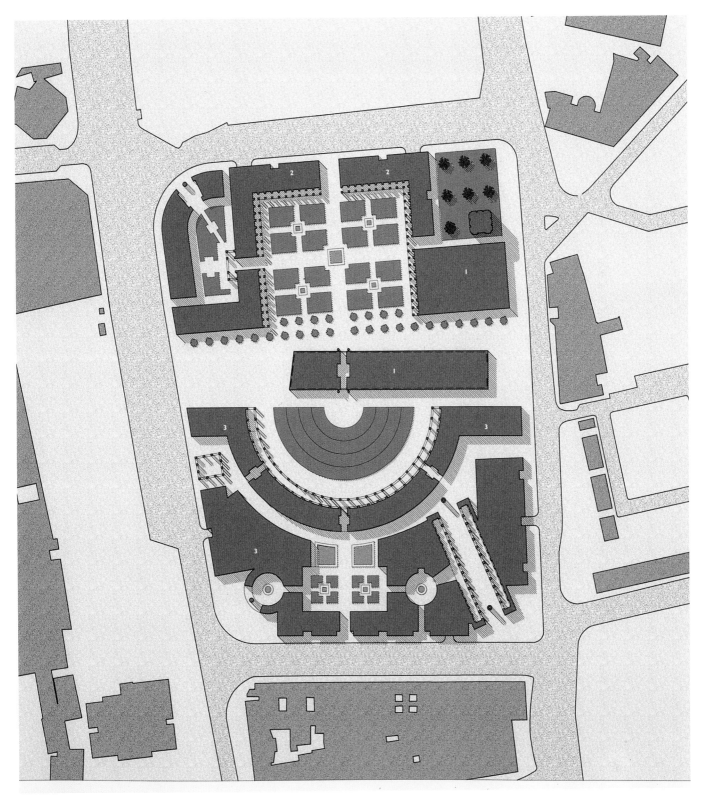

1 Existing building
2 New housing
3 New retail/housing

Site plan

0   12.5   25 m

425 Fifth Avenue

New York, New York, 2000

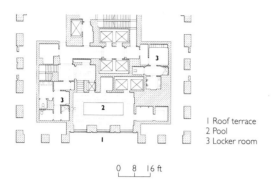

1 Roof terrace
2 Pool
3 Locker room

0   8   16 ft

Seventh floor plan

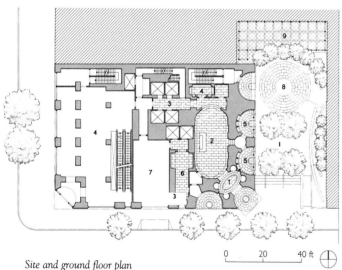

1 Plaza and garden
2 Residential lobby
3 Office lobby
4 Retail

0   20   40 ft

Site and ground floor plan

Residential lobby

This mixed-use tower rising to a height equivalent to 67 stories is located on the northeast corner of Fifth Avenue and 38th Street. Its massing reconciles New York City zoning regulations and the relatively small footprint of the site by placing a thin residential tower with setbacks on a six-story commercial base.

The scale, detailing and materials of the base of 425 Fifth Avenue complement historically significant buildings in the neighborhood and are reminiscent of traditional New York towers. The base contains two floors of retail and four floors of offices. The amenities for the residences are concentrated in the Fifth Avenue Club, which occupies the seventh and eighth floors. A major public terrace wraps around the building on the seventh floor. The eighth floor contains an extensive business center and the lounge for the Envoy Club, an extended-stay residence that rises through six floors. Upper-level apartments and condominiums feature a variety of studio, one-, two- and three-bedroom units, which offer protected views of uptown and downtown Manhattan, including an excellent view of the nearby Empire State Building.

View from Fifth Avenue and 38th Street

Famille-Tsukishima

Tokyo, Japan, 2000

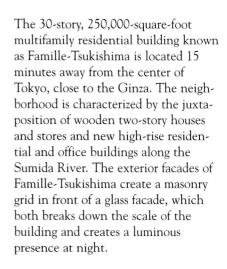

The 30-story, 250,000-square-foot multifamily residential building known as Famille-Tsukishima is located 15 minutes away from the center of Tokyo, close to the Ginza. The neighborhood is characterized by the juxtaposition of wooden two-story houses and stores and new high-rise residential and office buildings along the Sumida River. The exterior facades of Famille-Tsukishima create a masonry grid in front of a glass facade, which both breaks down the scale of the building and creates a luminous presence at night.

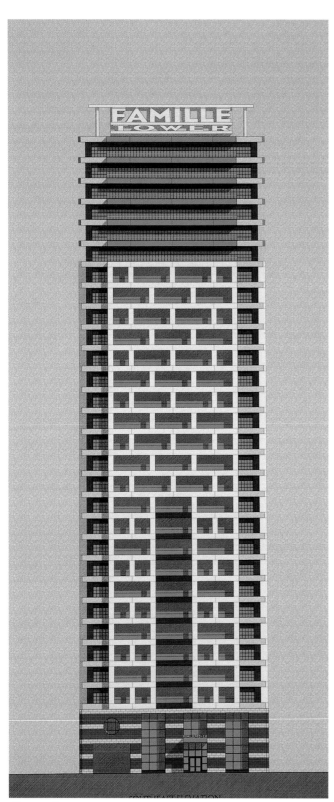

Primary elevation

Hart Productions Studio

San Francisco, California, 2000

Morris Street elevation

Third floor plan

Second floor plan

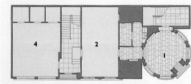

Ground floor plan

1 Lobby/reception
2 Studio
3 Meeting Room
4 Garage
5 Open to below

The studio building for the photography company Hart Productions is sited at the intersection of Morris and Bryant Streets in a district of San Francisco where many multimedia enterprises are located. The three-story, 5,300-square-foot building is entered at the corner through a large rotunda, which contains a reception room on the ground floor and meeting rooms above. The several levels of the working areas of the building are linked visually through a double-height space. Abundant natural light penetrates the interiors through large windows and skylights.

The simple massing of the building is sympathetic to the prevailing context of industrial buildings, whereas the lively coloration and articulation of the facades announce the artistic purpose of the studio.

Tallahassee Community Hospital

Tallahassee, Florida, 2000

View toward the entrance

The Community Hospital in Tallahassee is an eight-story replacement facility for Columbia ACH. Located on a prominent urban site, the hospital is envisioned to have a civic presence appropriate to its prominence in the community. The Tennessee-based firm, Thomas, Miller & Partners, planned the building technically and enlisted Graves' participation to develop the exterior character and the public interiors.

By emphasizing the entrance portico and central pavilion, the hospital is given a human scale and sense of accessibility. Taking cues from the design of hotel buildings, the entrance sequence and lobbies are given a comfortable, non-institutional character to improve the hospital experience for patients and their families.

Private Offices
Washington, D.C., 2000

Reception

The corridors of this suite of executive offices and conference rooms double as a library in order to enliven them and break down the scale of their lengthy elevations. Glass doors to perimeter offices allow daylight to penetrate the interior. The stained maple millwork and stone floor patterns provide a streetlike rhythm and richness. The main conference room, while equipped with sophisticated technical systems, is given a domestic character through its finishes, custom furnishings and artwork.

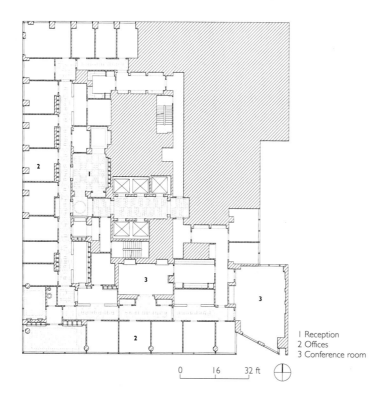

1 Reception
2 Offices
3 Conference room

Floor plan

0   16   32 ft

Executive office

Main conference room

Sportevo

North Charleston, South Carolina, 2000

Sportevo is a prototype for a series of family-friendly sports complexes that cater to fitness and activity needs of every age group. Each Sportevo center would contain general recreational facilities as well as venues for sports that are most popular in its particular geographic area, such as golf and tennis facilities and indoor rinks for soccer and in-line skating. A variety of eating establishments and retail shops make Sportevo an all-day destination for families. A consistent upbeat identity is provided by large-scale graphics and bold patterns and colors applied to the expansive building surfaces.

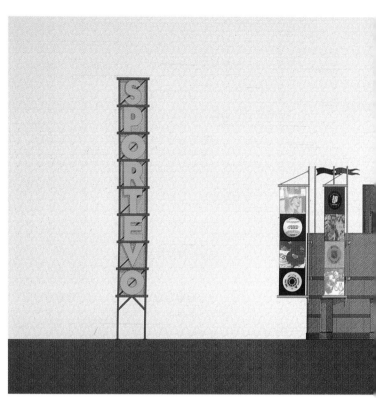

Sportevo retail center

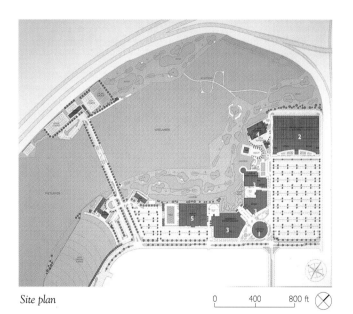

Site plan

0   400   800 ft

1 Retail center
2 Performance center
3 Retail
4 XPLEX
5 Life center
6 Golf center
7 Tennis center

Sportevo performance center

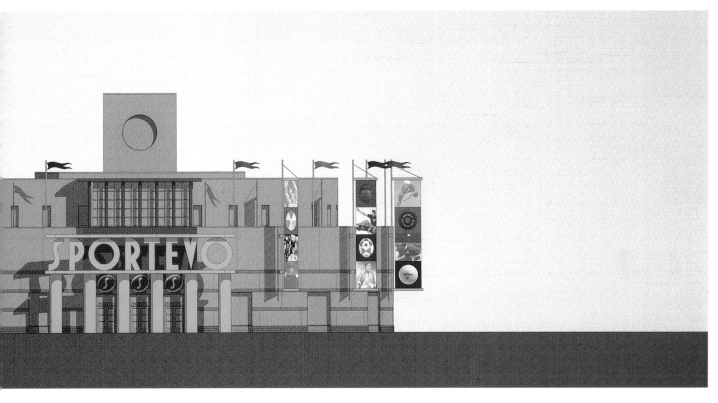

Stoa Olympica

Maroussi (Athens), Greece, 2000

Entrance elevation of retail center and office buildings

The selection of Athens as the site for the 2004 Olympic Games created opportunities for significant investment in the local infrastructure and facilities associated with the Games. Consequently, new locations for real estate development emerged in places such as Maroussi, a municipality northeast of Athens where the Olympic Stadium and other sport facilities are located. The site for the mixed-use development known as Stoa Olympica forms a link between the northern and eastern expansion of the municipal transportation system and the central part of the city. It therefore has the capacity to draw large numbers of people.

The program for the development includes 64,000 square meters of retail and entertainment facilities, 15,000 square meters of offices, and parking for 3,400 cars. The retail center is organized on several levels as an indoor-outdoor environment. In addition, a master plan was prepared for extensive residential development on an adjacent site.

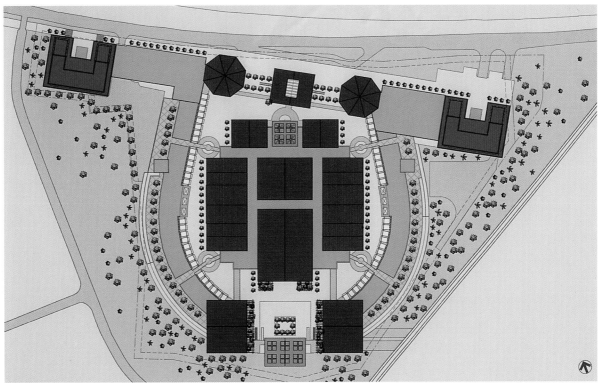

Site plan

Retail center entrance

Cinema complex

Retail arcade

Cinema complex and food courts

Piazza Duomo and Piazza Orsini

Benevento, Italy, 2000

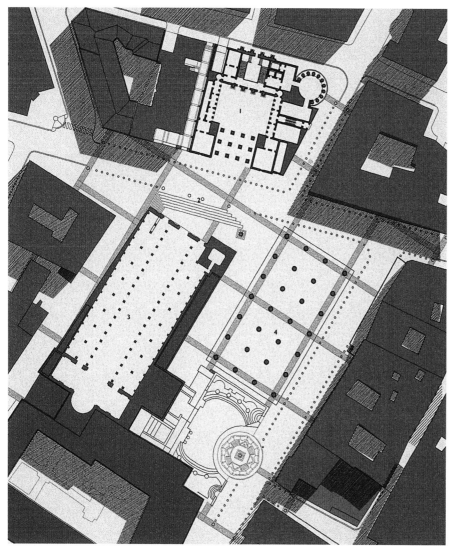

Site and ground floor plan

Referential sketches of Roman ruins

An international consultation was held to revise the urban plan of Piazza Duomo and Piazza Orsini in Benevento and to design a new museum. This proposal to treat the combined *piazze* as a precinct binds together these disparate urban sites while preserving their individuality. The *piazze* become more cohesive by strengthening the figural character of the open space and articulating the entire ground plane as a large-scale grid.

The location of Corso Garibaldi in Piazza Duomo immediately in front of the church creates a paradoxical urban condition in that one would normally expect a forecourt in that location. Thus, despite its name, there is in effect no defined piazza. The new museum is sited immediately opposite the church, completing the streetwall along Corso Garibaldi and creating a civic presence appropriate to the institution and its urban position. The museum is organized around an open-air courtyard, which can be thought of as an internalized forecourt for the church.

While the northern edge of Corso Garibaldi is seen as a continuous streetwall, the southern edge leading into Piazza Orsini is more informal and reflects a shift from the orthogonal of the street to the diagonal of the church. A new building is proposed for Piazza Orsini, a hypostyle hall reminiscent of market structures seen throughout Italy. While open-air, the hall has a volumetric presence sympathetic to that of the church and yet provides visibility and pedestrian circulation at the ground level.

Museum view from the hypostyle hall

Hypostyle hall

265

Private Museum in the Middle East

2000

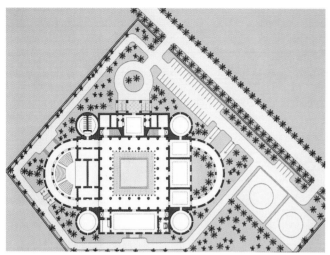

Scheme 1 ground floor plan

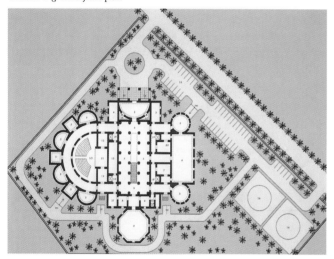

Scheme 2 ground floor plam

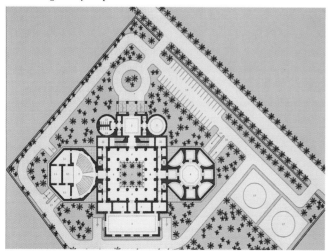

Scheme 3 ground floor plan

0 10 20 m

Three alternative conceptual designs were prepared for a speculative private museum and exhibition center to be located in the Middle East. The 15,000-square-meter program to be developed on three levels includes a major exhibition hall, galleries for a permanent collection of art and artifacts, a multipurpose theater, a reception hall, offices, private library, storage and support facilities. The architectural character of each of the schemes was intended to relate to the indigenous architecture of the region.

Scheme 1 elevation

Scheme 2 elevation

Scheme 3 elevation

267

Private Villa Compound in the Middle East

2000

A conceptual design was prepared for a private villa compound accommodating several related individuals and their families. The compound is oriented toward a body of water and includes common recreational facilities as well as private residences for each family. At the owners' request, the compound has an architectural character reminiscent of traditional buildings found in the Mediterranean region.

Site model

1 Villa 1
2 Majlis
3 Villa 2
4 Guest house
5 Swimming/tennis
6 Service
7 Wives' residences

Villa 1 elevation

Majlis elevation

Villa 2 elevation

Houston Branch of the Federal Reserve Bank of Dallas

Houston, Texas, 2000

Dining room

By drawing on the traditions of national bank buildings throughout the country and the architecture of the Southwest, this new building is intended to be easily identifiable as the "Houston Fed." In order to communicate the civic importance of the Federal Reserve Bank as a national financial institution, the design is intentionally timeless and conveys permanence and authority balanced with openness. By using local materials and colors, as well as loggias, terraces and pergolas typical of Houston architecture, the character is also rooted in its community.

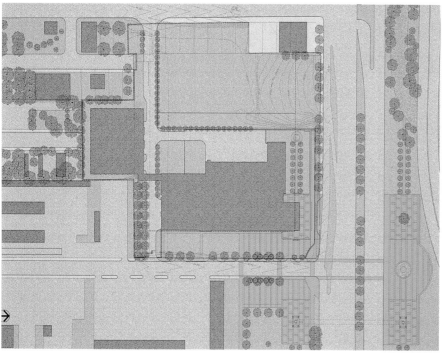

Site plan

0   80   160 ft

View from Gillette Street and Allen Parkway

View from Allen Parkway looking toward downtown Houston

Discovery Square Master Plan

Erie, Pennsylvania, 2000

The program for the Concept Master Plan for Discovery Square includes new galleries, support space and classrooms for the Erie Art Museum, new exhibit space and classrooms for the Children's Museum, and shared facilities such as a common lobby, enclosed courtyard and sculpture garden, orientation center, gift shop, café, collection storage areas, workshops and offices.

The master plan takes advantage of and reinforces the existing mixed-use nature of the area by retaining the three existing museum buildings and their individual identities when viewed from State and French Streets. The primary public access to Discovery Square is located on Fifth Street with a secondary pedestrian door on Fourth. These entrances, at approximately mid-block, are linked by a three-story spine — an interior street — that establishes a clear literal and figurative link among the three institutions and provides access to the central atrium and various common program spaces. The proposed materials and articulation are meant to tie Discovery Square to its context without specific stylistic reference.

View from Fifth and French Streets

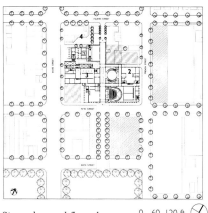

Site and ground floor plan

1 Theater
2 Children's Museum
3 History museum
4 Erie Art Museum

Fifth Street elevation

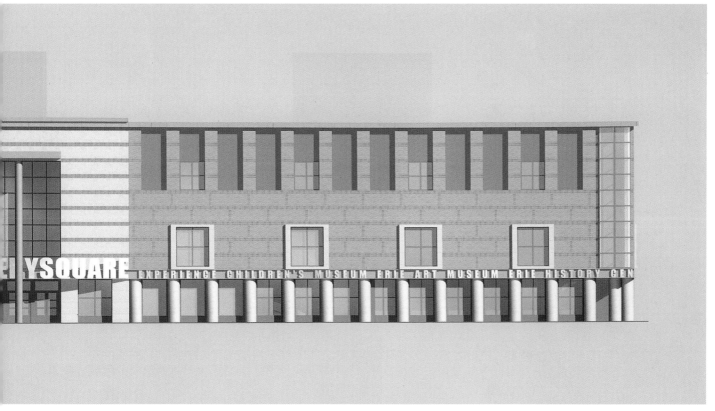

United States Embassy Compound

Seoul, Korea, 2000

The master plan for the United States Embassy Compound balances the need for modern, secure facilities with respect for the local environment and the historic Korean context. The location and massing of the buildings were determined by the topography of the site, traffic patterns, setbacks required for security and mandated viewsheds from two adjacent historic and cultural properties, the Russian Legation Tower and Duksoo Palace.

The first phase replaces out-of-date housing with an eight-story apartment building for diplomatic families. The buildings are compatible in scale with other mid-rise buildings adjacent to the site. The second phase involves construction of the chancery office building on the northern, flatter portion of the site. At 15 stories, the chancery fits within the context of tall modern commercial buildings at north edge of the site.

The entire site inside the walls of the compound is developed as a series of landscaped gardens. A large lawn provides common open space to resident families. Other more intimate picturesque spaces are reminiscent of traditional Korean gardens, acknowledging the local reverence for natural landscape.

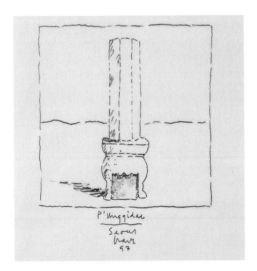

Referential sketches

Chancery office building view from the garden

Housing view from the garden

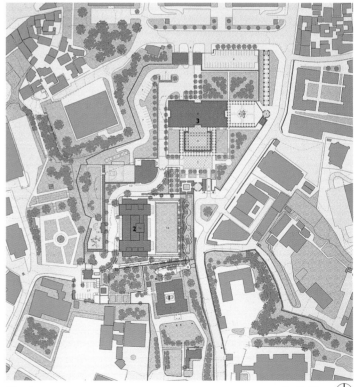

1 Existing ambassador's
  residence
2 Housing
3 Chancery office
  building

Site plan

0 15 30 m

Master plan model

Mahler 4

Amsterdam, Netherlands, 2000

Lobby

Mahler 4 is a mixed-use development on the Mahlerstrasse in Amsterdam. Nine different architects were asked to design buildings to be sited above a common 2,000-car parking garage. This project is an 110,000-square-foot speculative retail and office building with a predetermined wedge-shaped footprint.

The character and detailing of the building are reminiscent of the geometric interests found in Dutch architecture of the 1920s. The ground floor, double height to accommodate the retail portion of the program, is clad in red honed marble. The six office floors above are clad in a buff-colored attenuated brick known as "Dudok" brick after the Dutch architect. At the top of the two vertical facade elements flanking the entrance courtyard, copper-barrel-vaulted roofs create special spaces on the uppermost floor to be used for conference rooms or boardrooms.

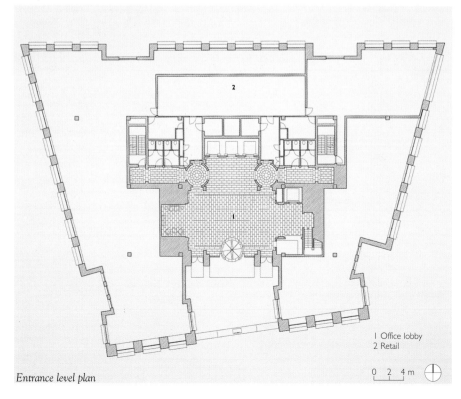

1 Office lobby
2 Retail

0 2 4 m

Entrance level plan

View toward building entrance

Competition for the West Palm Beach Library

West Palm Beach, Florida, 2001

This competition entry, which was not premiated, sites the new library along the intercoastal waterway at the terminus of Clematis Street, historically the main street of West Palm Beach. Surrounding the library are plazas, pergolas, an outdoor amphitheater and steps leading down to the water; all of which enhance public use of the site.

The first level of the library contains the main lobby, circulation desk and community spaces such as a café, auditorium, galleries, art studios, library store and bookstore, built above an on-grade service level. The mezzanine contains staff offices and workrooms, the genealogy collection and the seniors' area. The Children's Library and Multimedia Area occupy the second level, and the Adult Library is located at the top of the building.

The lower levels of the library have extensive windows that provide a transparent quality and allow views through the building to the water from upper Clematis Street. A dramatic frame in the form of a truncated cone rises in the center of the building, creating an iconic landmark on the water.

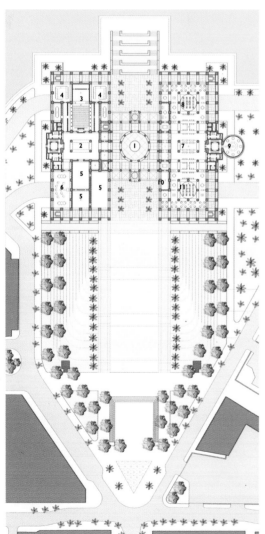

Upper library floor plan

First level floor plan

1 Lobby
2 Community Center reception hall
3 Auditorium
4 Meeting room
5 Gallery
6 Art studio
7 Adult Library new collections display
8 Adult popular fiction
9 Café
10 Library store
11 Adult popular non-fiction

0   32   64 ft

Model view from the water

Section

Dameisha Resort
Master Plan

Shenzhen, China, 2001

The master plan for this 260-room resort hotel in Shenzhen, China emphasizes the relationship between architecture and the natural landscape. The hotel is organized as a series of buildings sited along the beach and oriented toward the water. The main building surrounds an informal courtyard with various food and beverage functions.

Two seven-story buildings house the majority of guestrooms. Suites are located in the wings with presidential suites located in circular elements closest to the water. Additional guestrooms are provided in villas sited along the beach. This organizational strategy provides a sense of community at a domestic scale while preserving the privacy of individual quarters. The teahouse at the eastern end of the site is a quiet place reminiscent of Chinese traditions.

Throughout the resort, the buildings are given a distinctive identity through a playful architectural character that integrates the openness of a resort hotel with site-specific concerns to connect the development to the city and an adjacent park. Extensive landscaping with indigenous tropical vegetation provides shade and complements the buildings.

Aerial view of the resort

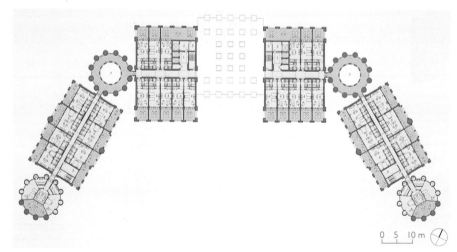

0 5 10 m

Main hotel building plan

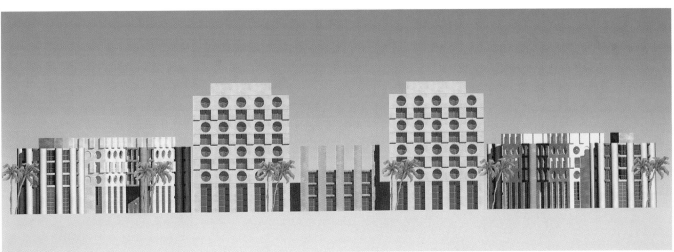

Main hotel building elevation

Guestroom group elevation

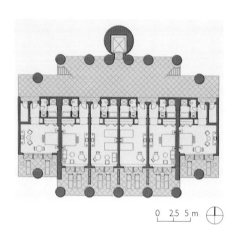

Guestroom group plan

0 2.5 5 m

Guestroom group elevation

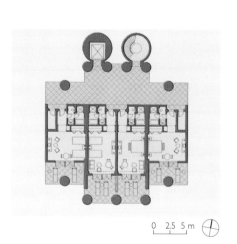

Guestroom group plan

0 2.5 5 m

284

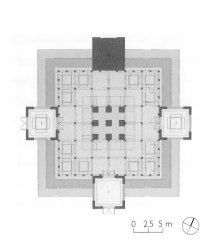

Teahouse plan

Teahouse elevation

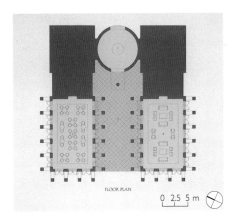

Marina restaurant pavilion plan

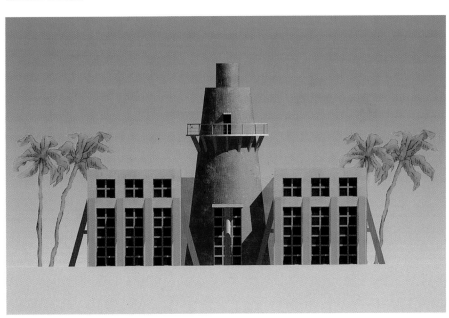

Marina restaurant pavilion elevation

Competition for the
United States Institute of Peace

Washington, D.C., 2001

The United States Institute of Peace, which sponsors exhibitions, education and conference functions, is sited on Constitution Avenue facing the Mall. An elliptical Peace Garden creates a forecourt and reconciles the symmetrical organization of the building with the triangular configuration of the site. The ellipse, which is also expressed in the glass dome above the entrance pavilion, embodies formal principles that contribute to the symbolism of the institution. As described by Thomas Jefferson, pre-eminent American President and architect, the ellipse is characterized by two centers that create one pure geometric form— in essence two entities resolved in a perfect whole—a paradigm for negotiating peace.

Central to the composition is a domed cylindrical pavilion containing the entrance lobby on the ground floor and a Great Hall for special events on the second floor. The glass dome, glistening by day and radiating at night, creates a recognizable and symbolic image for the institution. This scheme was not chosen for further development.

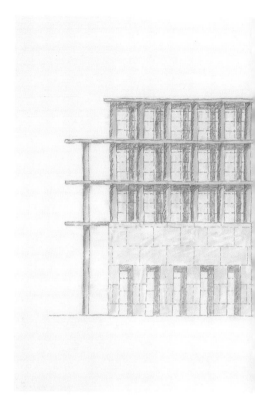

Constitution Avenue elevation

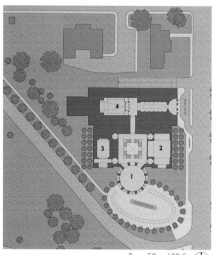

Site and ground floor plan

1 Lobby/exhibition
2 Exhibition
3 Multipurpose room
4 Auditorium

0   50   100 ft

View from Constitution Avenue

United States Institute of Peace

287

Minneapolis Institute of Arts
Minneapolis, Minnesota, 2001

Atrium lobby

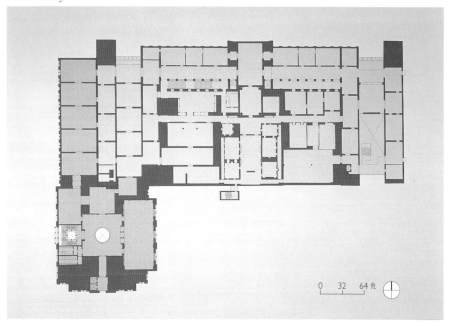

Gallery floor plan

The Minneapolis Institute of Arts occupies a 1915 neoclassical building designed by McKim, Mead & White, to which two modern wings by Kenzo Tange were added in the 1970s. The four-story, 117,000-square-foot museum expansion is organized in two sections facing Stevens Street. A linear addition is located in front of the Tange wing, and a square block is located to the south. The ground floor contains public study rooms for the library and collections of works on paper and a small gallery organized around a central skylit atrium. The top floor houses a reception hall and prefunction space. The intermediate levels contain galleries connected to renovated space in the existing building.

The design of the new facades addresses both the neoclassical character of the original building and the abstract modernism of the 1970s additions. Like the McKim, Mead & White building, the composition of the expansion uses rhythm, symmetry and surface relief to articulate the facades and make the architectural language accessible. Like the Tange additions, the surfaces are simple and unadorned. The light, monochromatic masonry materials are similar to both and help unify the appearance of the complex.

Preliminary garden elevation

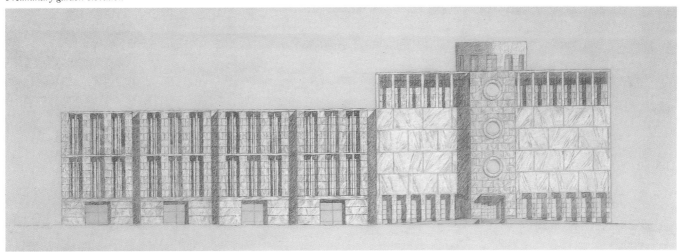

Preliminary Stevens Street elevation

Stevens Street elevation

Children's Theatre Company
Minneapolis, Minnesota, 2001

New theatre

The Children's Theatre Company occupies one of the wings designed by Kenzo Tange and added to the Minneapolis Institute of Arts in the 1970s. The program for the 45,000-square-foot expansion includes a 290-seat flexible theatre, rehearsal space, and educational facilities, as well as renovation of the existing 720-seat theatre and backstage areas. A new theatre lobby is planned adjacent to the Third Street entrance shared with the MIA. The lobby, a dramatic multi-story space with glass walls and a glass dome, assumes a luminous presence at the terminus of the Avenue of the Arts where it both enlivens the pedestrian level of the street and creates an iconic presence for the arts campus.

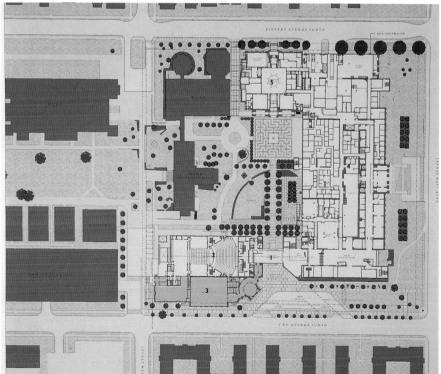

Site and ground floor plan of the MIA and CTC

1 Shared MIA/CTC lobby
2 Existing CTC
3 CTC expansion
4 Existing MIA
5 MIA expansion

Atrium lobby

Study for St. Charles Porte d'Aix

Marseilles, France, 2001

View from the west

This potential mixed-use project is located on a prominent site in the district known as St. Charles Porte d'Aix near the Arc de Triomphe in the Place Jules Guesde. A three-star hotel located in the center of the building holds the streetwall along Boulevard Charles Nedelec and creates a crescent-shaped public plaza for automobile drop-off along Boulevard Du Bois.

The hotel is flanked by retail stores on the ground floor and commercial office space above. These three functional sections are separated by arched openings on the ground floor, which provide pedestrian circulation through the building. The western end of the building culminates in a monumental rotunda that offers premier office and retail space and acknowledges the nearby Arc de Triomphe with the details of its design.

The massing and character of the building correspond with the prevailing architecture in this section of Marseilles. Its materials and detailing, including the tile roofs, exterior shutters, decorative metal railings and roof terraces, reflect building traditions in the region of the Mediterranean.

Model view facing Boulevard Du Bois

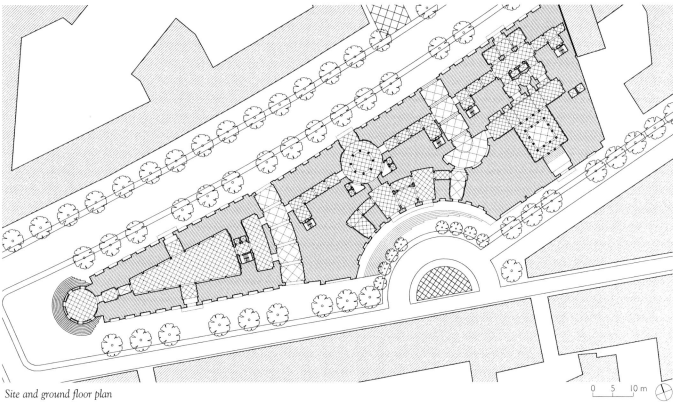

Site and ground floor plan

0 5 10 m

Three on the Bund

Shanghai, China, 2001

East atrium

East atrium

Following a meticulous exterior restoration of the seven-story landmark Beaux-Arts building known as Three on the Bund, the interior, which was dramatically altered over the years, is transformed into a modern, vibrant art and retail center. The lower three floors contain fashion retail stores and art galleries. The upper floors contain upscale restaurants for notable international chefs. A seventh-floor cafe and jazz club opens onto a landscaped roof terrace.

The renovation creates an open, public image by reorganizing internal circulation and introducing a central Grand Stair. The walls surrounding the skylit Grand Stair are clad in translucent alabaster, creating a diaphanous shaft of light through the building. Two full-height atria provide vertical orientation and allow daylight to penetrate to all floors. The east atrium, with its inwardly tilting walls and round columns backed by piers of richly figured green marble, is reminiscent of a mountain forest. In contrast, the quieter west atrium is clad in red stone and penetrated with circular windows into the private dining rooms of the restaurant levels.

Three on the Bund

West atrium

Preliminary view of a bar

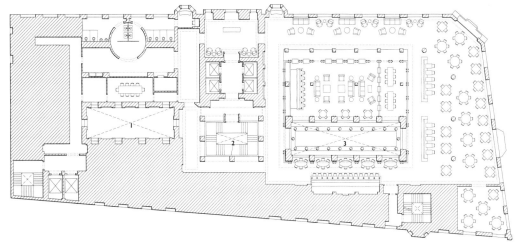

Typical restaurant level plan

1 West atrium
2 Grand stair
3 East atrium

0   2.5   5 m

Preliminary view of a dining room

Section through west atrium, grand stair and east atrium

0 5 10 m

House at Sagaponac

Southampton, New York, 2001

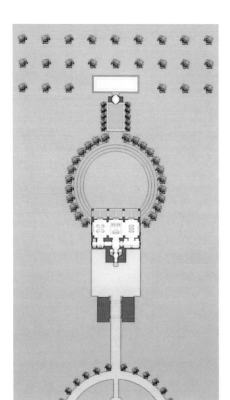

Site plan

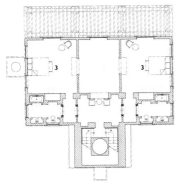

Second floor plan

1 Living/dining
2 Kitchen
3 Bedroom

0 4 8 ft

Ground Floor Plan

The Houses at Sagaponac, located in Southampton on Long Island, New York, is a unique development community of contemporary houses designed by 34 prominent international architects. The houses are all designed to create environmentally conscious single-family dwellings ranging in size from 2,000 to 4,500 square feet. They are intended to be modest without compromising artistic vision.

The Sagaponac house designed by Michael Graves & Associates is a retreat for weekends and vacations. The program includes a living room, dining room, library, kitchen and two bedrooms in the main house, with options for a studio and a garage flanking the house on either side. These three components form a central courtyard that creates a sense of arrival and also provides privacy for the house. The rear yard, with its sunken amphitheater, echoes the privacy of the front court. A circle of trees encloses this space, creating the feeling of an outdoor room. A small folly, perhaps a pool house or a gazebo, marks the end of the primary axis.

302

Entrance elevation

Garden elevation

303

St. Coletta's School

Washington, D.C., 2002

Independence Avenue elevation

The new campus for St. Coletta's School, nationally recognized for excellence in special education, is located in the Southeast District of Washington D.C. at the corner of Independence and 19th Street, near the Stadium-Armory Metro station. The site is also adjacent to a residential neighborhood of single-family homes. Three tile-clad multistory pavilions establish the school's identity on Independence and contain the primary public spaces, including a multipurpose room to be shared with the community.

The classrooms, designated as "houses," are designed with a scale and organization similar to the residential neighborhood along 19th Street, including those immediately across the street. The building is substantially set back from the sidewalk, which accommo-dates the Metro's right-of-way and creates a landscaped area for outdoor instruction. Each classroom "house" corresponds to a different age group and contains divisible instructional space, offices, tutoring rooms, bathrooms and an elevator. A central three-story skylit hall, called the "Village Green" organizes the scheme along a single axis. The gymnasium, available to the community, is located in an adjacent structure connected to the school.

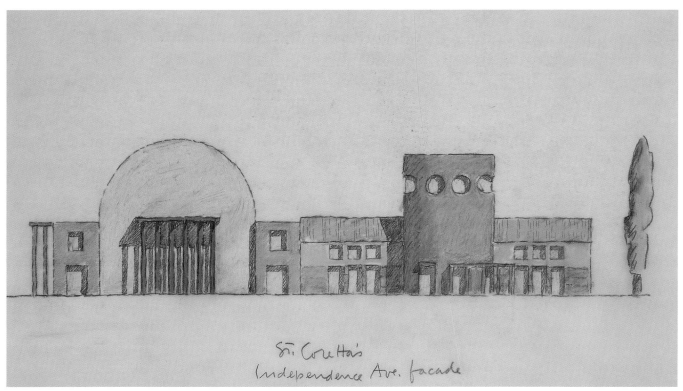

Preliminary Independence Avenue elevation

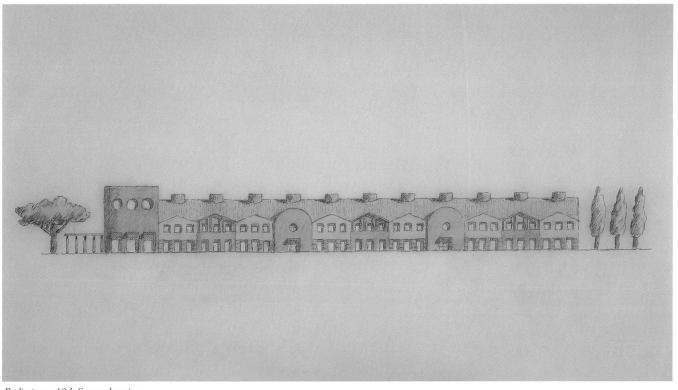

Preliminary 19th Street elevation

305

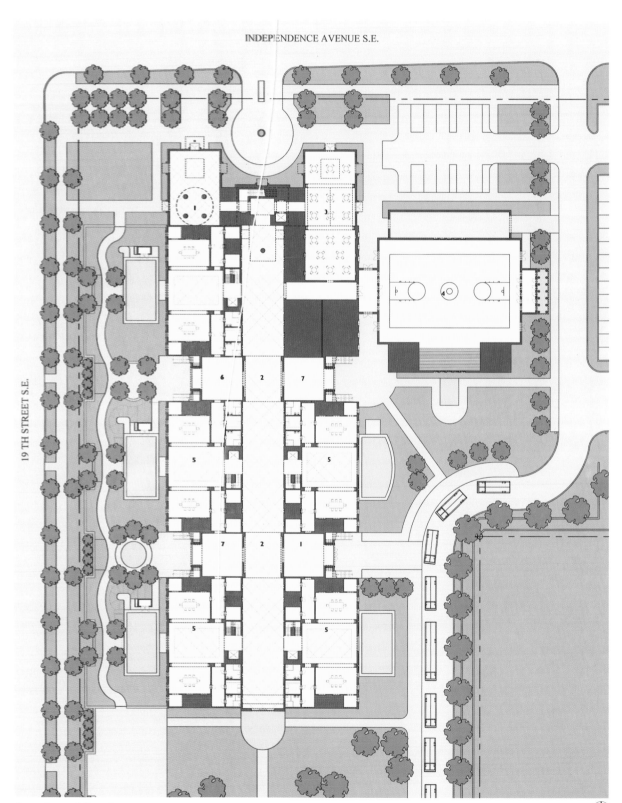

INDEPENDENCE AVENUE S.E.

19 TH STREET S.E.

Site and ground floor plan

1 Lobby
2 "Village Green"
3 Community room
4 Gymnasium
5 Classroom "houses"
6 Music studio
7 Health services

0   20   40 ft

Model view from Independence Avenue and 19th Street

Model view from Independence Avenue

Department of Transportation Headquarters

Washington, D.C., 2002

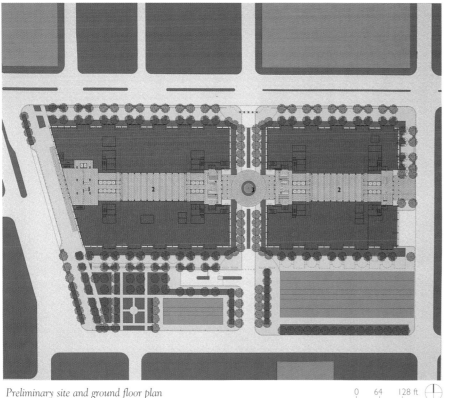

Preliminary site and ground floor plan

0   64   128 ft

1 New Jersey Avenue
  entrance
2 Atrium
3 Third Street

The headquarters of the United States Department of Transportation is sited in the Southeast Federal Center between federal and commercial Washington, adjacent to the Navy Yard Historic District and the Anacostia River waterfront. Spanning two full city blocks, the 1.35-million-square-foot project is developed as two separate but architecturally similar office buildings above a common below-grade parking garage.

Both buildings relate in character to the prevailing industrial context. The western building is nine stories high, while the eastern building occupies eight stories. The difference in height creates variety along M Street and emphasizes the primacy of the western building and its public entrance along New Jersey Avenue, a L'Enfant Plan boulevard within view of the Capitol Building. The New Jersey Avenue facade has a presence appropriate to the importance of a cabinet-level federal institution. The entrance portico and multistory lobby lead to adjacent first-floor space containing large departmental assembly and joint-use facilities. A central linear atrium is developed in each of the buildings. While the buildings are not physically connected across Third Street, the transparency of each building's atrium helps create a visual link between them.

Preliminary view from New Jersey Avenue

New Jersey State Police Headquarters Master Plan

West Trenton, New Jersey, 2002

Aerial view from the south

The master plan for the headquarters and training center for the New Jersey State Police creates a campus that integrates new construction with existing buildings and preserves the natural landscape. Several plateaus are established within the hilly terrain to accommodate new buildings and large-scale outdoor functions requiring flat sites, such as the parade ground, running track and driver training area.

The various functional components of the program are organized hierarchically from the most publicly accessible and visible activities to those requiring a greater level of privacy and security. Each functional group is organized around a formal open space, promoting a sense of common purpose and camaraderie. Although the buildings have individual identities

appropriate to their uses, the similarities of organization and consistent use of brick and wood materials create a unified campus.

The state-of-the-art training center comprises the Police Academy's administrative headquarters, dining hall, classrooms and auditorium grouped around a quadrangle to the east of the campus entrance. The headquarters complex, consisting of a 200,000-square-foot office building, two dormitories and a fitness center surround a tree-lined parade ground, the most significant ceremonial space within the campus.

1 Existing museum
2 Dining
3 Police Academy Training Center
4 Headquarters office building
5 Parade ground
6 Dormitories
7 Fitness center
8 Driver training

Site Plan

0 100 200 ft

Competition for the
Jacksonville Library

Jacksonville, Florida, 2002

Monroe Street elevatiom

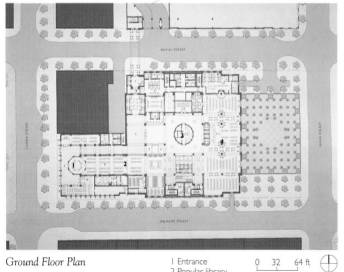

Ground Floor Plan

1 Entrance
2 Popular library
3 Theater
4 Children's library

0   32   64 ft

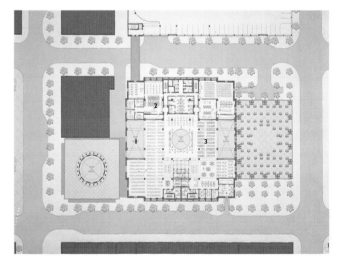

Third level mezzanine plan

1 Adult collection
2 Adult learning center
3 Young adult collection

The library is organized as two simple, legible volumes, a three-story entrance pavilion facing Hemming Plaza adjacent to the existing MOMA building, and a six-story building occupying the center of the site. The facades are proportioned to give the library a civic presence and yet, with its generous fenestration and sun control devices, the building is given a sense of openness appropriate for a public educational institution. As required by the program, the public spaces throughout the building are completely open. Vertical circulation among floors via escalators and glass elevators encourage the visual experience of the library's offerings. Positioning separate service cores for patrons and staff at the building's perimeter maintains the sense of transparency throughout the center of the building.

Lobby

Resort Master Plan

Canary Islands, 2002

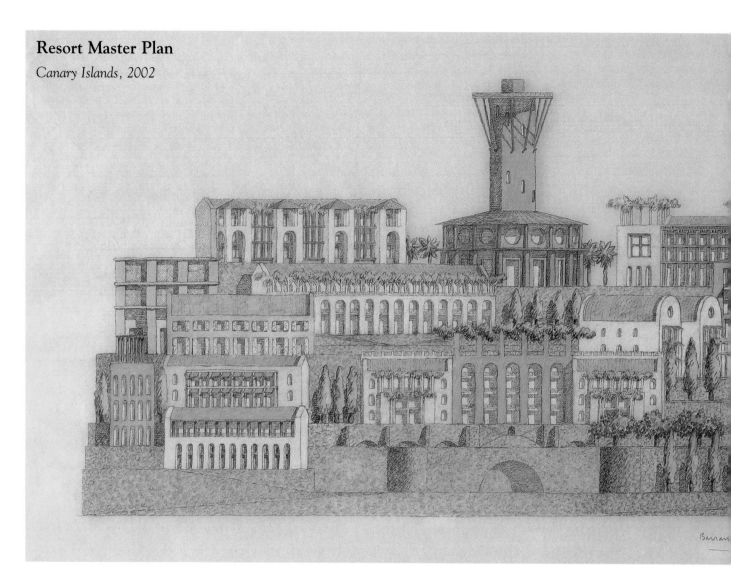

Hilltown elevation

Beachfront

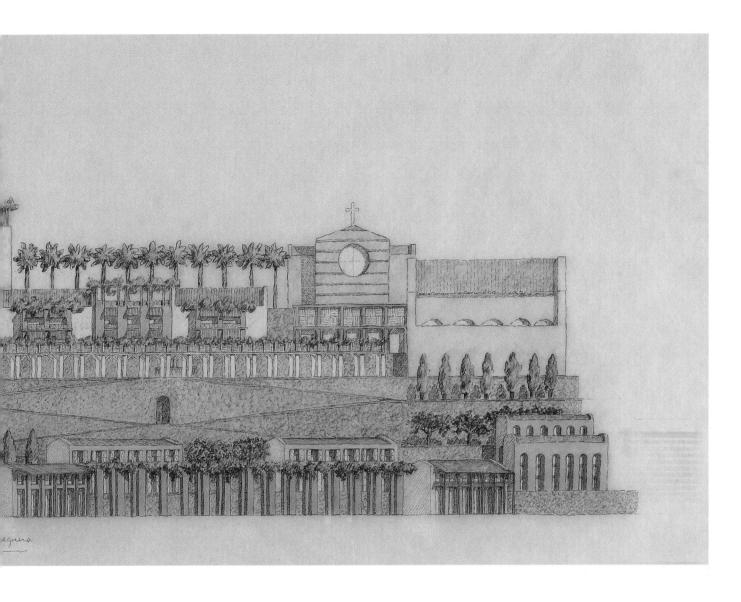

The master plan for a resort in the Canary Islands combines exciting recreational experiences with a sensible approach to land use and environmental issues. The character of the resort is inspired by the valley landscape and embraces traditional architecture of the region. One of the planning goals is to preserve the natural landscape and concentrate development to minimize disruption of the terrain. Therefore, instead of developing tennis courts, swimming pools and other recreational facilities requiring flat land throughout the resort, those facilities are concentrated in a Town Center sited on the naturally level terrain adjacent to the waterfront. An expanded beach with clubs, retail and cafes, a pier for ocean expeditions and a marina maximize opportunities for waterfront recreation. Golf courses following the contours of the valley floor

and lower ridges are selectively planted and irrigated with recycled gray water.

Various types of guest accommodations are provided in terraced hotels overlooking the ocean or the golf course, in upper levels of Town Center buildings and in hilltowns. In reaction to the proliferation of generic hotels with no ties to local context, the hilltowns are imbued with an architectural character particular to the terrain, climate and the building traditions of the region. Organizing the buildings in small-scale increments responsive to the topography creates a wide variety of courtyards, gardens and piazzas, which are lively and active in the public realm and intimate and peaceful in the private guest quarters.

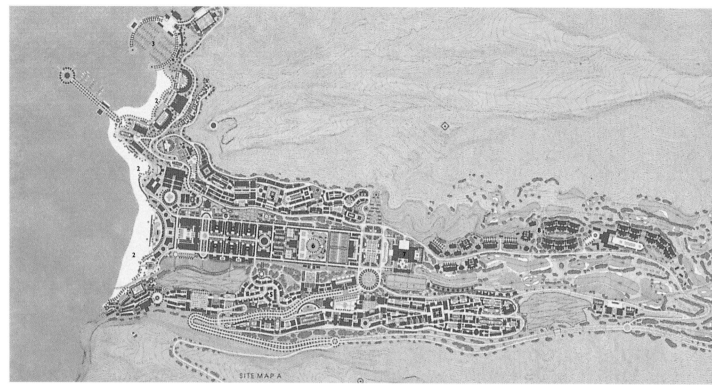

Site plan

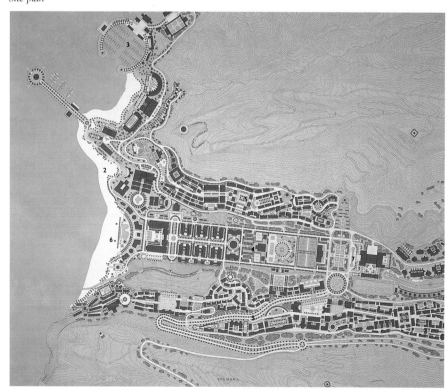

Alternative Town Center site plan

1 Beach club
2 Beach hotels
3 Marina
4 Town Center
5 Hilltown
6 Swimming/tennis centers
7 Conference center
8 Golf hotel
9 Golf club
10 Equestrian center

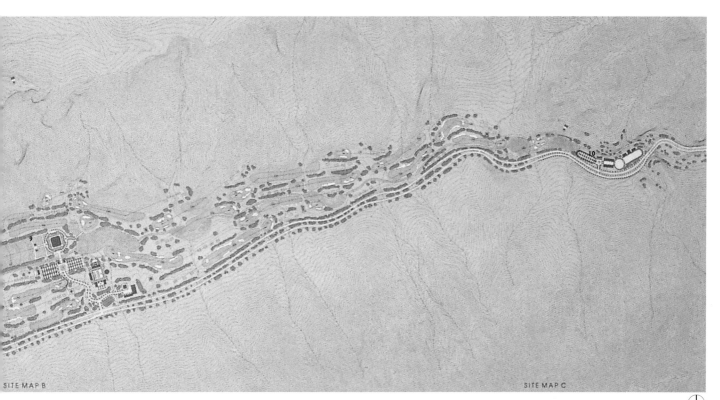

SITE MAP B

SITE MAP C

Resort entrance and equestrian center

Golf clubhouse

Town Center elevation

Beach club elevation

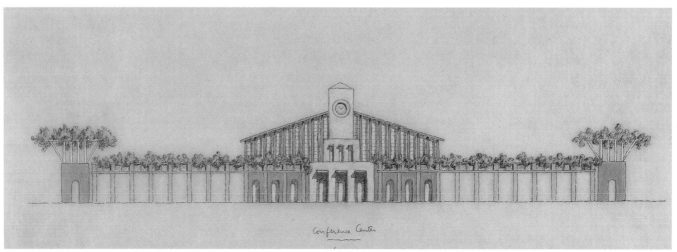

Conference center elevation

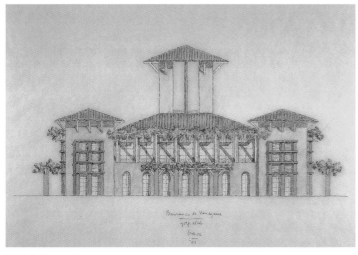

Golf clubhouse elevation

Water tower elevation

Town Center

Town Center

Beach club

Town Center

Kennedy Center
Expansion Study

Washington, D.C., 2002

View of civic plaza and exhibitions pavilion from the Kennedy Center

The expansion of the John F. Kennedy Center for the Performing Arts reconnects the institution to Washington's monumental core by building a deck over the adjacent highway and constructing a pair of buildings on top. In addition to providing much-needed program space, the project creates an opportunity to reaffirm the center as a living memorial to President Kennedy through the character of the new civic plaza and its architecture.

In both of the formal plan options the expansion consists of two buildings embracing a dramatic public space centered on the Kennedy Center. One of the buildings contains a café and gift shop, exhibits and educational facilities, and administrative offices. Its companion building contains restaurants on the plaza level and

rehearsal space and offices on other levels. A pair of flanking towers, which create a gate to the new plaza, accentuates the axis of E Street, the major connection to the city. Aligned with the existing Hall of States and Hall of Nations, the towers also frame the view toward Washington from inside the Kennedy Center. The civic plaza is developed as an urban garden for the arts, grand in scale but intimate in character. Two pavilions — one for exhibitions and the other for performances — pull some of the most visible activities of the program out into the public realm and, through their iconic forms, enhance the dramatic character of the place.

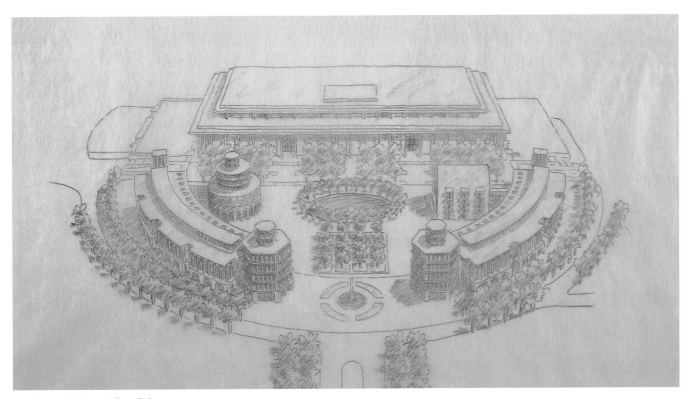

Aerial view of Option 1 from E Street

Aerial view of Option 2 from E Street

South Campus Master Plan
Rice University

Houston, Texas, 2002

This master plan studies the south and west portions of the Rice University campus, including the adjacent Main Street and University Boulevard, and assesses the impact of new development on the existing academic campus. It also considers urban relationships between the nearby Texas Medical Center and the university while addressing mass transportation, parking and automobile and pedestrian circulation in relation to both the campus and the surrounding neighborhoods.

A space utilization study for the entire campus of academic, administrative and residential components formed the basis for the physical master plan. This work included a more detailed program study for the School of Natural Science, the School of Engineering and the Athletics Department as well as for student recreation, arts-related programs and retail space. Major components of the master plan program comprise a 3,500-seat convocation center, student centers, four future residential colleges, research and academic facilities. The study follows the original Cram-Goodhue master plan by increasing the density of the existing campus through adding rooms to existing residential colleges and adding new residential colleges to existing residential quadrangles. The major and minor axes of the original master plan are extended as a new quadrangle is planned to the south, terminated with a new entrance to the campus opposite the Texas Medical Center on Main Street and reinforced by landscaping with the live oaks typical on the campus. Proposed long-term expansion of the campus is meant to extend the original plan strategies to new quadrangles similar in scale to those existing but which can also accommodate the more flexible floor plates needed in modern academic research buildings.

Site plan

MASTER PLAN
SCHEME A
RICE UNIVERSITY
HOUSTON, TEXAS

PATHS
FIELDS
STRUCTURED PARKING
EXISTING BUILDINGS
NEW BUILDINGS

NEW BUILDINGS:
1. CONVOCATION/RECREATION
2. NEW RESIDENTIAL COLLEGE
3. ACADEMIC EXPANSION
4. PERFORMING ARTS
5. SATELLITE CENTRAL PLANT
6. HOUSING
7. STUDENT CENTER
8. STRUCTURED PARKING
9. VARSITY TENNIS

DECEMBER 10, 2002
MICHAEL GRAVES & ASSOCIATES

Arts and Sciences Building
New Jersey City University

Jersey City, New Jersey, 2002

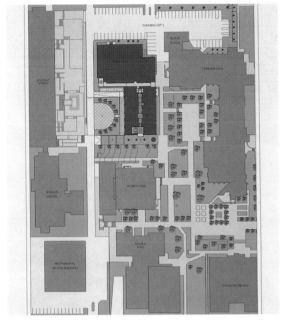

Site plan

0 30 60 ft

The Arts and Sciences Building largely replaces Fries Hall, an existing building on the site, and comprises six stories plus a lower level that opens to grade as the site slopes down to the west. The building program provides offices and teaching space for several departments, including 14 new classrooms and 10 computer laboratories.

The building's massing reflects its pivotal location on the campus. A two-story exterior colonnade along the south facade responds to major circulation paths connecting Hepburn Hall, the historic heart and symbol of the university, to the much-frequented Student Union. A distinctive entrance tower at the southeast corner of the building creates a new visual focal point for this section of the campus. The Dean's conference room is located on the upper floor of the tower beneath a pyramidal roof.

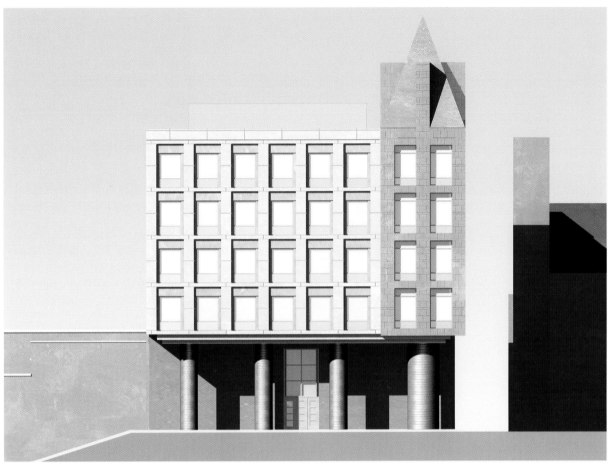

West elevation

South elevation

Expansion of the Kavli Institute for Theoretical Physics

University of California at Santa Barbara

Santa Barbara, California, 2002

The 11,500-square-foot expansion of the Institute for Theoretical Physics, designed by Michael Graves & Associates and completed in 1994, provides additional offices and meeting rooms, and a new 50-seat auditorium for a variety of conferences and presentations. The plan of the original building features two wings in a V-shaped configuration with a courtyard in the center. The expansion connects the two wings and fills in the western end of the courtyard with a first floor auditorium and second floor offices. The remaining area of the courtyard, now covered with a steel and glass roof canopy, becomes a prefunction space. The composition, character, colors and materials of the expansion are in keeping with the picturesque and informal nature of the original building.

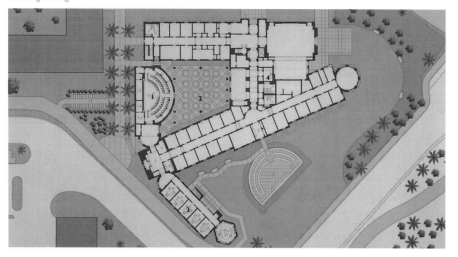

Site and ground floor plan

Enclosed courtyard

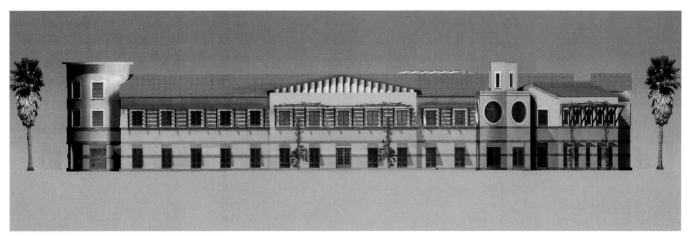

South elevation

East elevation

View from the south lawn

Kasteel Holterveste

Den Bosch, Netherlands, 2003

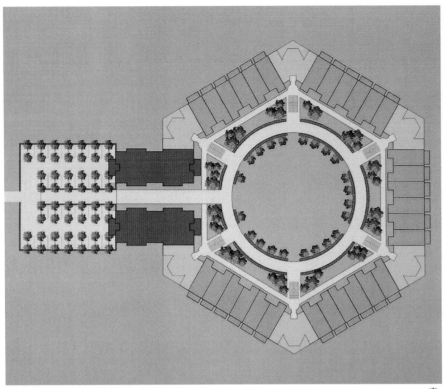

Site and ground floor plan　　　　0　5　10 m

Aerial view of the development

Kasteel Holterveste is the sixth of nine multifamily residential projects in Haverleij, a large development located in Den Bosch near Eindhoven. The program consists of 68 dwellings, including 48 single-family houses and 20 apartments, plus parking. Consistent with Haverleij's master plan, each development is characterized as a castle, the Dutch word for which is "kasteel." Kasteel Holterveste is organized as a hexagon. Five sides feature three-story houses, and the sixth side is designed as a gate flanked by apartment buildings and leading to the interior garden court. Four house towers with peaked roofs articulate the intersections of the sides of the hexagon and serve as iconic markers creating the image of Kasteel Holterveste as seen from the landscape of the surrounding golf course.

The architectural character is inspired by the Amsterdam School architectural movement of the 1920s, which featured a modern and somewhat abstract use of brick without sacrificing the scale and detail that provide a sense of domesticity.

Courtyard facade detail

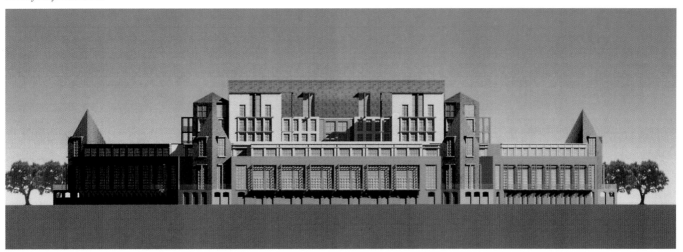

Rear elevation

Club Wedd House

2003

View of the entrance

Target Stores commissioned a house as the first prize in a sweepstakes for couples listed in the store's bridal registry. The house is designed to be flexible in the use of the rooms, the options for exterior materials and colors, and future expansion. The plan is organized symmetrically about the central entrance and a two-story living room. The house is designed as a kit home to be fabricated by Lindal Cedar Homes of Seattle, Washington. Its architectural character is derived from the wooden post and beam construction system and expressed through the timber frame detailing and wood siding.

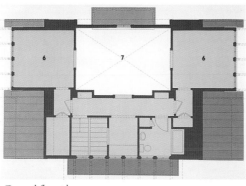

Ground floor plan

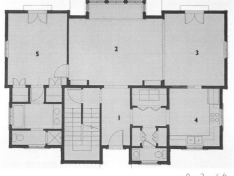

Second floor plan

1. Foyer
2. Living room
3. Dining room
4. Kitchen
5. Master bedroom
6. Bedroom
7. Open to below

0   3   6 ft

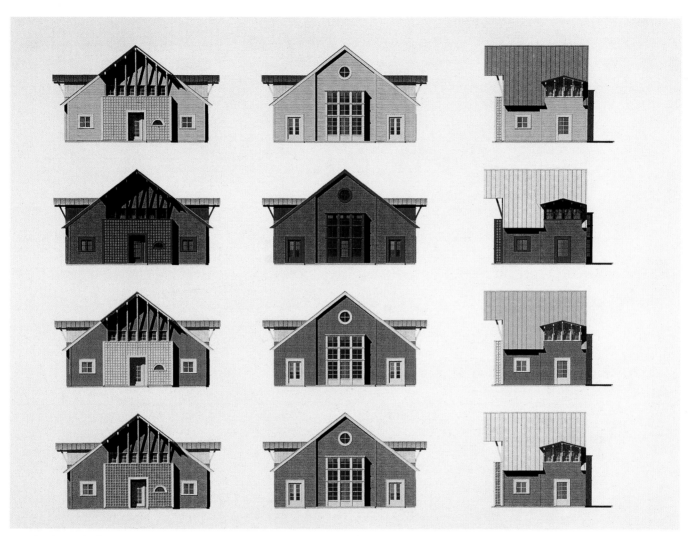

Facade siding and color options

Pavilions™

2003

The Pavilions™ continue a tradition of outbuildings as architectural accessories for the home. Customarily, a pavilion is an exceptional room in an estate, a whimsical complement to the residence proper. Thus it can vary in color and style from the main residence. The Pavilions™, developed in partnership with target.com and Lindal Cedar Homes of Seattle, Washington, are part of a long tradition of American kit homes shipped all over the country and assembled on site.

The impetus to design the Pavilions™ came from the desire to offer homeowners the option of adding flexible space to a house without the inconvenient disruption often associated with adding a room. A Pavilion either can be built as a freestanding structure or, using a door or window opening, can be attached to an existing house via an "extended threshold."

The Pavilions™ are available in three models with a variety of options for colors and siding design: Brighton, an octagonal pavilion useful as a breakfast room, dining room, garden room or studio; Heathcote, a square room useful as a media room, home office, game room or library; and Sherwood, an open-air or screened room ideal for a garden room or a porch.

Brighton pavilion

Brighton pavilion study

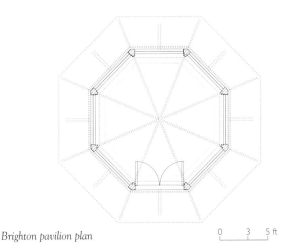

Brighton pavilion plan

0   3   5 ft

Sherwood pavilion

Heathcote pavilion

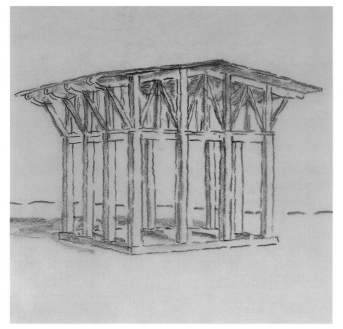

Sherwood pavilion study

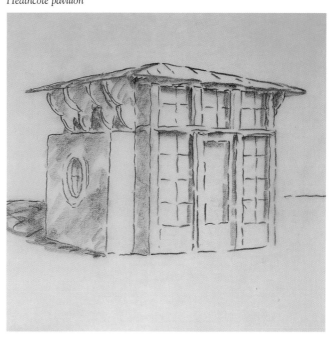

Heathcote pavilion study

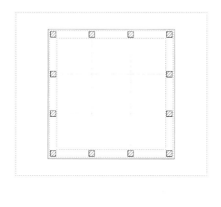

Sherwood pavilion plan   0   3   5 ft

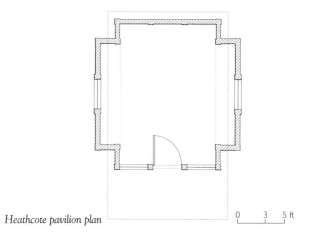

Heathcote pavilion plan   0   3   5 ft

Campus Master Plan
Florida Tech

Melbourne, Florida, 2003

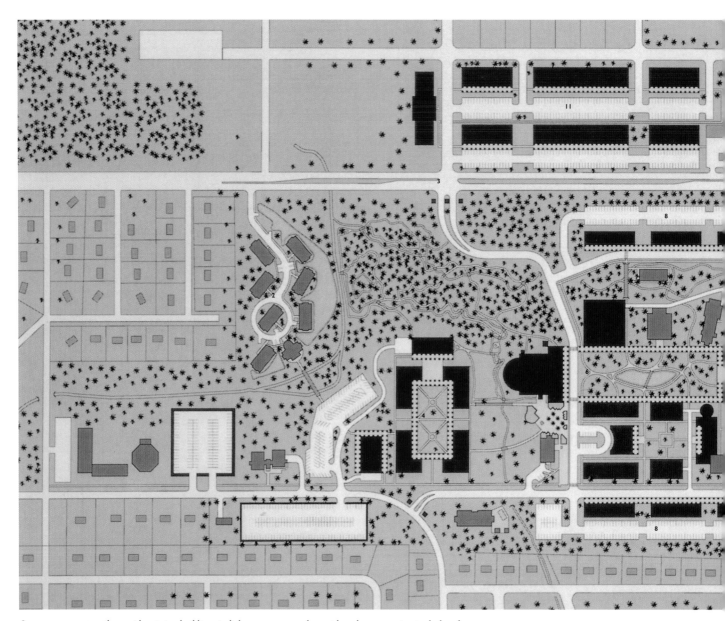

Long-range master plan, with existing buildings in light terra cotta and new phased construction in dark red

In order to accommodate future growth in university programs and student population, Florida Tech commissioned a master plan for its 130-acre campus that provides managed growth in four major phases over a 20-year period. The master plan proposes a hierarchical system of internal roadways and walkways that encourages the development of a coherent campus integrating academic, residential and recreational activities. The plan also proposes reinstatement of the original entrance to the campus adjacent to an extraordinary 25-acre botanical garden containing more than 200 species of palm trees. Relocating the campus entrance and developing a central quadrangle in the first phase will create a strong and immediate presence for the school. A consistent palette of exterior colors and materials for the buildings will reinforce the relationships among buildings and contribute to the campus's sense of place.

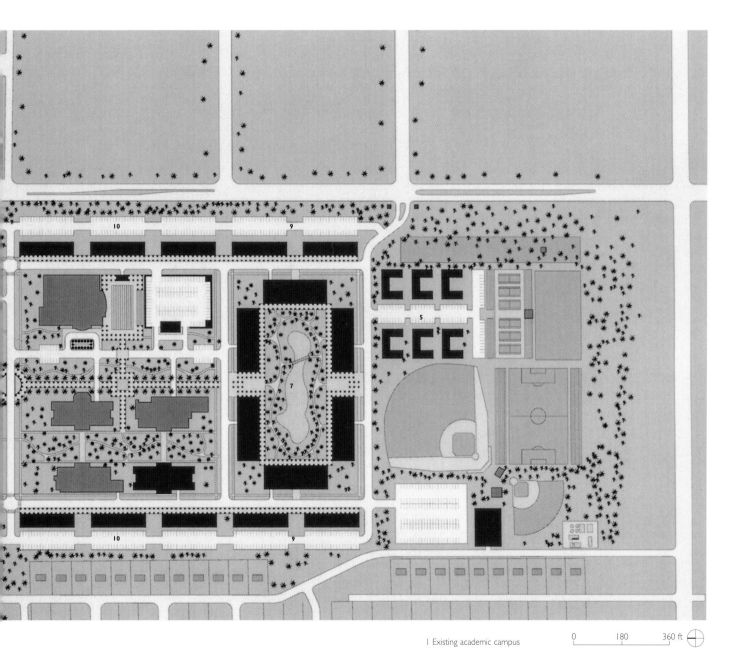

1 Existing academic campus
2 Existing student housing
3 New campus entrance
4 Phase 1 student housing
5 Phase 1 fraternity/sorority houses
6 Phase 2 academic buildings and
  dining hall, new construction and
  renovation
7 Phases 2 and 3 academic
  quadrangle
8 Phase 2 student housing
9 Phase 3 student housing
10 Phase 4 student housing
11 Phase 4 research complex and
  commercial development

0   180   360 ft

National Automobile Museum

The Hague, Netherlands, 2003

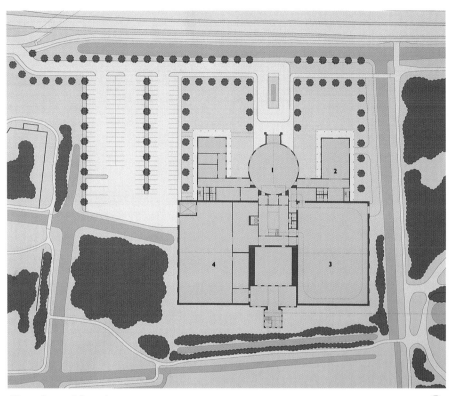

Site and ground floor plan

1 Entrance
2 Auditorium
3 Exhibition
4 Workshop

0   25   50 m

The National Automobile Museum is a new institution to preserve and display an extensive collection of new and vintage automobiles. It is located in a park near the Queen's residence and faces the Leidsestraatweg. Its architectural character responds to the traditional nature of the context through massing, detailing and consistent use of brick materials. In order to mitigate the large scale of the exhibit space and workshops, the smaller scale public activities are organized in a U-shaped configuration facing the street. The central rotunda, the main entrance to the museum, doubles as a temporary exhibition gallery for featured pieces. To either side, the roof overhangs and columns surrounding the auditorium and reception hall impart a domestic scale to the composition in deference to the neighborhood.

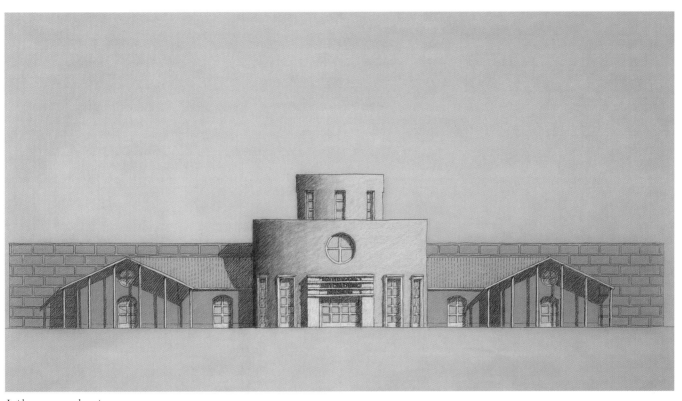

Leidsestraatweg elevation

View of the entrance

Biographies

Michael Graves, FAIA

Michael Graves, FAIA, has been at the forefront of architectural design for nearly four decades. Cited by Paul Goldberger, former *New York Times* critic, as "the most truly original voice American architecture has produced in some time," Graves has influenced the transformation of urban architecture from a focus on abstract modernism to more contextual design. He has received many prestigious awards, including the 1999 National Medal of Arts and the 2001 Gold Medal from the American Institute of Architects.

A native of Indianapolis, Graves received his architectural training at the University of Cincinnati and Harvard University. In 1960, Graves received the Rome Prize and studied at the American Academy in Rome, of which he is now a Trustee. He is the Robert Schirmer Professor of Architecture, Emeritus, at Princeton University, where he taught for 39 years.

Michael Graves & Associates

Michael Graves founded his firm in Princeton, New Jersey in 1964. Today, Michael Graves & Associates, with offices in Princeton and in New York City, has a diversified worldwide architectural practice encompassing many building types as well as a highly successful product design practice. In addition to Graves, the principals of the firm: (in order of seniority) are: Karen Nichols, Patrick Burke, Gary Lapera, Thomas Rowe, John Diebboll and Susan Howard. The firm is organized in studios: four architecture studios, an interior design studio and several product design studios. The architecture studios are led by principals who collaborate with Michael Graves on project design.

Karen Nichols, FAIA

Since joining the firm in 1977, Karen Nichols, FAIA, has had overall responsibility for managing Michael Graves & Associates' practice in architecture, interior design and product design. As an architect, she has been the Principal-in-Charge of multiple phases of renovation and expansion of The Newark Museum in Newark, New Jersey, the master plan of the Detroit Institute of Arts, and the Riverbend Music Center in Cincinnati, Ohio. She received her education at Smith College and the Massachusetts Institute of Technology.

Patrick Burke, AIA

Principal and Studio Head, Patrick Burke, AIA, received his architectural degrees from University of Illinois, Chicago Circle and Princeton University and joined Michael Graves & Associates in 1982. Representative projects included in this monograph are: four resort hotels in Egypt; the Brussels headquarters of the international insurance company, Fortis AG; expansions of the Minneapolis Institute of Arts and the Children's Theatre Company; the Museum of the Shenandoah Valley in Virginia; and a master plan for a resort in the Canary Islands.

Gary Lapera, AIA

Principal and Studio Head, Gary Lapera, AIA, joined Michael Graves & Associates in 1983. Representative projects included in this monograph are: the United States Embassy Compound in Seoul, Korea; the NovaCare Complex for the Philadelphia Eagles football team; Castalia, the Ministry of Health, Welfare and Sport in The Hague; the New Jersey State Police Headquarters Master Plan; several apartment towers and mixed-use buildings in Japan; and the Pavilions and Club Wedd House. He received his education at Cornell University and Harvard University.

Thomas P. Rowe, AIA

Principal and Studio Head, Thomas Rowe, AIA, received his architectural education at Catholic University and Princeton University and joined Michael Graves & Associates in 1984. Representative projects included in this monograph are: the NCAA Headquarters and Hall of Champions in Indianapolis, Indiana; the headquarters of the International Finance Corporation in Washington, D.C., the O'Reilly Theater in Pittsburgh; the Houston branch of the Federal Reserve Bank of Dallas; two residential towers in New York; and several projects for Rice University in Houston.

John Diebboll, AIA

John Diebboll, AIA, is the Principal-in-Charge of the firm's New York studio. He was educated at Bennington College and Princeton University and joined Michael Graves & Associates in 1984. Representative projects included in this monograph are public libraries in Alexandria, Virginia and Topeka, Kansas; the Taiwan National Museum of Pre-history; the Indianapolis Art Center; 1500 Ocean Drive in Miami Beach, Florida; St. Mary's Church in Rockledge, Florida; the master plan for Florida Tech; and several private residences.

Susan Howard

Susan Howard has advised Michael Graves & Associates on financial and legal matters since 1987. She has played a key role in developing MGA's employment practices and business plans. She has focused her attention on diversification of the practice, in particular on the development of the interior design and product design practices. She received her undergraduate degree from Beaver College, a J.D. from Seton Hall and an L.L.M. in Taxation from New York University.

Associated Architects and Designers

Academy-Groupe Atelier de Genval
Arcadis
Architecture & Planning Group
Atelier d'Art Urbain
Baum Associates
Buro Hoen Architecten
Burt Hill Kosar Rittelmann Architects
Crowner/King Architects
Dalton, Moran & Robinson
Daniel, Mann, Johnson & Mendenhall/Holmes & Narver
ECADI
EDAW Inc.
Rami El Dahan & Soheir Farid Architects
Grabowsky & Poort BV
HACBM
Haigo Shen & Associates
Yasuhiro Hamano
Ahmed Hamdy
Hammel Associates
HKS Inc.
Horst, Terrill & Karst, Architects
INA
Arch. Michel Jaspers & Partners
KBJ Architects
Kunwon International
Vlastimil Koubek, Architect
Maeda Construction Company, Ltd.
Massive Design Group
Min Associates
H. Thomas O'Hara, Architect
Amr Omar
Alain Poncet & Patrick Schwarz
Pierce, Goodwin, Alexander & Linville
Franco Possemato
Rafferty Rafferty and Tollefson Architects
Rolland, DelValle & Bradley
RSP Architects
Ryckaerts, Peeters and Partners
S & P Ltd.
Schmidt Associates
SERA Architects
Jose Siao Ling & Associates
SmithGroup Incorporated
STV Architects
Robert Swedroe, Architects and Planners
Tongi University
Mart van Schijndel Architect
Thomas, Miller & Partners
TSP Architects & Planners
Van den Acker Architekten
Van den Oever, Zaaijer, Roodbeen and Partners
URS Corporation
WHL-Archasia Consultants

Project Staff

The following list represents professional and administrative staff members and professional interns employed by Michael Graves & Associates from 1995-2003. We would like to thank the numerous individuals not mentioned here who assisted our administrative staff on a short-term or part-time basis during this period.

Principals
Michael Graves
Patrick Burke
John Diebboll
Susan Howard
Gary Lapera
Karen Nichols
Thomas Rowe

Senior Associates & Senior Directors
Michael Crackel
William Harrington
Roisin Heneghan
Don Menke
Robert Miller
Peter Neilson
Stephen Panzarino
Pim Robberechts
Donald Strum
Edward Tuck
Gregg Wielage
Mary Yun

Associates & Directors
J. Craig Babe
Jesse Castaneda
Adina Chouequet
Hillary Ellison
Robert Fahr
Keoni Fleming
Saverio Manago
Diana Nelson
Lyndon Neri
David Peschel
Mark Proicou
Barry Richards
Joseph Sullivan
Mark Sullivan
Joshua Zinder

Senior Designers
Katherine Ambroziak
Heidrun Beck
Robert Blaser
Eric Bogner
Christopher Brown
Russell DiNardo
Katherine Dy
Arturo Herscovici
Antoinette Jackson
Matthew Ligas
John Orgren

Shih-fu Peng
Jil Peters
Erika Schmitt
Tony Wilson
James Wisniewski
John Wriedt

Design Staff
Anne Adams
Sabra Albert
Brian Ambroziak
Michael Ammerman
Patricia Anahory Silva
John Anastasiadis
Kim Armour
Kristopher Artz
Emily Atwood
Giovanna Balarezo
Robert Bander
Meryl Blinder
Brian Bock
Anthony Boczkowski
Stefanie Brechbuehler
Randi Brookman
Jeffrey Brunner
David Cabianca
Antonija Campbell
Chris Campbell
Philip Chan
Grace Chen
Lin-Ann Ching
Marco Cimatti
Dorothy Colavecchio
Mark Cox
Tiffany Curtis
Lara Daniel
Jerome del Fierro
Jerome Dell'Olio
Roxanne de Prado
Elizabeth DeTeresi
Paul De Voe
Matthew Dockery
Scott Doty
Julie Dowling
Leslie Dowling
Urszula Duda
Emily Estes
Maria Fedorchenko
Elizabeth Ferrara
Justin Ferrick
Jamie Fleming
Jennifer Flume
Alex Garzon

Daniel Gatto
Danielle Gingras
George Hauner
Travis Hicks
Karen Hilde
Anthony Hron
Jiayur Hsu
Rossana Hu
Newman Huh
Earl Jackson
Brooke Johnson
Derek Jones
Joshua Jones
Esther Kardos
Tambi Kat
Michelle Kaufmann
Christine Kelley
Brook Kennedy
Christine Kennedy
Justus Kessler
Norine Kevolic
Nelson Kim
Lorissa Kimm
Xandra Kohler
David Kubik
Jason Kuhnle
Tae Wook Lah
Alan LaZare
Sangzo Lee
Hu Li
Tiffany Lin
Stephanie Magdziak
Lucy Malone
Andrew March
Karen McEvoy
Yuka Midorikawa
Coleman Mills
Shelley Miracle
Christina Noble
Kara Nykreim
Julie Nymann
Brian Pawlowski
Damon Pearson
Thomas Pen
Lisa Perrine
Richard Perry
Brendan Peters
Arturo Ponciano
Hortensia Quevedo
Raquel Raimundez
Doug Reitmeyer
Brian Revoir
Pablo Riestra

Stephanie Rigolot
Edwin Rivera
Andrew Roman
Ani Rosskam
Maria Ruiz
Kyle Ryan
Savvas Sarafidis
Annatina Schneider
Christina Seo
Stephen Skelly
Roger Smith
Jason Smith
Christopher Starkey
Dortha Starling
Shanmei Sun
Michael Sweebe
Susan Szymanski
Venina Tandela
Genie Tang
Jacqueline Teo
Teresa Thiele
Heidi Toll
Ludwing Vaca
Robert Van Varick
Kindra Welch
Irina Wong
Bonni Yelin
Ashley Yoon
Erhmei Yuan

Senior Administrative Staff
Deborah Baker
Kathleen P. Cherry
Nancy Festa
Caroline Hancock
Linda Kinsey
Kenneth Zauber

Administrative Staff
Carlos Acevedo
Dean Acquaviva
Kathryn Aptner
Karin Beauregard
Catherine Boerner
Marek Bulaj
Lisa Burke
Linda Burton-Hammell
Robert Cifelli
James Cifelli
Allison Clancy
Donna Clifton
Christina Dallas
Nicole DeCongilio

Katherine Dixon
Lisa Dockray
Elise Dodeles
Audrey Eisenstein
Andrea Ellis
Royce Epstein
Patricia Frik
Judith Gawlowski
Jennifer Geoghan
Anmei Goldsmith
Carolyn Goodridge
Adam Graves
Courtney Havran
Laura Hawkins
Janet Hickey
Holly Hyde
Janna Israel
Cara Jacobson
Eric Janson
Beatrice-Rose Johnson
Ann Johnston
Stacy Kelley
Elizabeth-Anne Kilkenny
Kathryn-Anne Kilkenny
Joel Koenigsberg
Bryan Kubik
Jason Lazarz
Payal Luthra
Eileen Mathes
Andrew Merz
Deborah Miller
Carole Nicholson
Patrick O'Leary
Kristen Palkovich
Tracy Panzarino
Ann Protinick
Christana Puzio
Emily Reeves
Suzanne Reiss
Renee Robichaud
Cary Ryan
Marc Sanchez
Jennifer Scappatura
Tiffany Schrader
Lori Sherman
Lori Stagnitto
Ron Stow II
Heather Strauber
Kathleen Tchorni
Allison Unruh
Dorothy Urquhart
Krista Van Ness
Eleanor Voorhees

Robert Walker
Laura Warner
Carol Wasielewski
Tara Waters
Maura Whang
Benjamin Wintner
Maryellen Zingarini
Regan Ziobro

Selected Honors and Awards

The following list includes selected honors and awards given to Michael Graves as an individual and to the firm, Michael Graves & Associates.

American Academy in Rome: Centennial Prize, 1996; Rome Prize, 1960-1962; Brunner Fellowship, 1960

American Academy of Arts and Letters: Induction as a Member, 1991; Arnold W. Brunner Memorial Prize in Architecture, 1980

American Institute of Architects: 2001 Gold Medal

American Institute of Architects: 10 National Honor Awards, 1975–1992

AIA and American Library Association: Award of Excellence, 2001

AIA–New Jersey and other state AIA chapters: 60 design awards, 1967–2002

AIA– New Jersey: special recognition award, 1982

American Federation of Arts: Graphic design award, 1990

American Sculpture Society: Henry Hering Medal, 1986

Architectural Digest: "AD 100 Best Architects and Designers": 1990, 1995, 2000, 2002

Boston University: Silver Spoon Award, 1984

Chicago Athenaeum: 2 American Architecture Awards, 1999 and 2000

Chicago Athenaeum Good Design Award: 11 awards, 1997–2002

Christopher Columbus Fellowship Society, Frank Annunzio Award, 2001

Design Alliance: Most significant contribution to the design industry, 2000

Design Zentrum, Nordrhein Westfalen: Red Dot award for design quality, 2000

Downtown New Jersey, Inc.: Urban design award, 1990

Euster Merchandise Mart: Outstanding leadership in architecture and design, 1983

Friends of The Hague Citation for Improvement to the City, 1998

Fukuoka Building Contractor's Society Award, 1995

Fukuoka Urban Beautification Award: 2 awards, 1995 and 1997

GQ Magazine: Man of the Year, 1997

House Beautiful Magazine "Giants of Design" award, 2000

Industrial Designers Society of America: IDEA Award, 3 awards: 1999, 2001, 2003

Institute of Business Designers: 3 design awards, 1982–1990

International Furnishings & Design Assoc.: 33rd Annual Trailblazing Award, 2000

Interiors Magazine: 3 design awards; Designer of the Year, 1981, Hall of Fame, 1991

Japanese Society of Commercial Space Designers Design Award, 1994

Manitoga, Russel Wright Center: First Russel Wright Award, 2000

Metropolitan Home Magazine: Design 100 Award, 1990

National Medal of Arts, conferred by President Clinton, 1999

New Jersey Business & Industry Association: Firm Award for Achievement, 1990 and Good Neighbor Award, 2000

New Jersey Center for Visual Arts: Arts Person of the Year, 2000

New Jersey Governor's Pride Awards: Walt Whitman Creative Arts Award, 1991

Philadelphia Museum of Art: COLLAB Award, 1995

Progressive Architecture Magazine: 13 design awards, 1970–1989

Progressive Architecture Magazine: 2 furniture design awards, 1982 and 1983

Resources Council Commendations: 2 design awards, 1980 and 1982

Rhode Island School of Design and Bryant College: Success by Design Award, 2003

Tau Sigma Delta Honor Society in Architecture and the Allied Arts: The Tau Sigma Delta Gold Medal, 2003

University of Cincinnati Alumni Association: William Howard Taft Medal, 1998

Selected Bibliography

ARCHITECTURAL MONOGRAPHS

Dobney, Stephen. *Michael Graves: Selected and Current Works*. Musgrave, Australia: Images Publishing, 1999.

Kudalis, Eric. *Michael Graves*. Minneapolis, MN: Capstone Press, 1996. [young adult textbook]

World Architecture Review Agency. *Michael Graves, Architect: World Architecture Review 96:04/05* Special Issue. Beijing, China, 1996.

Nichols, Karen, Lisa Burke, and Patrick Burke, eds. *Michael Graves: Buildings and Projects 1990–1994*. New York: Rizzoli International Publications, Inc., 1995.

Powell, Kenneth. *Graves Residence: Michael Graves*. Architecture in Detail series, London: Phaidon Press, 1995.

Brown, Theodore L. and De Vita, Maurizio, eds. *Michael Graves: Idee e projetti 1981–1991*. Milano: Electa, 1991.

Nichols, Karen Vogel, Patrick J. Burke, and Caroline Hancock, eds. *Michael Graves: Buildings and Projects 1982-1989*. New York: Princeton Architectural Press, 1990.

Wheeler, Karen Vogel, Peter Arnell, and Ted Bickford, eds. *Michael Graves: Buildings and Projects 1966–1981*. New York: Rizzoli International, 1983.

Dunster, David, ed. *Michael Graves*. London: Academy Editions, 1979.

Museum of Modern Art, New York. *Five Architects: Eisenman, Graves, Gwathmey, Hejduk, Meier*. New York: Museum of Modern Art and Oxford University Press, 1975.

PRODUCT DESIGN MONOGRAPHS

Iovine, Julie. *Compact Design Portfolio: Michael Graves*. Design Briefs series. San Francisco: Chronicle Books, 2001.

Bertsch, Georg-Christof. *Design Classics: The Water Kettle by Michael Graves*. Frankfurt am Main: Verlag form, 1997.

Buck, Alex and Matthias Vogt, eds. *Michael Graves: Designer Monographs 3*. New York: Saint Martins Press, 1994.

WRITINGS, INTERVIEWS AND ILLUSTRATIONS
BY MICHAEL GRAVES

"The Figural City." Introduction to *Town Spaces: Contemporary Interpretations in Traditional Urbanism: Krier·Kohl·Architects*, by Rob Krier. Basel: Birkhäuser, 2003.

"Henry Hornbostel." In *Invisible Giants: Fifty Americans Who Shaped the Nation but Missed the History Books*. Edited by Mark Carnes. New York: Oxford University Press, 2002.

"Michael Graves on Le Corbusier." In *Architects on Architects*. Edited by Susan Gray. New York: McGraw-Hill, 2001.

"Le Corbusier at Princeton." In *OCULUS* 63, no. 9 (May–June 2001).

"A Monumental Task." Interview by Margaret Warner. *NewsHour with Jim Lehrer* (2 March 1999).

Cover illustration. *Italy in Mind*. Edited by Alice Leccese Powers. New York: Vintage Books, a division of Random House, Inc., 1997.

"Architecture of the Michael C. Carlos Museum." In *Handbook*. Atlanta, GA: Michael C. Carlos Museum, Emory University, 1996.

"Commentary by Michael Graves." Preface to *World Architecture Review: Michael Graves*, April/May 1996.

"Humana Building a Louisville." *Paesaggio urbano*, July–October 1996.

"Sketches – An interview with Michael Graves." Edited by Alex Buck and Mathias Vogt. *Michael Graves: Designer Monographs 3*. Berlin: Ernst & Sohn, 1994.

"Michael Graves." Interview by Stanley Collyer. *Competitions*, Winter 1994.

Illustrations for *Mr. Chas and Lisa Sue Meet the Pandas*, by Fran Lebowitz. New York: Alfred A. Knopf, Inc., 1994.

"Michael Graves." Interview by Gordon Simmons. *Practices: Journal of the Center for the Study of the Practice of Architecture* (University of Cincinnati) 2 (Spring 1993).

"A Conversation with Michael Graves." Interview by John R. Kirk. *Modulus: The Architectural Review of the University of Virginia*. New York: Princeton Architectural Press, 1989.

"Has Post-modernism reached its limit?" *Architectural Digest Supplement*, April 1988.

"Graves/Schmidt: Competition Statement." In *Art + architecture + landscape: The Clos Pegase Design Competition*. San Francisco, CA: San Francisco Museum of Modern Art, 1985.

Illustrations for *The Great Gatsby*, by F. Scott Fitgerald. San Francisco: The Arion Press, 1984.

"A Case for Figurative Architecture." In *Michael Graves: Buildings and Projects 1966–1981*. Edited by Karen Vogel Nichols, Patrick J. Burke and Caroline Hancock. New York: Rizzoli International Publications, Inc., 1983.

"Ritual Themes in Architecture." *The Princeton Journal*, 1983.

"Michael Graves on Michael Graves." *GA Document*, 1983.

"Representation." In *Representation and Architecture*. Edited by Omer Akin and Eleanor F. Weinel. Information Dynamics, 1982.

"Le Corbusier's Drawn References." In *Le Corbusier: Selected Drawings*. London: Academy Editions, 1981.

"Michael Graves." In *Architectural Drawing: The Art and the Process*. Gerald Allen and Richard Oliver, editors. New York: Whitney Library of Design, 1981.

"The Wageman House and the Crooks House." In *Idea as Model*. New York, Institute for Architecture and Urban Studies: Rizzoli International Publications, Inc., 1981.

"Michael Graves." In *Speaking a New Classicism: American Architecture Now*. Smith College Museum of Art, 1981.

"Porta Maggiore." In *Roma Interrotta Incontri Internazionale d'Arte*. Rome, 1978.

"Toward Reading an Architecture." Interview by Douglas Ely. *Nassau Literary Review*, Princeton University, Spring 1978.

"Thought Models." *Great Models*, North Carolina State School of Design, Fall 1978.

"Referential Drawings." *Journal of Architectural Education*, September 1978.

"The Necessity of Drawing: Tangible Speculation." *Architectural Design*, June 1977.

"The Swedish Connection." *Journal of Architectural Education*, September 1975.

ARTICLES

Pugh, Clifford. "Rice refreshed: New campus buildings expand on tradition." *Houston Chronicle*, 10 March 2003. [Rice University North College residence halls]

Rich, Motoko. "Michael Graves Enters his Post-Teapot Phase." *Wall Street Journal*, 26 March 2003. [Target Pavilions]

Margolies, Jane. "Good Design Means Business." *House Beautiful*. Giants of Design issue, June 2003. [Product design]

Goldberger, Paul. "Cincinnati Synthesis: Turning Disparate Design Elements into a Unified Whole." *Architectural Digest*, April 2001. [Residence at Indian Hill]

Ivy, Robert. "Michael Graves: The Road to Gold." *Architectural Record*, May 2001. [Cover: AIA Gold Medal]

Davidson, Cynthia. "Michael Graves: O'Reilly Theater, Pittsburgh." *Architecture*, May 2001.

Catinella, Rita. "Michael Graves: Man of the House." *Architectural Record*, April 2000. [Products design]

Clines, Francis X. "A Washington Cover-Up With Aesthetic Appeal." *New York Times*, 17 January 2000. [Washington Monument Restoration Scaffolding]

Gibney, Frank, Jr. and Belinda Luscombe. "The Redesigning of America." *Time Magazine*, 20 March 2000.

Pittel, Christine. "Giants of Design: An Intimate Look at Seven Who Changed Our World; Michael Graves, Product Design." *House Beautiful*, June 2000.

Goldberger, Paul. "Architecture: Malibu Composition: A Play of Grids and Circles Embraces its Oceanfront Site." *Architectural Digest*, October 2000. [Malibu Beach House]

Naegele, Daniel. "We Dig Graves – All Sizes." *Harvard Design Magazine*, Fall 2000.

Schmertz, Mildred F. "Egyptian Mirage: Michael Graves' Sheraton Miramar Rises on the Red Sea." Photography by Erhard Pfeiffer, *Architectural Digest*, January 1999. [The Miramar Hotel, El Gouna Egypt]

Forgey, Benjamin. "The Monument's New Winter Coat: Temporary Transformation of Obelisk Is Quite a Treat." *The Washington Post* Style section, 23 January 1999. [Washington Monument Restoration Scaffolding]

Sogg, Daniel. "Classic Harmony: Architect Michael Graves and His Collections." *Art & Antiques*, April 1999. [Graves Residence - The Warehouse]

Kamin, Blair. "A D.C. '10': Elegant scaffolding on Washington Monument captivates capital city." *Chicago Tribune Arts & Entertainment*, 4 July 1999.

Goldberger, Paul, with photograph by Todd Eberle. "Postmodern Pillar." Showcase section, *The New Yorker*, 4 October 1999 [Washington Monument Restoration Scaffolding]

Curtis, Eleanor. "Intonaco: Michael Graves in Egitto: Miramar Hotel." *Abitare*, February 1998. [The Miramar Hotel, El Gouna Egypt]

Russell, John. "Architect Gives a Library Space to Read and Dream." *New York Times*, 4 November 1998. [The French Institute Library]

Rozhon, Tracie. "Michael Graves: The Prince of Princeton." *Graphis 312*, Volume 53 (November/December 1997).

Allen, Jenny. "The 1996 LIFE Dream House." *LIFE*, May 1996.

Brown, Patricia L. "At Home with Michael Graves: How the Pearl Designed his Oyster." *New York Times*, 14 March 1996. [Graves Residence – The Warehouse]

Goldberger, Paul. "A Little Book That Led Five Men to Fame." *New York Times*, 11 February 1996. [retrospective look at Five Architects]

Goldsmith, Barbara. "Architecture: The American Academy's Rare Book Room: A Michael Graves Design Enhances Preservation in Rome." *Architectural Digest*, December 1996.

Hoyt, Charles. "Hyatt Regency Hotel." *Architectural Record*, October 1996. [Hyatt Regency Hotel, Fukuoka, Japan]

Hoyt, Charles. "Joining Hands to Connect a Campus." *Architectural Record*, July 1996. [University of Cincinnati Engineering Research Center]

Prisant, Carol. "Graves' New World." *World of Interiors*, May 1995. [Graves Residence – The Warehouse]

Fukuwatari, Isao. "The Tajima Building" (*in Japanese*). *Shin-kenchiku*, July 1994. [Tajima Office Building, Tokyo, Japan]

Goldberger, Paul. "Rural Revisited: Working Wonders on a New Jersey Farm Property." *Architectural Digest*, May 1994. [Dairy Barn Renovation, NJ]

Goldberger, Paul. "A Remembrance of Visions Pure and Elegant." *New York Times*, 3 January 1993. [on lecture: "Five Architects 20 Years Later"]

Hamano, Yasuhiro. "Onjuku Town Hall and Health Center." *Shin-kenchiku*, July 1993. [Article in Japanese on Onjuku Civic Center]

Russell, Beverly. "The Hotel New York." *Interiors*, May 1992. [Hotel New York: Disneyland Park – Paris]

"Momochi District Apartment Building." *Architektur + Wettbewerbe*, September 1991.

Sutro, Dirk. "Classical Animation." *Architecture*, June 1991. [Team Disney Building, Burbank, CA]

Branch, Mark Alden. "Design Feature: Fish Story." *Progressive Architecture*, October 1990. [Walt Disney World® Swan and Dolphin Hotels]

Branch, Mark Alden. "Story Time." *Progressive Architecture*, March 1990. [Walt Disney World Swan® and Dolphin Hotels]

Lavin, Sylvia. "Michael Graves, Architect: Growth and Diversity." *Progressive Architecture*, March 1990.

Brown, Patricia L. "Disney Deco." *New York Times* Magazine, 8 April 1990. [Team Disney Building, Burbank, CA]

Goldberger, Paul. "And Now, an Architectural Kingdom." *New York Times* Magazine, 8 April 1990. [Walt Disney World® Swan and Dolphin Hotels]

Goldberger, Paul. "Raising the Architectural Ante in California." *New York Times*, 14 October 1990. [The Aventine Hotel and Business Center, La Jolla, CA]

Papademetriou, Peter. "Four Not-so-easy Pieces." *Progressive Architecture*, March 1990. [The Newark Museum]

Schreiner, Judy. "Irrepressible Michael Graves." *Engineering News Record*, 6 September 1990.

Stein, Karen D. "Gravesian Images." *Architectural Record*, February 1990. [Cover: Crown American Headquarters, Johnstown, PA]

Glueck, Grace. "A 'Yellow Brick Road' Brightens a Museum." *New York Times*, 12 November 1989. [The Newark Museum]

Pastier, John. "An Intimate Sequence of Spaces." *Architecture*, December 1989. [San Juan Capistrano Library]

Byron, Elizabeth S. "The Prince of Princeton." HG, July 1988.

Viladas, Pilar. "Mickey the Talent Scout." *Progressive Architecture*, June 1988. [Disney projects]

Filler, Martin. "A Shrine to Wine." *House & Garden*, September 1987. [Clos Pegase Winery, Calistoga, CA]

Giovannini, Joseph. "Designers' Showrooms That Reflect Architectural Trends." *New York Times*, 29 January 1987. [Sunar Showrooms]

Stein, Karen D. "On the Waterfront." *Architectural Record*, October 1986. [Riverbend Music Center for Cincinnati Symphony Orchestra]

Gandee, Charles K. "Humana." *Architectural Record*, August 1985. [The Humana Building, Louisville, KY]

Viladas, Pilar. "Full Circle." *Progressive Architecture*, September 1985. [Emory University Michael C. Carlos Museum of Art and Archaeology]

Jordy, William H. "Aedicular Modern: The Architecture of Michael Graves." *New Criterion*, October 1983.

Goldberger, Paul. "Architecture of a Different Color." *New York Times Magazine*, 10 October 1982.

Gandee, Charles. "Sunar Houston: The Allusive Language of Michael Graves." *Architectural Record*, June 1980.

Filler, Martin. "Better and Better." *Progressive Architecture*, September 1979. [Sunar Showrooms, Los Angeles and Chicago]

Filler, Martin. "Grand Illusions." *Progressive Architecture*, June 1979. [Sunar Showroom, New York City]

"Five on Five." *Architectural Forum*, May 1973. ["Stompin' at the Savoy" by Robert A.M. Stern; "Machines in the Garden" by Jacquelin Robertson; "In Similar States of Undress" by Charles Moore; "The Lurking American Legacy" by Allan Greenberg; "The Discreet Charm of the Bourgeoisie" by Romaldo Giurgola]

BOOKS

US Design 1975–2000. New York: Prestel Verlag in association with the Denver Art Museum, 2002.

Fentriss, Curtis W. *Civic Builders*. New York: John Wiley & Sons, 2002.

Futagawa, Yukio. "Plocek House, Warren, New Jersey, USA." *GA Houses Special, Masterpieces 1971–2000 Edition*. Tokyo: A.D.A. Editor Tokyo, Ltd., 2002.

Gronin, Pierrette. *Cyberculture et objects de design industriel*. Laval, Canada: Les Presses de l'Université Laval, Fall 2000.

"Michael Graves & Associates." *Architects of the New Millennium*. Mulgrave, Australia: Images Publishing, 2000.

Powell, Kenneth. "Michael Graves Architect." In *Architecture Reborn: The Conversion and Reconstruction of Old Buildings*. London: Laurence King Publishing, May 1999.

Liu Erming/Yi Feng. *International Architects in China*. Beijing: China Planning Press, 1999.

Wiseman, Carter. *Shaping A Nation*. New York City: W.W. Norton & Company, Inc., 1999.

Byars, Mel and Arlette Barré-Despond. *Cent Objets: Un Siècle de Design*. Les Editions de l'Amateur, 1999.

Pearman, Hugh. *Contemporary World Architecture*. London: Phaidon Press Limited, 1998.

Bertsch, Georg Christof. *The Water Kettle by Michael Graves*. Frankfurt am Main: Design-Klassiker Verlag form, 1997.

Riewoldt, Otto. *Intelligent Spaces: Architecture for the Information Age*. London: Laurence King Publishing, 1997.

Myerson, Jeremy. "The Denver Central Library." *New Public Architecture*. London: Laurence King Publishing, 1996.

Lebowitz, Fran. "The Warehouse." In *Building Sights*. Edited by Ruth Rosenthal and Maggie Toy (100–105). London: Academy Editions, 1995.

University of Maryland. *Five Architects: Twenty Years Later*. Introduction by Steven W. Hurtt. College Park: University of Maryland, 1992.

Spencer, Dorothy. *Total Design: Objects by Architects*. San Francisco: Chronicle Books, 1991.

Papadakis, Dr. Andreas C., ed. A.D. (*Architectural Design*) Profile No. 88: "*Post-Modernism on Trial*." London: Academy Group Ltd, 1990. [Walt Disney World® Dolphin and Swan Hotels (cover), Newark Museum]

Papadakis, Andreas and Watson, Harriet, eds. *New Classicism: Omnibus Volume*. New York: Rizzoli International Publications and London: Academy Editions, 1990.

Tapert, Annette. *Swid Powell: Objects by Architects*. New York: Rizzoli International Publications, Inc., 1990.

Collins, Michael and Andreas Papadakis. *Post Modern Design*. New York: Rizzoli International Publications, Inc., 1989.

Shoshkes, Ellen. *The Design Process*. New York: Whitney Library of Design, 1989.

Fleischmann, Melanie. *In the Neoclassic Style*. New York: Thames and Hudson, 1988.

Papadakis, Dr. Andreas C. AD (*Architectural Design*) Vol 58 No 1/2 – 1988; "*Michael Graves: Two Recent Projects*." London: Academy Group Ltd., 1988. [Clos Pegase Winery & WVU Alumni Center]

Merkel, Jayne. *Michael Graves and the Riverbend Music Center*. Cincinnati: Contemporary Arts Center, 1987.

Stephens, Suzanne, et al., eds. *Building the New Museum*. New York: The Architectural League of New York, 1986.

Poling, Clark V. *Henry Hornbostel/Michael Graves*. Atlanta: Emory University Museum of Art and Archaeology, 1985.

GA Document 10, Tokyo: May, 1984. [Cincinnati Symphony Summer Pavilion; The Humana Building; San Juan Capistrano Public Library (cover); Liberty State Park Environmental Education Center; The Portland Building; others.]

Jencks, Charles. *The Language of Post-Modern Architecture*, Fourth Revised Enlarged Edition. London: Academy Editions, London, 1984.

Jencks, Charles. *Kings of Infinite Space: Michael Graves and Frank Lloyd Wright*. London: Academy Editions, 1984.

Arnell, Peter and Ted Bickford eds. *A Tower for Louisville: The Humana Competition*, New York: Rizzoli International Publications, Inc., 1982.

"Michael Graves: Sunar." *GA Document 10*, Tokyo: 1982.

Jensen, Robert, and Patricia Conway. *Ornamentalism: The Return of Decorativeness in Modern Design and Art*. New York: C.N. Potter, 1982.

Turner, Judith. *Judith Turner Photographs Five Architects*. New York: Rizzoli International Publications, Inc., 1980.

Emanuel, Muriel. *Contemporary Architects*. Edited with Architectural Consultant Dennis Sharp. New York: St. Martin's Press, 1980.

Cerruti, Marisa, ed. *Roma interrotta*. Rome: 1978.

Gebhard, David, and Deborah Nevins. *200 Years of American Architectural Drawing*. New York: Whitney Library of Design for the Architectural League of New York and The American Federation of Arts, 1977.

Jencks, Charles. *The Language of Post Modern Architecture*. London: Academy Editions, 1977.

Stern, Robert A.M. *New Directions in American Architecture*. New York: George Braziller, 1977.

Photography Credits

All photographs in this monograph are copyrighted and may not be reproduced without prior written permission. The following credits refer to photographs of completed buildings. Photographs of the drawings and models and photographs of completed buildings not credited below are by Michael Graves & Associates (MGA). We would like to acknowledge Courtney Havran, our images librarian, Marek Bulaj, our in-house photographer, and Taylor Photo, which provided reproduction and processing services.

1500 Ocean Drive, 44-47: ©Steven Brooke Studio

Astrid Park Plaza Hotel, 24–27: ©Luc Polfliet, except 25 top, 26 bottom, MGA

Castalia, 28–33: ©Daria Scagliola and Stijn Brakkee

Cedar Gables, 208–213: ©Susan Gilmore

Charles E. Beatley, Jr. Central Library, 116–119: ©Eric Taylor Photography

Disney's Garden Pavilion, 43: ©William Taylor/Taylor Photo; with permission of The Walt Disney Company

El Gouna Golf Hotel and Club, 134–145: ©John Donat

Elephant Fountain at Target House, 227: courtesy of Target House

Famille-Tsukishima, 250–251: courtesy of Maeda Corporation

Fortis AG Headquarters, 132–133: ©Luc Polfliet, except exterior image, MGA

Golf Villas, 146–149: ©John Donat, except 148 top, MGA

House at Coolidge Point, 50–55: ©John Bellenis Photography

House at Indian Hill, 106–113: Scott Frances (Photographs on pages 109 and 112, courtesy of Architectural Digest, ©2001 Condé Nast Publications, Inc.)

Hyatt Regency Hotel, 82–89: ©John Donat, except 88, Erhard Pfeiffer (Photograph courtesy Architectural Digest ©1999 Condé Nast Publications, Inc. This image was photographed by Erhard Pfeiffer at a different location, the Miramar Hotel in El Gouna, a companion project for the same developer. It shows a guestroom design that was replicated at the Hyatt Regency Hotel in Taba Heights.)

Indianapolis Art Center, 22–23: ©William Taylor/Taylor Photo

International Finance Corporation Headquarters, 14–19: ©Andrew Lautman/Lautman Photography

Lake Hills Country Club, 98–101: ©Seung Hoon Yum

Laurel Hall, New Jersey Institute of Technology, 66–67: ©William Taylor/Taylor Photo

Library of the French Institute/Alliance Française, 102–103: ©Cervin Robinson

LIFE Magazine Dream House, 104–105: cover image courtesy of LIFE Magazine

Main Library of Topeka and Shawnee County, 68–71: ©Douglas Kahn Photography

Martel, Jones and Brown Colleges, Rice University, 194–203: ©Jud Haggard Photography

Miele Americas Headquarters, 92–95: ©William Taylor/Taylor Photo

Miramar Resort Hotel, 56–63: ©Daniel Aubry, except 62 top, Erhard Pfeiffer (Photograph courtesy of Architectural Digest, ©1999, Condé Nast Publications, Inc.) and 63, ©John Donat

Mixed-use Building, 160–161: courtesy of Fukuoka Jisho Co.

Museum of the Shenandoah Valley, 242–245: 245 bottom courtesy of Glen Burnie and the Museum of the Shenandoah Valley

NCAA Headquarters and Hall of Champions, 126–131: 126–127, 129 top, ©William Taylor/Taylor; 130, 131, ©Greg Murphey

Nexus Momochi Residential Tower, 34–35: courtesy of Maeda Corporation

North Hall, Drexel University, 156–159: ©Matt Wargo

NovaCare Complex, Philadelphia Eagles Training Center, 220–223: ©Matt Wargo

O'Grady Library, Saint Martin's College, 168–169: ©Doug Walker

One Port Center, 48–49: ©Matt Wargo

O'Reilly Theater, 72–79: ©Ed Massery, except 75 top, 79, ©Barney Taxel

Private Offices, 254–257: ©Robert Lautman/Lautman Photography

St. Mary's Church, 188–191: ©Steven Brooke Studio

Taiwan National Museum of Pre-History, 36–37: 40 top, ©Jeffrey Cheng; 40 bottom, 41, ©Peter Mauss/ESTO

Target Stage at Harriet Island Park, 226: courtesy of Rafferty Rafferty Tollefson Architects

The Impala, 170–173: ©Norman McGrath, except 173 bottom, MGA

Uffelman Country House, 120–123: ©George Kopp Photography

United States Post Office, 42: ©William Taylor/Taylor Photo; with permission of The Walt Disney Company

Washington Monument Restoration, 176–179: ©Robert Lautman/Lautman Photography

Watch Technicum, 228-231: ©Larry Lefever